# Crossing the Boundaries

## A COMMENTARY ON MARK

Chi Rho Commentary Series

# Crossing the Boundaries

## A COMMENTARY ON MARK

*Rick Strelan*, BA(Hon) DipTh

WIPF & STOCK · Eugene, Oregon

Wipf and Stock Publishers
199 W 8th Ave, Suite 3
Eugene, OR 97401

Crossing the Boundaries
A Commentary on Mark
By Strelan, Rick
Copyright©1991 by Strelan, Rick
ISBN 13: 978-1-5326-5825-9
Publication date 5/1/2018
Previously published by Lutheran Publishing House, 1991

*To my teachers
and companions in Christ*

# PREFACE

There has been a notable growth in the desire and determination of many Christian people to know the truth and to find direction for their lives through a deeper study of the Scriptures. This desire deserves encouragement in the face of the strident efforts of humanism, atheism, and exotic religious movements to offer 'another gospel'.

The Chi Rho Commentary series has been undertaken to serve this earnest Christian public. The present editorial committee planning and guiding the project comprises J.G. Strelan, DTh, V.C. Pfitzner, BA DTh, J.T.E. Renner, BA DipEd DTh (all lecturers in biblical studies at Luther Seminary, North Adelaide), R.W. Mayer, BA DipEd STM (lecturer at Lutheran Teachers College, North Adelaide), and the undersigned (the Director of Publications of the Lutheran Church of Australia). It is planned that at least two volumes will appear annually. Books from both the Old and the New Testament are being treated.

The series aims to provide a commentary on Scripture which is popular, but not superficial. The language is simple and clear, and technical terms are avoided wherever possible. References to the original Greek or Hebrew have been kept to a minimum, but careful and solid study of the text is still required.

The basic text used for the commentary, and printed out at the head of each section, is that of the Revised Standard Version of the Bible (RSV). However, other Bible versions as well as the original languages are used where these are considered necessary to illuminate the scriptural message. Short essays are included in some commentaries to provide additional material on important themes related to the study. A basic reading list for the average student, and a wider bibliography for the more scholarly, are given at the end of each commentary for those who want to pursue further study on the book in question.

The writers chosen for the Chi Rho Commentary are Lutheran scholars who accept 'without reservation the Holy Scriptures of the Old and New Testaments, as a whole and in all their parts, as the divinely inspired, written, and inerrant Word of God, and as the only infallible source and norm for all matters of faith, doctrine, and life' (Constitution of the Lutheran Church of Australia), and who also stand under personal commitment to the Lutheran Confessions. This confessional commitment enables them to use the best of modern biblical scholarship, but also frees them from the errors and excesses of biblical criticism which are often abroad today even in popular commentaries.

Deep reverence for the text as God's revealed Word to human beings, a warm love for Christ the incarnate Word, and the aim to rightly divide Law and Gospel, mark these commentaries. They offer an explanation of the text which is sound and reliable, which can deepen understanding and faith, and can equip the Christian to apply it to life.

May each volume enjoy a warm response in the church, open up the Scriptures to many, and give glory to the God of our salvation.

*John Pfitzner,*
*Editor.*

In the Commentary proper, words and phrases that are being explained and commented on are set in bold type. The numbers in the right margin indicate the verse or verses under review.

For the sake of convenience the following abbreviations are used to define the various Bible translations being referred to in the commentary: AV (King James or Authorized Version); JB (Jerusalem Bible); NEB (New English Bible); NIV (New International Version); RSV (Revised Standard Version); TEV (Good News Bible – Today's English Version).

The Bible text used in this Commentary is the Revised Standard Version of the Bible, copyright 1946, 1952, and 1971 by the Division of Christian Education, National Council of Churches, USA. Permission to use this version is gratefully acknowledged.

# CONTENTS

Preface .................................................. 6

Introduction ............................................ 11

The Commentary:
  Part I: 1:1 - 4:34 ................................. 24
  Part II: 4:35 - 8:21 ............................... 82
  Part III: 8:22 - 10:52 ............................ 121
  Part IV: 11:1 - 13:37 ............................. 156
  Part V: 14:1 - 16:20 .............................. 182

Further Reading ....................................... 232

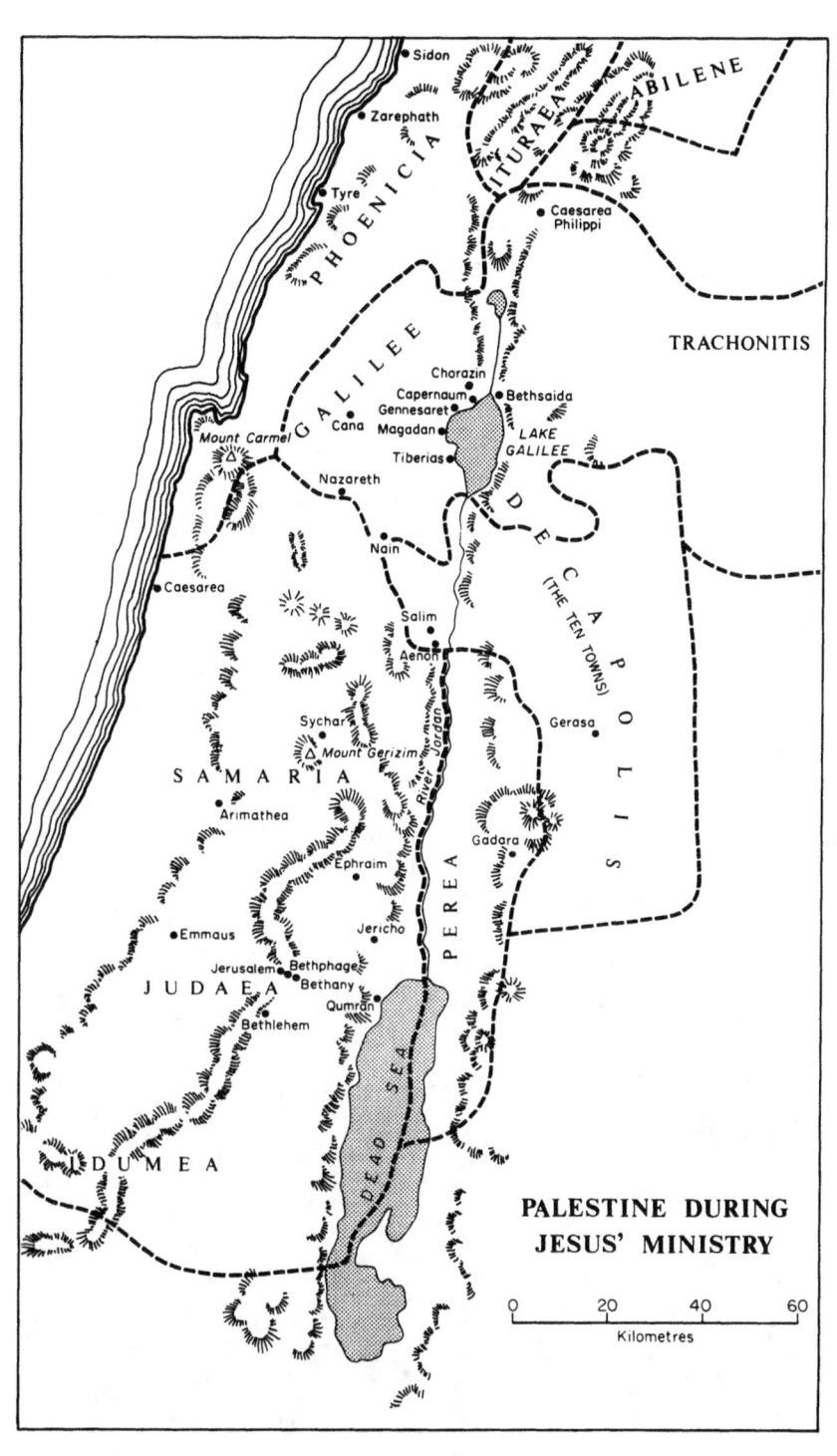

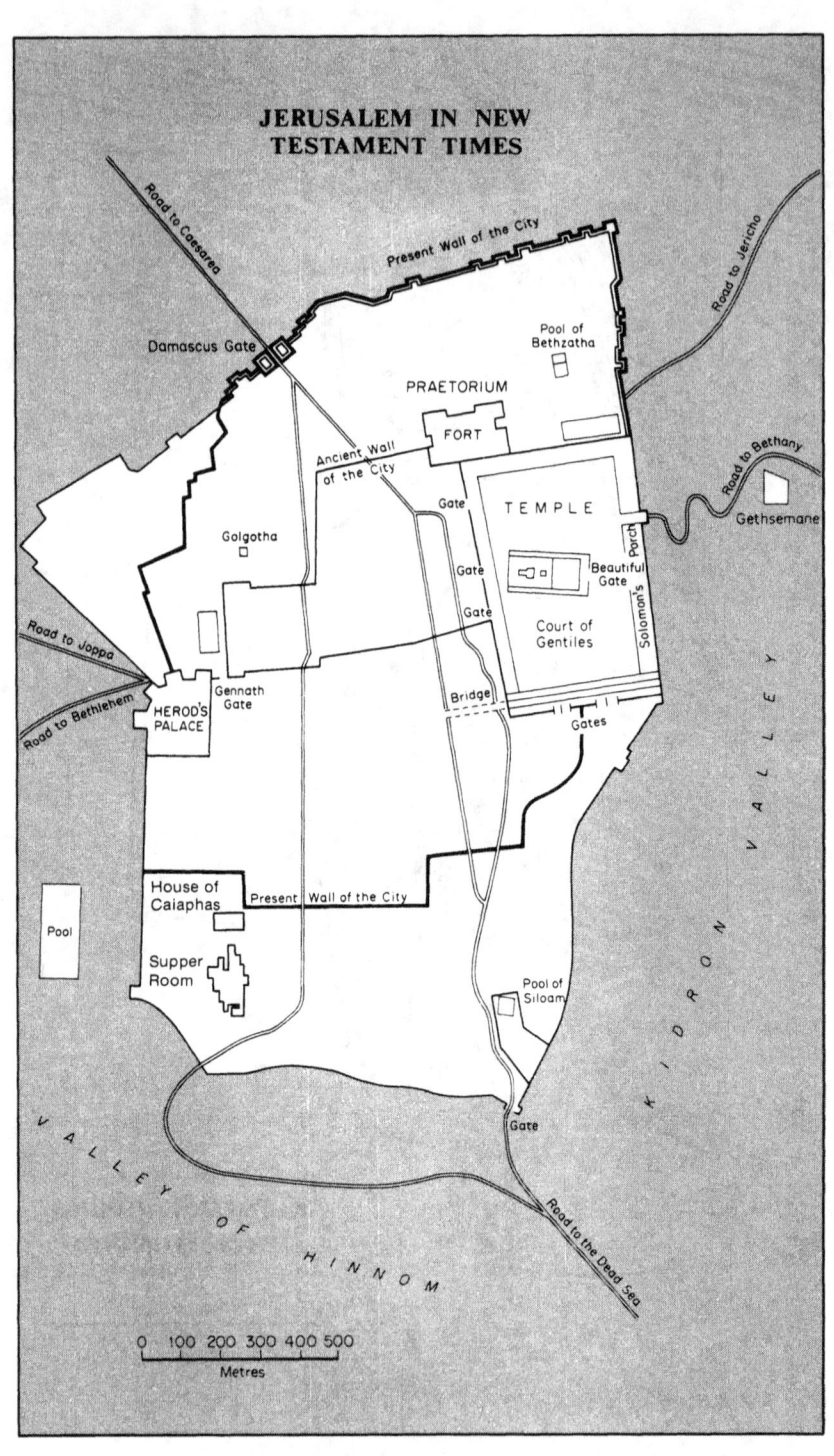

# INTRODUCTION

**A Story To Tell**

Everyone loves a good story; it fires the imagination. Unlike a movie, which does much of the imagining for you, a written or spoken story allows readers or listeners to imagine the characters and events for themselves. A story lets the audience be part of the creative interpretation process, that is, events and characters can be interpreted and given significance according to the imagination of the audience. This is partly what Jesus had in mind when he said: 'Those who have ears to hear, let them hear'.

Words are pictures, which people in all societies can also play with. In many non-Western societies, words are often used to protect the bald and naked truth, almost like walls. Westerners, on the other hand, are often quite blunt with words, a characteristic sometimes viewed with amazement by people of other cultures. In his gospel, Mark often uses words very much as pictures, as creative and stimulating symbols for his readers. People from other cultures who use words in this way can be frustrating for Westerners, who find themselves confronted by a logic and a way of using words that are different from what they are used to. Interpretation becomes more difficult where deeper levels of meaning exist beneath the surface words of the text. After all, how can we ever be sure that we have understood what the author meant? Westerners who have worked in other cultures will appreciate the problem.

Mark tells a story about Jesus. Of course, the word 'story' is not used in the sense of something that has been made up, but to indicate the *form* of writing that Mark chooses to use in communicating to his audience. Paul writes letters; Mark writes a story.

However, looking at the gospel of Mark as a story raises certain problems. Studying a text is not dissimilar to what anthropologists do when they study, observe, and ultimately interpret, a particular culture. Like anthropologists, interpreters of the Scriptures come to the text with their own preconceived ideas and expectations, formed by experience and their own cultural background and conditioning. It is impossible to deal with a text without any bias or subjectivity. This means that every interpreter comes with a particular method of interpretation, or even a particular goal. Christian interpreters are not immune from theological and other biases.

For some interpreters it may be important to view the text in a *political* light. This is likely to happen with people living, and doing their thinking, in a community suffering injustice and oppression. In recent times, such a theology, or method of interpretation, has been called liberation theology. For these interpreters, the significance of Jesus is seen in his radical opposition to the forces of oppression and injustice, and his message is understood as offering freedom for the oppressed. In this case, the experiences of the interpreter, and of those for whom the text is interpreted, influence the way in which the text is understood and applied.

Others wish to understand the text from a *sociological* viewpoint, claiming that it is impossible to interpret any piece of literature without taking into consideration the sociological circumstances of the text, its author, and its audience. This is a valid approach, since neither writing nor interpretation takes place in a sociological vacuum.

The *feminist* understanding of the Scriptures has provided new and distinctive kinds of interpretation in a field previously dominated by males, and by assumptions that males tend to bring to a text. Very often this approach is used with a *literary* interpretation, in which the text is studied as a literary text, a piece of literature. This common modern approach is extremely valuable, because we do have a text before us, and, as the literary critics tell us, a text only has meaning as it is read and interpreted, in much the same way as a score of music only makes sense when it is played.

Others again take a *theological* approach, and interpret the text as a theological document. Theology, however, is not done in a vacuum, either. Very often our experiences and circumstances – sociological, political, and other – have an effect in shaping our theology.

Some readers approach the biblical text from an *historical* perspective. This is often the case particularly with the gospels, because of people's desire to find out what the historical Jesus was really like. This is a legitimate interest, but again it needs to be remembered that our understanding of history is also culturally determined. Our Western Anglo-Saxon view of history will not be the same as that of the Australian Aborigine or the Melanesian.

Two main dangers are common to all approaches. The first is to read present circumstances back into the text. To put it simply, the danger is to assume that Mark thinks and writes, and understands the world, as we do. Although we can never get inside Mark's head, we do need to make the effort to understand him as he would have wanted to be understood. We need to try to 'see the joke', while always acknowledging that we are doing so as outsiders. The other danger is to adopt only one approach in interpreting the text, as if that were the only legitimate approach. Things are never as simple as that! There is something to be learnt from *all* approaches, and this commentary will make at least some use of those that have been mentioned.

In a way it is right that the gospel of Mark should be approached and understood in many different ways. What Mark gives us is Word of God, and that word is always very much a living word, not one confined to letters and words on a printed page. As a living word, it speaks to people in various ways, with special significance or meaning, depending on their particular circumstances. God's word wraps itself in the language, circumstances and experiences of the people for whom it is meant.

To go further: Just as the interpreter comes to the text wearing blinkers of various kinds, the biblical authors also write within a particular social and cultural context. Their writing is not done in a vacuum, either. They write with a certain view, a certain background, certain preconceptions, which all have an effect on the way in which they write. It is important not only to view the text against the background of the original cultural and social environment, but also to see the text itself as being embedded in that environment. Language itself is a cultural phenomenon. In addition, all the gospel writers have experienced in some way the risen Christ, and so they understand and interpret the pre-Easter Jesus in the light of that faith-creating experience. So the language of Mark does not simply inform, but also performs. It proclaims, and it evokes a response. The author hopes that the word will engage his audience in the same way as it has engaged him. He wants his readers to come under the domination of him who dominates his story: Jesus.

Questions must also be asked about those who originally heard or read this gospel: What are their circumstances? How did they understand the text? What was the relationship between the author and his listeners or readers? These questions make the interpreting of the biblical text a highly exciting and interesting exercise! And when the text comes to us in the form of a story – with all that is involved in the telling and interpretation of stories – then the excitement is sharpened and intensified.

We do not have the original manuscript of Mark's gospel. In

the text that we do have, it is obvious that translation has taken place. Jesus spoke mainly Aramaic, but the gospels are written in Greek. A linguistic change has taken place, and all such change involves interpretation; it is simply not possible to translate without interpreting. This is not to say that Mark translated from a *written* text. The tradition that he received would have come to him, at least in part, in oral form, and some of that material would have been in Aramaic. At some stage, this material was translated. Translation, and even simply the writing down of oral traditions, involves interpretation of some kind.

Mark's story is not that of an eyewitness: he makes use of material received from tradition. This is not to say that he is simply an editor. It is what he does with the tradition which makes his gospel unique. Some scholars spend much of their energy trying to uncover the sources and traditions behind the written text as we have it. This is a valid and important exercise, but this particular commentary does not follow this approach.

Mark's gospel intends to help readers and listeners come to terms with Jesus and the significance of his life, particularly his death and resurrection. It is clear that the latter two events were central in the teaching that took place in Christian communities, and that they were meant to shape the lives of Christians. About a third of Mark's gospel is devoted to the events of the last week of Jesus' life. Questions about Jesus were important for those of the Jewish tradition who had to come to terms with a Messiah who had suffered and died, and had then become a model for the Christian community in their suffering and dying. At the same time, these questions were important also for those coming from a Gentile tradition, who would not have expected a 'son of God' (an idea not foreign to Greeks) to come from the backwaters of Palestine, let alone die as a criminal on a Roman cross, and then be proclaimed as the living, resurrected Lord. Those who had seen and heard the Jesus of history had to explain him to those who had not. But once those original followers of Jesus had died, then the Christian communities, and others who were interested in the Christian message, were left with only the tradition. As previously mentioned, Mark was in this position himself, and the rather strange ending of his gospel can perhaps be understood in the light of this situation, which applied also to his listeners or readers (see commentary on 16:1-8).

Mark's gospel is not a biography of Jesus; there are too many gaps! Mark crowds everything into one year of Jesus' life, and ultimately concentrates on one week! It is a story, and a good story, because it is good news. It is, therefore, a kind of *preaching*. Mark is not only interested in telling a story about Jesus, but also wishes to proclaim Jesus as the good news of God. As in all good proclamation of God's word, Mark wants his audience to see themselves in the story: it is their story too. This story is for them, and it concerns and involves them.

Like all good stories, Mark's gospel can be read or heard at various levels. It is possible that the author himself was not always aware of the depths in his gospel. When reading a commentary such as this, one might sometimes be tempted to ask: 'Did Mark consciously think of all these things?' So much seems to be wrung out of the text! The situation can be compared to that of anthropologists when they observe another culture. If they ask a local person, 'Why do you do things like this?' almost invariably the answer will be, 'Because we have always done it this way'. This is not helpful to the anthropologist! People in any culture seldom know *why* they do things: that is just the way they do them.

A similar situation exists in relation to literary texts. Authors are not always able to explain why they wrote as they did, and are not always conscious of the various forces which shape their writing. An outsider, however, can sometimes detect these things more clearly. In the case of New Testament writers, there is always the strong possibility that the Old Testament is the source of many ideas, even when it is not directly quoted or referred to. It is therefore legitimate for interpreters of Mark to look for Old Testament references, images, and illustrations in the text. Mark may not have consciously used these references, but his thinking would have been so steeped in the Old Testament, that it unconsciously formed his images, and his language generally. Other writers may be so influenced by Greek philosophy, for example, that their writing is expressed, unconsciously, in those terms. In the same way, when pastors preach, they draw on all sorts of sources, consciously and unconsciously. They cannot help but be influenced by what they have read and heard.

It has been mentioned a number of times that Mark is writing or telling a good story. It would be interesting to know how the gospel was first used. The first hearers certainly did not all have their own copies! Was it read aloud? Was it even acted out in some way? Was it read or heard in the way that we often read or hear it: in shorter sections at a time? Or was it told and heard in its entirety? I suspect the latter. Mark was writing to Christians who already knew the story, and who enjoyed hearing it again and again. There are points in the story where one can almost imagine the readers or listeners smiling or laughing to themselves, because they know how the story goes, they know the ending! As in the case of many good stories, the more they would have heard it the more they would have got out of it, and in this way it would have increasingly become *their* story.

The skill of Mark as a storyteller is shown in his structuring of the plot. He repeats certain key elements in the story, which serve as clues to the audience. This repetition does not occur along a straight line, but rather in a circular fashion. It has been called the echo system. But the circles are progressive, that is, readers are not brought back to the same place they were before, but are led to a new point which provides a clearer understanding. Mark often introduces a character, or an important thought, in a rather casual way. However, these apparently offhand references to a character or event sometimes become an important motif for readers to watch out for later in the gospel. For example, in 3:14 Mark mentions the twelve as those whom Jesus chose 'to be with him'. This is a seemingly insignificant phrase, but Mark wishes his readers to remember it in relation to the failure of the twelve to 'be with' Jesus in his time of testing and trial. In 14:67 Peter is accused of having been 'with' Jesus, an accusation which he vehemently denies.

Another storytelling device that Mark makes good use of is that of contrast. Jesus stands in contrast to Peter; the disciples stand in contrast to the crowds; people from Galilee stand in contrast to those from Jerusalem. The structure of the gospel as a whole can be seen as being based on a series of contrasts: between Jesus and those who are opposed to him; between the disciples and Jesus; between those who are insiders and those who are outsiders. Contrast and conflict are very old storytelling techniques, which are often used by writers to build dramatic tension.

A third storytelling skill demonstrated by Mark is that of movement. He writes in the present tense, and his gospel moves along at a brisk pace. He makes frequent use of the word 'immediately'. There are swift changes of scene. The events which are recorded appear at first to be only loosely connected, or even unrelated, but closer examination shows that they are often quite tightly knit. There is a strong movement toward a climax, and the story has a clear goal. The narrative does not drag. The story also has strong tragic elements. Jesus, the hero, is faced with opposition, but he defeats the opposition, and leaves them shaking their heads in wonder. But just when he seems to be on top of everything – literally on top of the mountain, where he is revealed in glory as Son of God – he becomes acutely aware that, despite all the glory and success, he must go to Jerusalem, and there meet his death at the hands of violent and wicked forces. The hero is rejected. He must die. The readers of the gospel, of course, are aware right from the beginning that this is his fate, and they also know that this fate is one which they themselves might have to face.

Finally, Mark's gospel makes good use of irony, a frequent feature of good stories, especially those with an element of tragedy. Irony is only effective, however, when the readers already know the story. Mark's readers are able to relish the irony of much of what happens and is said, because they already know the story; they have heard it before. This sometimes brings a touch of humour, even fun, into the telling and hearing of the gospel story. Oppressed people and minority groups are known for their sense of humour; it keeps them sane!

## Author! Author!

Mark's gospel itself tells us nothing about the author. The title that we now use is a later addition. It is an early tradition which identifies the author as a person called Mark. He is not one of the twelve disciples or apostles. The tradition recorded in Papias (second century) says that Mark worked with Peter, and that his gospel is an interpretation of material received from that apostle. In his first letter, Peter makes reference to someone with the words 'my son Mark' (5:13). There is a John Mark mentioned in Acts 12:12,25, and a Mark mentioned in Colossians 4:10; 2 Timothy 4:11; and Philemon 24. Mark, however, was a common Latin name, and so we are left, in the end, with only the early tradition. The text itself gives us no clue regarding the author. Since apostolic authority became important for Christian writings, it is not surprising that the gospel was linked with an apostle. The idea that the gospel was written from Rome is based mainly on the tradition of the link between Peter and Mark, and this leaves room for doubt as to whether it really did originate in that city.

## More Than One Story

It has been recognised for a long time that there is a close relationship between the gospels, especially the first three, Matthew, Mark and Luke. These are called the synoptic gospels, because they present a very similar picture of Jesus, often in the same or similar words. If the three are placed side by side in parallel columns, it can quickly be seen that they are linguistically very similar in many passages, too much so for it to be coincidental. Either there is a dependency of one or two on the other, or all three have made use of a common source. The following situation exists: Mark and Luke have material in common which is not found in Matthew; Mark and Matthew have material in common which is not found in Luke; there is material that all three have in common; and, in a few cases, Matthew and Luke have material in common which is not found in Mark.

By far the majority of modern scholars believe that Mark was the first gospel to be written, and that Matthew and Luke independently used Mark as a source for their accounts. Dr H.P. Hamann, in his commentary on Matthew in this series, argues that Matthew's gospel was the first to be written, and that the others are dependent on it. His is a valid, but minority, opinion. These are matters of theory, but it is a highly plausible view that Mark is the first gospel, that Matthew and Luke made use of him independently of each other, and that Matthew and Luke had access to another common source which was not available to Mark. This special source is often called Q, the first letter of the German word for 'source'. This source is said to have consisted mainly of Jesus' sayings. It is only an hypothesis that such a source existed. No document has ever been found, although the discovery of the Gospel of Thomas, which contains alleged sayings of Jesus not found in the New Testament, suggests that a collection, or collections, of Jesus' sayings may have existed.

Stories in Mark's gospel are usually longer and more detailed than the parallels in Matthew and Luke. It would appear that the latter two have abbreviated and polished Mark, rather than that Mark has expanded their accounts. Mark's rather colloquial way of writing has been changed into a more polished literary style by Matthew and Luke. A study of the texts placed side by side also reveals that additions, alterations, and omissions have been made by Matthew and Luke in relation to Mark, in order to develop their own particular themes and directions.

The theory that Mark is the original gospel raises the question of why Matthew and Luke decided to write their own gospels when Mark was already available to them. A simple answer would be that they wished to communicate the story of Mark's Jesus in their own way, and for their own situations.

Mark's relationship with John is quite different from that with Matthew and Luke. They have very little vocabulary and style in common, and their understanding of Jesus also differs quite significantly. The material that they do have in common centres on the last week in Jesus' life, which is not surprising, since that story must have been very well known in all Christian communities.

## The Man's Got Style

Mark's style is popular, rather than polished and literary. His Greek is popular Greek, possibly reflecting the kind of language used by people living in ghettos, which may indicate something of the social and political position of his readers. Possibly they were a minority group being subjected to a certain amount of pressure, both from within their own group, as well as from outside. Mark's sentence structure is simple, and his narrative technique straightforward. His miracle stories, for example, invariably follow the same pattern: a person in a hopeless situation is brought to Jesus, who gives help or effects a cure, which produces a reaction from the observers.

Stories are often narrated in the present tense. This has the advantage of drawing readers into the action, so that they become participants, at least in imagination, in the story. The use of the past tense, on the other hand, can have the effect of distancing readers from the characters in a story. Mark uses the Semitic narrative practice of beginning nearly every new incident with the word 'and'. It functions in a similar way to the English 'and then', which we use very much in our oral storytelling. This commentary tries as much as possible to follow Mark's story along the lines (or around the circles!) that he himself has used. He has a simple technique for making changes of scene in his drama: he simply moves his character, Jesus, from one place to another, while other people follow or crowd around. In chapter 3, for example, Mark links each episode with some movement of Jesus: to the synagogue (v 1), the sea (v 7), a mountain (v 13), a house (v 20). Each movement sees Jesus accompanied by a group of people, often a large crowd. This is a standard literary device which Mark uses in telling his story.

Jesus is very much to the fore throughout the gospel. So central is he, that it is possible for Mark to tell long sections of his story without once mentioning him by name.

## When and Where?

On the basis of Mark 13, it would seem best to date the gospel at about the time of the destruction of Jerusalem by the Romans, which took place during the war of 66-70 AD. If Matthew and Luke used Mark as a source, his gospel has to be dated before them, which leaves us with 65-75 AD as the likely period in which Mark was written. Some scholars think that Jesus' prediction of the destruction of the temple was put into his mouth after the event, but it is not necessary to take this view. Jesus did not have to have divine foreknowledge in order to make such a prediction. Conditions were such in Palestine that many a prophet was predicting the end-days. John the Baptist, for example, was one who saw the writing on the wall, as did others like the Essenes, who left Jerusalem for the desert in preparation for the end. This suggests that there is no need to date the gospel after the destruction of the temple.

Mark's association with Peter, according to tradition, has led to the view that his gospel originated in Rome. This theory gains support from Mark's use of Latin words, and his explanation of Jewish customs and translation of Jewish terms, which suggests that some of his readers, perhaps the majority, were not Jews. Others have suggested Alexandria in Egypt as the gospel's place of origin: Eusebius records the tradition that Mark was the first bishop of that city. However, the absence of an account of Jesus' flight to Egypt would seem strange in a gospel supposedly originating from that country. Other places, such as Antioch, have also been suggested. Rome seems to be the most widely favoured possibility. However, the obvious bias that Mark shows toward Galilee suggests that he might well have been a spokesperson for the Galilean Christians, who found themselves in conflict with the more traditional and influential Jerusalem Christian community. In this case, Galilee may well be the gospel's place of origin.

## The Reason for Writing

As already mentioned, the readers of this gospel are Christians who already know the story, so it is not written to convert or convince them. Its purpose is rather to give encouragement to a minority group being subjected to pressure, and facing the threat of persecution, presumably from the Roman authorities, but possibly also from others, such as Jewish groups in their local community.

But there is also another kind of pressure which is affecting the group, one that is internal rather than external. It is interesting to note that the gospel does not vilify the opponents of Jesus, shows little evidence of an 'us versus them' mentality, and does not see the world as being evil. The problems are seen as coming from within the Christian community itself, rather than from some external opposition. Mark's purpose, then, is to set matters straight within the community. The questions are: How are members of the community to relate to one another? More importantly, how is the community to make the transitions that need to be made, if they are to take the message of Jesus seriously? What is it that is distinctive about being Christian in contrast to following Judaism? These are crucial questions. Mark's community is making a transition and, like a sea crossing, the journey is not always plain sailing, but is often rough.

Jesus is the example and, above all, the leader, as the community faces these complex difficulties. He is central in the story, and everything focuses on him. He is seen as the one who has already made the transition, and who stands with those who are still rowing against the wind. He is also the model of a martyr: the one who gives the good confession, remains faithful, and is the true disciple. The theme of discipleship is strong in this gospel, but the disciples themselves stand in contrast to Jesus, rather than as models of discipleship for the readers. They often represent what Christians should avoid!

One of Mark's central concerns is the vexing question, for Christian communities, of what is clean and what is unclean in the light of Jesus' message, and particularly in the light of his death. Mark's story can be simply stated as that of the Clean One who associates with the unclean. This theme will form one of the focuses for this commentary. It was the understanding of this matter which ultimately caused the separation between synagogue and church. Exactly when that separation actually took place is very difficult to determine; no doubt it occurred at different places at various times and in various ways. Mark wishes to encourage his readers to make the transition from synagogue to church, and to know that Jesus is present with them as they do so. He also wants to show that Christians no longer need to look to Jerusalem as their place of revelation and authority. Jerusalem Christians still wished to maintain their links with Judaism and, by their standards, many in Mark's community were probably regarded as unclean. Mark underlines the authority of Jesus, who is with them in their community, in opposition to the authority of those from Jerusalem. His is an authority which extends the boundaries of God's mercy, and his call to be his people, to include those who are unclean by Jerusalem standards.

At this stage, an explanation of the terms 'clean' and 'unclean' needs to be given. These terms do not relate to matters of morality. In our Western tradition, we tend to think of holiness and purity in moral terms. However, when Mark talks about an unclean spirit or the spirit of holiness, he is not primarily thinking in terms of morality. In biblical terms, there are three things which profane or make unclean: leprosy (which is believed to affect objects and houses, as well as people); sexual emissions (whether of male or female), sexual intercourse, and menstrual blood; corpses, and any place, person or thing associated with a dead body. Certain foods are also regarded as being unclean, and are therefore forbidden, the most well-known being meat from pigs. Certain people are also regarded as unclean: Gentiles, people who do not observe the rituals and traditions, and people who live and act beyond the boundaries in any way. Some people are virtually permanently unclean. Some, however, may be made clean by the performance of certain rituals, and/or the observance of certain prohibitions.

Something is unclean if it is outside the boundaries; something is clean or holy if it is within the boundaries. Gentiles, for example, are seen as being outside the boundaries of what is clean, because they do not observe such things as circumcision, the sabbath, and the other laws and traditions which come from the holy God. Holiness is determined by God and his will. He is seen as setting his people apart, and drawing the boundaries for them. Anyone who steps across the boundaries becomes unclean. An unclean spirit is a spirit which causes a person to be on the outside. In Mark's story, those who are, according to a literal translation, 'in an unclean spirit' are often *outside* of their village, town, or community. During Israel's journey to the promised land, whatever was unclean was expelled from their camp. The unclean *belongs* outside. Impurity excludes a person or thing from the divine presence. The 'spirit of holiness', however, brings a person inside. Leviticus 11-17 gives examples of what being clean and unclean meant in practice.

## The Shape of the Story

It seems best to talk about the shape of the story, rather than giving an outline of its contents. An outline suggests a logical, straight-line development or progression. Mark's story does not follow that pattern. Like all stories, however, it has a beginning, a middle, and an end. The beginning of the story is Jesus' baptism, the middle is chapter 9 with the account of his transfiguration, and the end is his crucifixion and resurrection. At each of these three points in the story the declaration is made: Jesus is Son of God (1:11; 9:7; 15:39).

Jesus dominates the story, but other characters are introduced along the way. All these people misunderstand Jesus to some degree: the authorities, the disciples, the crowds. In relation to the three confessions of Jesus as Son of God, the question that is raised is: Who is Jesus? The answers that are given are all seen as being inadequate: Jesus is more than a prophet, more than the Christ, more than the Son of David, more than a man of God. Other crucial themes occur: Who is inside, who is outside? Who is clean, who is unclean? Who hears and sees, who still does not understand? Who has authority, who must be silent?

The story revolves around the three confessions. Readers know right from the beginning that Jesus is Son of God, so there is not really a progression, but rather various ways of saying the same thing. This results in repetition. In the first half of the story, for example, there are two accounts of Jesus feeding large numbers of people, two healings of people who are blind, a number of crossings of the lake, and two exorcisms.

After chapter 9 and the transfiguration, the story-line (story-circle might be a better expression) changes. There are less accounts of miracles, and more situations of people questioning Jesus. The scene also shifts from Galilee to Jerusalem, and the tension rises. Jesus' struggle is now not so much with the unclean and demonic powers of sickness, and the chaotic forces in nature, but rather with the unclean and demonic forces in the institutions of power: the temple and the Roman legal system. Here again, the story follows a circular path rather than proceeding in a straight line. Jesus is involved in debates on various issues, predictions are made about the future of the temple, and clues are given about the final outcome of Jesus' visit to the centre of power. The cross, which already casts its shadow over the first eight chapters, does so in a different way in the last eight.

The rather strange ending to the story could well suggest to the original readers or hearers, and also to us, that this story is not yet finished. Jesus, the Son of God, goes ahead of his people, and calls them to meet with him, and to follow him. It is the never-ending story, the living Word which has to be appropriated anew in different times and different situations.

# THE COMMENTARY

## PART 1: 1:1-4:34

*The beginning of the gospel of Jesus Christ, 1:1-8*

¹ **The beginning of the gospel of Jesus Christ, the Son of God.**[a]
² As it is written in Isaiah the prophet[b]
'Behold, I send my messenger before thy face,
who shall prepare thy way;
³ the voice of one crying in the wilderness:
Prepare the way of the Lord,
make his paths straight —'
⁴ John the baptizer appeared[c] in the wilderness, preaching a baptism of repentance for the forgiveness of sins. ⁵ And there went out to him all the country of Judea, and all the people of Jerusalem; and they were baptized by him in the river Jordan, confessing their sins. ⁶ Now John was clothed with camel's hair, and had a leather girdle around his waist, and ate locusts and wild honey. ⁷ And he preached, saying, 'After me comes he who is mightier than I, the thong of whose sandals I am not worthy to stoop down and untie. ⁸ I have baptized you with water; but he will baptize you with the Holy Spirit.'

[a] Other ancient authorities omit *the Son of God*
[b] Other ancient authorities read *in the prophets*
[c] Other ancient authorities read *John was baptizing*

The gospel begins and ends very abruptly, that is, if we take 16:18 to be the original ending. This abruptness has led some scholars to speculate that there was another beginning to the gospel, as well as another ending, which have somehow been lost, and that 1:1 is simply a later editorial comment, a heading to mark the beginning of the book. There is no direct manuscript evidence for this, however. Some would argue that the manuscript variations in 1:1 suggest a lost original beginning to the gospel, but this remains speculation. We simply have to work with the text that we have before us.

Mark says that the gospel begins with **Jesus Christ**. 1 This is the only time that Mark refers to Jesus with this full title, which gives some support to the idea that this introduction was added later. Jesus dominates Mark's story. He is the beginning of the good news. The word **gospel**, in a secular context, often conveys the idea of an announcement of victory, and the idea that a better life is on the way. It can refer not only to the proclamation itself, but also to the effect of that news or proclamation.

**The beginning** can be understood in several ways. It can be seen as standing in contrast to the 'bad news' of the old Jewish order which was centred on Jerusalem and the temple. That order is finished, and it is the good news that is now beginning. Or it can mean that this is merely the beginning of the gospel, and that for Christians there is still much more to come. Or, finally, it can be seen as referring to what preceded the presence of Jesus, namely, the work of Isaiah and John the Baptist. In some way, they and their work are seen as the beginning of the gospel.

**Christ** is a very early title for Jesus which was soon also used as a name. That is how Mark uses it here. For non-Jews the title would not have meant very much. In relation to Jewish readers, Mark's use of the term appears to clearly reject any idea of Jesus as a nationalistic Messiah. (The word 'Christ' is Greek. The Hebrew term is 'Messiah'. The literal meaning of both words is 'the anointed one'.)

Some manuscripts omit the phrase **the Son of God**. Even if it did not originally appear in this verse, the title is very significant and important for Mark: it occurs in three key passages, at crucial points in the story (1:11; 9:7; 15:39). Although the exact phrase is not used at 14:61, the identification of Jesus as the Christ who is 'the Son of the Blessed' (God) is very significant there in Mark's account of the trial of Jesus. The expression is the climax to the implied question throughout the gospel: What kind of Christ is Jesus, if he is Christ at all? A similar identification of Jesus is made by unclean spirits or demonic powers, but they are commanded to be quiet (see 3:11; 5:7). The irony of Mark's story is that those outside the boundaries know him, while those inside do not.

Mark has included no stories about Jesus' birth. Did he know them? If he did, why did he omit them? Perhaps Mark is trying to indicate that Jesus is not simply of human origin, but that he has his origins already in the word and prophecy of Isaiah. This would mean that the gospel does, in some way, already begin with Isaiah's prophecy. Or does Mark wish to express some continuity between the Old Covenant and Jesus? Certainly, many New Testament writers see Jesus as the fulfilment of Old Testament prophecy.

In Mark this is particularly apparent in his account of Jesus' suffering and death. By mentioning Isaiah, however, Mark may be wishing to link John the Baptist more directly with Jesus. The most likely reason for referring to Isaiah is simply to introduce John the Baptist. Isaiah is very much the prophet of the new age which God is about to bring in for his people, a time in which also Gentiles will come under God's favour.

John the Baptist is important because his work involves washing, making clean what is unclean. Mark clearly sees John merely as the forerunner of the Clean One. His gospel climaxes with the confession of the Gentile, an unclean person, at the foot of the cross (15:39). John the Baptist, then, by being linked with Isaiah, the prophet of God's mission to the Gentiles, also is the one who prepares the way for this confession by the Gentile soldier.

It is interesting that Mark begins his story with an Old Testament quotation introduced with the words: **As it is written**. The Jews believed in a God who writes! This became especially significant for them when their temple was destroyed, and they wanted to rediscover their roots. We can recall how, in Josiah's reform, the written word of God was found again, and read to the people, who then renewed their commitment to Yahweh. The scrolls of the sacred Torah, God's law, are still central today in Jewish worship, and it is not uncommon for tears to come to the eyes of worshippers as their hands reach out to touch the sacred text. In writing this gospel, Mark may unconsciously be claiming that the God who writes is here writing again.

The first part of the quotation itself does not actually come from Isaiah. Perhaps Mark sees Isaiah as *the* prophet, under whom all other prophets, and their message, can be subsumed. The first part of the quotation is from Malachi 3:1, and the second part from Isaiah 40:3. What the two passages have in common is the important phrase **the way**. Isaiah's words about preparing the way of the Lord are applied to John the Baptist, who now prepares and announces the way of the Lord. John prepares the way not only in his message, but also in his suffering and execution. Mark speaks of **the way** especially in connection with Jesus' suffering and death. John's suffering and execution announces and prepares the way that Jesus will follow. His way leads to Jerusalem, and to the cross (see 8:27; 9:33; 10:32). Being a disciple – an important theme in Mark's story – means following **the way**. We know from Acts that the Christian movement, at least in some centres, was known as 'the Way'. Mark's gospel is the story of Jesus' movement along the way, and his calling of followers to fall in behind him as he leads. Judaism was very much a way of living, rather than a way of thinking or believing. It did not have a dogmatic theology in which doctrines were important. We are always tempted to impose our own Western penchant for doctrines onto first century Judaism, but to do so would be to misrepresent it. Similarly, Christians were offering, first and foremost, a new way of living, rather than a new set of doctrines.

The way of **the Lord** means the way of God, rather than the way of Jesus. Significantly, and remarkably, Mark never has the disciples call Jesus 'Lord'.

The **wilderness**, or desert, was highly significant in Israel's history. It was seen as the place of testing, of preparation, of intimacy between God and his people. It was the place where God acted to save and protect. It was also often seen as the place for new beginnings, for getting ready, for getting one's life in order, in preparation for some great saving act of God. Perhaps most importantly for Mark, it was the place where God chose Israel as his son. Yet, at the same time, it was seen as the place of the unclean spirits! It lay outside God's boundaries of what was holy. God's great act of salvation for his people begins in unclean territory! A similar thing happened when God's people were in Egypt, that unclean place. Their saviour, Moses, came from outside, from the desert, where he had been for forty years with Jethro, the priest of Midian. Now Jesus, the new deliverer of his people, is proclaimed in the desert as bringing in the way of God. Israel's unclean origins are also referred to by the prophet Ezekiel: 'Your father was an Amorite, and your mother a Hittite' (Ezek 16:3).

The desert features prominently in Mark's understanding of Jesus and his mission. It is the place outside, the unclean place, yet it is the place to which God's people are called to return, and where they hear his call to be his people. It is where Jesus hears the voice of God declaring him to be his Son.

There was a community living in the area of the Dead Sea, at the time of Jesus, usually identified with the Essenes, but best known as the Qumran community. Their writings, the so-called Dead Sea Scrolls, which were discovered in 1947 and during the early 1950s, are still in the process of being published and translated. These writings are extremely valuable in helping scholars gain a clearer picture of the circumstances in which Christian communities came into existence. The community at Qumran (about 20 kilometres from Jerusalem) was a group who rejected the traditions of Jerusalem, and lived in the desert in anticipation of the coming Messiah and Teacher of Righteousness. Washings were an integral part of their ritual. It is possible that John the Baptist belonged at some stage to this community, although there are significant differences between him and Qumran.

In any kind of baptism, and certainly as it is understood **4** by Christians, the idea of a new beginning is very much to the fore. John probably understood his baptism more as a preparation, a ritual cleansing, in readiness for the way of the Lord.

John is in the desert **preaching**. This may not be the best way of expressing the Greek verb. The word refers to the public pronouncement made by a prophet who has been called by God. What he says is an announcement from God.

**Repentance** is a turning away from one's old life, and a movement toward the new life that comes from God. The literal meaning of the Greek word is to 'change one's mind'. However, Mark probably has in mind the Hebrew background, where 'repent' means 'return'. John's call, and also Jesus' call, is for Israel to return to its roots and origins in the desert, where God first called Israel to be his son, and from where the final great saving action of God will begin. It is the call to go out beyond the boundaries of the city, and to return to the desert.

**Forgiveness of sins** was seen as one of the characteristics of the new, messianic age. It involves the re-establishing of relationships. It is the mark of the new covenant which God promised to make with Israel (Jer 31:31-34).

John's baptism, which is part of the old order, is a preparation for the new, as is the whole mission and work of John himself. Yet it offers something which is regarded as being unique to the Christian sacrament: the forgiveness of sins. Matthew seems to deliberately avoid mentioning this aspect of John's baptism (Matt 3:11). We know that Paul came across Christian communities who knew only the baptism of John (Acts 19:1-7). Did they believe that they had received forgiveness through that baptism?

All the people from Judea and Jerusalem went out to **5** John. Mark does not record any condemnation of them by John, as there is in Matthew 3:7-12 and Luke 3:7-9. These people followed John's call to go out into the desert, and there return to their roots, but they were not able to go along with the one to whom John pointed: Jesus. Judea and Jerusalem turn out to be the centre of opposition to Jesus. It may be that there were some in Mark's community who were in agreement with John's call to repent, and who had even gone out to live in the desert as John did, but who could not accept the call of Jesus. Mark is gently, but firmly, drawing the line between Jesus and John, a line which the scribes and Pharisees were unprepared to cross, even though some of them may have been in basic agreement with the call of John. Clement of Alexandria speaks of the scribes and Pharisees as having been associated with John the Baptist.

At first glance it appears that Mark is concentrating on John the Baptist in the introduction to his gospel, but a closer examination reveals that the focus of attention is not John but Jesus, who is greater than John. What the two have in common is their belief that a critical time has arrived, a time which calls for decisive action. Judgment is imminent. Both Jesus and John are apocalyptists, that is, they call for faithfulness and for a change of life-style, because God is about to break in upon Israel in judgment and create a new kingdom. Both of them call people to go outside the boundaries again, to return to the desert, and there find the call of God for them to be his people.

John plays an important role in Mark's understanding of **6** Jesus. John's similarity to Elijah, in dress and in the task he performs, is also important. Elijah was the messenger of the covenant, who was expected to appear on the eve of the Messiah's coming. John's clothes (**camel's hair** and a **leather girdle**) symbolise his message and his role: that he is Elijah, who was expected to come to prepare the way of the Messiah. Malachi 4:5,6, the very last words of the Old Testament, tell of the sending of Elijah 'before the great and terrible day of the Lord comes', and how he 'will turn the hearts of fathers to their children and the hearts of children to their fathers'. It is quite likely that Mark had this passage in mind, and that he associated it with John. Elijah is an important figure in Mark's gospel, more important, for example, than Moses. The return of Elijah, which was a strong theme in apocalyptic thinking, played a role in shaping Mark's outlook and message.

The people come out to hear John, and they repent, confess their sins, and are baptised in preparation for the

Coming One. But it is this Coming One that John wishes to highlight, not himself. He makes it clear that he is the servant, and that Jesus is the master: **After me comes he who is mightier than I, the thong of whose sandals I am not worthy to stoop down and untie.** To carry someone's shoes, or to undo them, was the distinctive work of a slave. Not only is John clearly depicted as Jesus' servant, but also his baptism is shown to be a forerunner to the baptism of Jesus. It appears that some communities held John in very high esteem, regarding him even as a messiah, or at least as *the* prophet, the new Moses (see Deut 18:15). Maybe Mark was aware of this.

The baptism of John is **with water**, and so it is a ritual washing, similar to the ritual washings of Jewish tradition. It is a washing which signifies the coming age, a washing of preparation. The baptism of Jesus, however, is not a ritual which makes one clean simply in preparation for the coming kingdom of God, but is a baptism in the **Holy Spirit**, the Spirit of holiness. It is the Spirit which makes clean, not the ritual washings. The Spirit is the sign that the kingdom has come. Here we have the first clue from Mark about the work that Jesus will perform: he will bring the Spirit of holiness, the Clean Spirit. This Spirit who makes clean does not come through rituals and observance of traditions, but through Jesus himself. John is clean, and he calls people to become clean through his washing, but in comparison with Jesus, the Clean One, the holiness of John is worth nothing.

## *Jesus comes clean, 1:9-11*

⁹ **In those days Jesus came from Nazareth of Galilee and was baptized by John in the Jordan.** ¹⁰ **And when he came up out of the water, immediately he saw the heavens opened and the Spirit descending upon him like a dove;** ¹¹ **and a voice came from heaven, 'Thou art my beloved Son;ᵈ with thee I am well pleased.'**

ᵈ Or *my Son, my* (or *the*) *Beloved*

**In those days** is not an insignificant expression. They are the exact words that were used by the Old Testament prophets when they spoke about the final actions of God to judge, redeem, and restore his people. John the Baptist is the forerunner to these days. These days are now here because of the presence of Jesus. He himself is the great act of God in the last times.

Jesus comes **from Nazareth**. This is how he is identified here, as also at his resurrection (16:6). There was an early group of Christians called Nazarenes, but whether Mark was aware of them is hard to say. Later in the gospel (6:1-6), Jesus is rejected in his home town, an event that would not have reflected favourably on those who called themselves Nazarenes. Mark makes no reference to a birth in Bethlehem as Matthew and Luke do (Matt 2:1; Luke 2:4).

Nazareth, which is in Galilee, was of little significance. As far as Jerusalem was concerned, Galilee was unclean territory. In 4 BC the kingdom of Herod the Great was divided into three, with Galilee forming the northern section. The region as a whole had been converted to Judaism only in 120 BC, so it was a relatively recent addition to Judaism. Mark makes the point here, very early in his gospel, that Jesus comes from unclean territory, not from the 'holy' area of Jerusalem. People from Galilee could not know God's law as well as those in Jerusalem, and were not expected to. What good thing could come from Nazareth? So Jesus is depicted, right here at the beginning, as the outsider, the 'law-less' one. Mark sees Galilee as standing in opposition to Jerusalem. It is very much a matter of the lone Galilean against all of Judea and Jerusalem.

Jesus joins the penitents in going out into the desert, to the region outside, where God first made his promises to his people, and called Israel his son (see Exod 4:22; Jer 2:2; Hos 11:1). Jesus shows solidarity with his people, by hearing the call of John and going out to the desert. But only Jesus himself hears the declaration that he is the Son of God: **Thou art my beloved Son; with thee I am well pleased**. This is not a word spoken to Israel, but to Jesus.

Jesus is baptised by John, but no reason for this is given. Mark does not focus on the baptism itself, but on the voice of God heard in connection with the baptism. For John and the crowds this is just another baptism. It is only Jesus who sees **the Spirit descending upon him like a dove**, and hears the voice from heaven. Only those Christians who are incorporated into Jesus can hear and see. Mark begins to develop his recurring theme: Jesus is only understood, heard, and seen by those who are 'inside'. On the other hand, to those *claiming* to be inside, he remains hidden, a riddle. This is often called the 'messianic secret', but it is not so much a secret as a riddle or mystery.

Jesus comes up **out of the water**. Being overwhelmed with water was a common way of expressing the judgment of God. God used water to execute judgment on his creation

(Gen 6,7) and on the Egyptians (Exod 14). The expression is used in a figurative sense in the Psalms (see Ps 18:4,16; 42:7; 69:1,2). Jesus' baptism, in one sense, means that he comes under the judgment of God. Yet the judgment, finally, is in his favour! He is Son of God, and is given the Spirit of holiness, which now sets him apart to be the Holy One of God.

Here at the beginning, Mark provides a pointer to the end of his story, where Jesus is again declared to be Son of God (15:39). There is a clear link between Jesus' baptism and his death. In both events he is shown to be under the judgment of God, and at the same time is declared to be holy and God's Son. There may also be a parallel between the heavens opening, or ripping, and the opening or ripping of the temple curtain at Jesus' death (15:38). His baptism, like his crucifixion, indicates who Jesus is: the Son of God. His death is also his 'cleansing'. The presence of the Spirit at his baptism is paralleled by the Spirit's presence at his death.

This account of Jesus' baptism, tantalising in its brevity, is a vital clue to the mystery of who Jesus is. It also encourages those in Mark's community, who have been baptised, to know that God's validation of them has been spoken to them too, and that the baptism of death, which they face, will be *their* ultimate cleansing in the Spirit of holiness.

The Spirit is the promised gift of God for the new covenant, the new day that God would bring in, as Isaiah prophesied (32:15; 44:3; 63:10-14).

**11** The reader is informed, right at the beginning, that this person Jesus has been declared Son of God **from heaven**, that is, from God. Who is Jesus? is the underlying question that is constantly asked. To Mark's readers, all the answers that people give are ironical, because they have already been told what *God's* answer to this question is! Jesus goes out, with his fellow-Israelites, to the desert, the place of Israel's origins as the son of God. But only Jesus hears the voice of God calling him to sonship. The title, Son of God, no longer applies only to people of a particular race or ethnic background, is no longer tied to particular traditions, but now refers to a new Son, a new Man, Jesus Christ. As Son of God he reunites all of humanity with God, making possible also the return of those who are outside of Israel. The opening of the heavens possibly echoes Isaiah 64:1, where the prophet expresses the hope that God will come breaking in with some new saving action.

The **voice** comes **from heaven**, that is, from God. The confession that Jesus is Son of God can come ultimately only from God. Here God acknowledges Jesus as his Son. Later, Peter, as the representative of the community of Christians, acknowledges Jesus as the Christ (8:29), but does not get it quite right, because he does not see that Jesus is the Son of God. He is put right on the mountain where Jesus is transfigured, and God's voice declares the true identity of Jesus (9:7). Finally, the centurion at the foot of Jesus' cross, as the representative of the Gentile community, acknowledges him as the Son of God (15:39). This Gentile knows what even Peter, a pillar of the Jerusalem church, had not properly comprehended.

As Son of God, Jesus has all the characteristics of God, chief of which is holiness. He is acknowledged by God as the Clean One. That is why the Holy Spirit, the Spirit of holiness, is given to him. It is interesting that for Mark the announcement of Jesus as Son of God occurs in his baptism, and not, as for Paul, in his resurrection (see Rom 1:4 where 'Son of God' and 'Spirit of holiness' are again linked).

Mark may have had Psalm 2 in mind, seeing Jesus' baptism as his messianic coronation. Alternatively, he may have been thinking of Isaiah 42:1, in which case Jesus' baptism is seen as that of the Suffering Servant, and is connected with his death. Both are possible, but it would seem that the focus in Jesus' baptism is not so much on him as king or prophet, but as the one who is clean, the one who is declared in the desert to be the new Son of God. This is accentuated in the episode that follows.

## *The unclean tests Jesus, 1:12,13*

**¹² The Spirit immediately drove him out into the wilderness. ¹³ And he was in the wilderness forty days, tempted by Satan, and he was with the wild beasts; and the angels ministered to him.**

Jesus is immediately cast out into the desert. His expulsion is the work of the Spirit, who creates new boundaries between what is clean and what is unclean. The Spirit of holiness leads Jesus into the desert, the place of the unclean and anti-God forces, the place that is outside. The Spirit of holiness leads the Holy One across the lines, across the boundaries. The language here consists of terminology associated with demonic exorcism. Jesus is 'driven out', or 'cast out', the same word that is used when Jesus himself exorcises! Already the cross looms, for there Jesus dies as the one who is expelled, the one who is outside. To be on the outside is death.

Jesus goes out into the desert to begin the battle with Satan on Satan's own ground. He is thus initiated into his ministry, which involves overcoming the powers of evil, by facing temptation in the desert. Temptation, or testing, is not to be understood in a moralistic sense. It is not Jesus' morals that are under attack, but his very claim to be the holy Son of God. Here in the desert, Satan attempts to make Jesus unclean. But the Clean One of God is chosen by God to become the leader of his new people, a people who are called out of the unclean region into his kingdom. This is the new and saving action of God which is about to take place in and through the life of Jesus.

13 The **forty days** that Jesus was in the wilderness brings to the readers' mind the forty years of testing that Israel, the son of God, went through while travelling in the desert. Israel failed that test and became unclean. There in the desert, at Sinai, God gave them his laws which distinguished between what was clean and unclean. The forty days also call to mind Elijah, the great prophet of God, who spent forty days in the wilderness as a result of the uncleanness of the people who had contaminated themselves through worship of Baal. There was also Moses, who spent forty days with the Lord, without food or drink, while the covenant was made between Yahweh and Israel (Exod 34:28).

**Satan** is the obstructionist, the adversary, the accuser. At first the word was used for the evil spirit or desire which existed in all humans. Later, this was objectified as a separate being outside of the human psyche.

Mark mentions **wild beasts** as being with Jesus. The beasts represent the desolation and anti-God forces of the desert. However, passages such as Isaiah 11:6 and Hosea 2:18 speak of the expectation that in the messianic age the Messiah and the wild beasts would coexist in peace. The rather peaceful impression of the words, **he was with the wild beasts**, suggests that this is the intended understanding. Support for this interpretation is provided by a remarkable passage in the Testament of Naphtali at 8:4: 'If you do good my children, both men and angels will bless you, and the devil shall flee from you, and the wild beasts shall fear you, and the Lord shall love you'. The beasts are subject to the Righteous Man as they were to the original Adam. The unclean, the demonic, stands under the authority of the Clean One.

This is reinforced by the mention of **the angels** who, as messengers from God, minister to Jesus. God stands beside his holy Son, who has not lost his holiness in the face of temptation. In spite of stepping across the boundary into the realm of the unclean, Jesus remains clean, and so breaks down the boundary. This little episode sets the stage, in very simple but dramatic fashion, for Mark's story. Jesus is the Man possessed by the Spirit of holiness, and he does battle with the spirits who are unclean and unholy, and who dehumanise the human beings who are possessed by them. Jesus extends the boundaries by bringing also the unclean powers under his authority. This means that the followers of Jesus are also called to struggle with the demons, with all those diabolical powers which threaten to destroy the creation of God and his purpose for his world. They are called to extend the boundaries of God's holiness into the unclean realm, which has been overcome and bound by Jesus. This is why the risen Jesus tells his disciples that he goes ahead of them into Galilee, which involves crossing the borders set by Jerusalem, and going into unclean territory (16:7).

It can be noted that Mark does not explicitly state that Jesus won the fight out in the wilderness. It is important to read Mark first of all for himself, without making comparisons with Matthew or Luke. Two things can be said. First, Mark sees Jesus' whole life as being a temptation or testing by Satan, a struggle with the evil powers, which is only completed with the great exorcism on the cross. Secondly, Mark's interest at this point is as much in the fact that Jesus is outside in the desert, as it is in his temptation by Satan.

## *Jesus picks up the theme, 1:14,15*

**¹⁴ Now after John was arrested, Jesus came into Galilee, preaching the gospel of God, ¹⁵ and saying, 'The time is fulfilled, and the kingdom of God is at hand; repent, and believe in the gospel.'**

John is spoken about in similar terms to Jesus: both are **arrested** or, more literally, handed over or betrayed. John's fate foreshadows that of Jesus, who is greater than his servant John. The action of the betrayer was regarded by many early Christian communities as *the* unclean act against the Clean One. Mark is preparing his readers for what is to follow later in the gospel. This verse also suggests the possibility that it was the arrest of John which triggered something in Jesus, causing him to begin his ministry against the unclean powers. John's arrest was an act of gross injustice perpetrated by a political figure, and this may have been a turning point for Jesus, an event which stung him into action.

The ministry of Jesus begins and continues predominantly in **Galilee** until the very last week. This places Jesus out in 'the sticks', far away from the holy city and its sacred temple, distant from the centre of the Jewish world, the place of the holy revelation and presence of God. It puts him beyond the boundaries of holiness into the area of the unclean. Socially, Galilee was constantly exposed to foreigners, those who were outside of Israel and did not observe the law of Moses. Through this simple geographical device of locating the events of his gospel in Galilee, Mark encourages his readers by saying that even if they are on the fringes, even if they are a minority group, the marginalised of their society, or the unclean of their religious community, in Jesus they have someone who is with them out there on the edge. The gospel is proclaimed to those on the edges, those, in fact, whom some would regard as having gone over the edge! The gospel is God's good news for them, that in Jesus they are in the centre of God's grace and mercy. This liberates them from the oppression of other systems, because they are now called to live and walk in the way of Jesus. This is the way of the kingdom of God, which is not based on power and oppression, but on creating a new order where the powers of chaos are broken. The Clean offers fellowship to the unclean. The Son of God offers the kingdom to the powerless, the rejects. They are called to go back into the desert, to struggle with the evil powers there, to share Jesus' victory as the Son of God.

Verse 15 presents the theme of Jesus' proclamation. **The gospel of God** which he preaches, is the message that in Jesus himself, and his word, **the time is fulfilled,** and God's rule, or **kingdom**, is present. This message of good news calls for a response of repentance and faith.

Jesus is the fulfilment of time, the fulfilment of God's saving promise. All the Old Testament prophecies about the special day of the Lord – the day when God would restore his people and create a new covenant, destroy the powers which dehumanise and oppress, and free his people to live in a new creation of peace and justice – all these prophecies are now fulfilled in Jesus, in his work and words and, ultimately, in his death and resurrection.

**The kingdom of God** is clearly central to Jesus' preaching, teaching and miracles. Ultimately, his death and resurrection are to be understood as bringing in the kingdom of God. **Kingdom** is a poor choice of English word, because it suggests a locality. 'The rule of God' is much better and more accurate. This rule of God is not confined by ethnic or political boundaries, but is found in his Son, and in all those who are called to be with him. God's way of doing things, of being God, of ruling as king, is demonstrated and seen in Jesus, in his word and work. We need not spiritualise this kingdom, as if it were something only for the spirit or soul, or only for the next life. Jesus proclaims a kingdom in which broken bodies are healed, and where boundaries are extended to include the physically unclean and those who are not accepted in the social and religious communities. This kingdom is present now, with his coming.

**Kingdom** has political connotations in Jesus' preaching, and deliberately so. What distinguished Israel in the Old Testament from other nations was that they saw God as their king – that is, until they wanted to have a king like the other nations (see 1 Sam 8). Jesus brings a radically new thought into the society of his day. He does not preach a Jewish kingdom, one which would see the Jews liberated and independent of Rome. Nor does he preach a kingdom dominated by Rome or any other power. This means that his message of the kingdom is not politically quietistic, or supportive of the status quo. He preaches a kingdom of *God*, a kingdom where all power and authority, whether Jewish or Roman, is responsible to God, and where all abuse of power is rejected as demonic. It is a kingdom which brings good news, not bad news. All aspects of human existence, including money, sex and political power, come under the authority of God in this kingdom. It is when people live under God's rule and authority in his kingdom that they live in peace, receive and practise justice, and enjoy security and safety.

Like all saving acts of God, the establishing of this kingdom calls for a change of mind, a turning from the old to the new, to faith in the good news which God offers. To **repent** means much more than merely feeling sorry for one's past actions. The call to repent is a call for a completely radical change of mind and way of life. It involves a return to God's original will for us. It is a practical matter, and not simply something 'spiritual'. It is a call to move away from mere obedience to the sabbath law and the laws of ritual purity, and to move to a new life, with new attitudes, as lived and taught by Jesus from Galilee. It is a call to not give support any longer to powers which oppress and destroy, but to give support to the way of Jesus which is opposed to such powers. To repent means to return to the desert, across the boundaries drawn up by the power systems, to the God who establishes his people in the desert. It means that any lines that are drawn are to be drawn by the Spirit of holiness, who has also given authority to the Son of God to do this. Repentance, then, means coming under the direction of God and his Holy Spirit.

To **believe** is not to be understood as referring to something inward and passive. In the Bible the term often includes the idea of faithfulness, and of courage and daring. The call of Jesus is a call to be faithful to the gospel. It is a call to be courageous, to have confidence in the gospel. It is even a call to suffer and die. Believing means having the courage to walk the way of Jesus, who 'came not to be served but to serve, and to give his life as a ransom for many' (10:45). This is the radical nature of the call of Jesus in bringing in the kingdom of God.

So the scene is set for Mark's story. He has introduced the main character, Jesus, and has fitted him into a geographical and religious setting, and into the setting of God's history. We know who Jesus is, from God's viewpoint, and the responses to him of the other characters in the story will stand in ironical contrast to God's own acclamation of his Son. We also know the mission of Jesus: to announce that, in his coming, the kingdom of God is here. We know that his mission involves doing battle with the evil powers, the unclean spirits, and that Jesus himself has not been profaned by the evil spirit, but has remained faithful to the calling of the Spirit of holiness to be the Son of God. What we are left with is an expectancy that something radically new and different is going to happen as this Jesus now moves to carry out his mission.

## Follow me, 1:16-20

¹⁶ **And passing along by the Sea of Galilee, he saw Simon and Andrew the brother of Simon casting a net in the sea; for they were fishermen. ¹⁷ And Jesus said to them, 'Follow me and I will make you become fishers of men.' ¹⁸ And immediately they left their nets and followed him. ¹⁹ And going on a little farther, he saw James the son of Zebedee and John his brother, who were in their boat mending the nets. ²⁰ And immediately he called them; and they left their father Zebedee in the boat with the hired servants, and followed him.**

Movement is a striking literary feature of Mark's story. Each of the remaining episodes in this chapter begins with the movement of Jesus from one place to another, which brings him into contact with different people (vv 16,21,29,35,40). The story moves along as it follows the responses of the people who hear the word and call of Jesus. In this particular episode, his proclamation of the gospel meets with a response from four fishermen. His call, **Follow me**, is really a call to repentance, as shown by their action of leaving their old way of life and following Jesus. They are also called to a life of faithfulness, by trusting this unknown one, who has broken into the security of their lives with his radical call to leave and to follow. **Immediately**, which occurs twice, is Mark's way of showing his readers that the message of Jesus has the power of the Spirit of God to change the direction of the disciples' lives. The Clean One calls fishermen who, according to certain standards, were not clean. Because they were not instructed in God's law, they were not considered clean enough to be exposed to the holy revelation of the holy God.

The **Sea of Galilee** is called Chinnereth in Numbers 34:11 and Joshua 12:3; Gennesaret in Luke 5:1; and Tiberias in John 21:1. It is approximately 20 kilometres long and 13 kilometres wide at its longest and widest points, and lies 210 metres below sea-level. It is bordered by steep slopes which rise to about 200 metres on its west coast and 300 metres on the east. It features prominently in Mark's story, and the various crossings of the lake that occur can be said to symbolise the transitions which Mark sees as resulting from the call of Jesus. To follow Jesus means having to make transitions. Mark's introduction of the Sea of Galilee here prepares his readers for the significant role that it will play later in the gospel.

Mark calls the lake a **sea**, even though there is a very common word in Greek for 'lake' which he could have used. This suggests that the word was deliberately chosen. The probable reason for this choice of word is that, for the people of Israel, the sea was a threatening place of chaotic and demonic powers, something which becomes significant later in the gospel.

Note the verb of movement again: it is as Jesus is **passing along** that he calls his disciples. Simon and Andrew are fishermen, but they are called by Jesus to follow him. They are called to be part of the movement along the way that Jesus travels.

17 The imagery of fishing was not taken up by the church as was the imagery of the harvest, or of shepherding sheep. The thought behind the imagery of becoming **fishers of men** is that of rescuing people from the sea of chaos and the evil powers, by gathering them into the safe net of the kingdom of God.

18 When Mark tells of the saving actions of Jesus, he does so using the language of power and authority; the terminology he uses is very strong. Jesus speaks, and the disciples follow. There is no need to speculate about psychological reasons for their reaction, or to suggest that they were somehow 'ready' for this call. Mark simply wants to say that following Jesus means obeying his call, being willing to fall into step behind him. Discipleship means leaving and following. Mark's characteristic **immediately** illustrates the power and authority of Jesus' call.

19 The brothers James and John are almost always linked together. They are called to leave their father. It can be noticed that the call is not given to everyone, but only to those whom Jesus chooses. Leaving one's family is often necessary for the follower of Jesus. It happens to many Christians today that the family becomes a barrier to true following of Jesus. In some cases, being 'for the family' is held up as a Christian ideal, when in fact it is preventing true following of the way of Jesus. Jesus' call to leave family was radical, and must have been socially unsettling, since the family was an economic unit as well as a social one. In the case of these four fishermen, leaving their family meant leaving their business, and that would have had drastic effects on the family's economy! But the call of Jesus takes precedence over all other claims.

20 Some commentators find significance in Zebedee being left with the **hired servants**, a term that is used in early

Christian tradition in a derogatory sense (for example, John 10:12,13). Is Mark suggesting that there are those who hold back from following the call of Jesus for mercenary reasons? There may, however, be a simpler reason for mentioning these servants. Simon and Andrew are depicted as simply leaving their nets, while James and John have also a boat and hired servants. It may be that the family of Zebedee represents a wealthier class of people, from which Jesus also calls disciples, in contrast to poorer fishermen such as Simon and Andrew. Later in the gospel, James and John show that they are not averse to seeking power and position (10:35-41).

It is important to note that following Jesus is not a call to imitate him, but a call to walk along his way, to fall into step behind him as he leads. It is a movement. It means leaving the old and the secure, and taking the risk of falling in behind this person. The readers know where the one who calls is going, and they know that they are called to follow that same way.

## *The unclean spirits, 1:21-28*

**[21] And they went into Capernaum; and immediately on the sabbath he entered the synagogue and taught. [22] And they were astonished at his teaching, for he taught them as one who had authority, and not as the scribes. [23] And immediately there was in their synagogue a man with an unclean spirit; [24] and he cried out, 'What have you to do with us, Jesus of Nazareth? Have you come to destroy us? I know who you are, the Holy One of God.' [25] But Jesus rebuked him, saying, 'Be silent, and come out of him!' [26] And the unclean spirit, convulsing him and crying with a loud voice, came out of him. [27] And they were all amazed, so that they questioned among themselves, saying, 'What is this? A new teaching! With authority he commands even the unclean spirits, and they obey him.' [28] And at once his fame spread everywhere throughout all the surrounding region of Galilee.**

The scene shifts to **Capernaum**, a town that was later razed by Vespasian and his Roman troops in the rebellion of 66-70 AD. It is the **sabbath**. Jesus has come **into** the town, probably in preparation for the sabbath, since there was a prohibition on walking more than 1000 metres on the sabbath. He is found in the synagogue. As the Holy One, he is in the holy place, at the holy time, with the holy people. But in the midst of this holiness, he confronts for the first time what is unclean. Zechariah, a prophet who clearly has a significant influence on Mark, had said in prophecy: 'I will remove the unclean spirit' (Zech 13:2).

What follows is a typical miracle story, in which there is a situation of need, Jesus is present and effects a wonderful cure, and the people then react to what happens. The **synagogue** was mainly a place of teaching and preaching. Any honourable rabbi or distinguished Jew could be asked to read the Scriptures or teach in the synagogue, or to discuss with those present the meaning of the readings or other matters. After the destruction of the temple, the synagogue came to be seen as the place where God was now present. Only ten men were needed to constitute a synagogue, and a town of any size would have had quite a number of them. Many were houses, while others were more elaborate buildings. All of them were used also for other purposes besides worship and instruction.

There is little doubt that Mark has the particular situation of his readers in mind. It is very likely that they no longer attended the synagogue, although it is difficult to know just when the break finally occurred between Christian community and synagogue. It is fairly certain that Christians in some areas, at least for a while, maintained their synagogue connections. Mark probably has in mind those of his readers who still wish to maintain their connections with the synagogue, together with everything that that means. It is possible that some of these are insisting on this for their fellow-Christians. If this is correct, it is not a struggle between Jews and Christians which underlies this story, but an internal struggle among Christians themselves.

The reaction of the pro-synagogue people to Jesus is one of surprise and wonder because of his **authority**, which is not like that of the **scribes**. This is not necessarily a put-down of the scribes, but is rather a differentiation between their authority and that of Jesus. The scribes are often part of the opposition against Jesus, but not always. They were secretaries who played a significant role in the cities, the courts, and in synagogue meetings. They were also part of the Jewish ruling body known as the Sanhedrin (see, for example, 8:31; 10:33; 11:18). More importantly in this context, they were teachers who had authority to interpret the law of God. Whenever the Torah (God's law) was read it was interpreted, and these interpretations were called the 'Words of the Scribes', and were often read out together with the public reading of the Torah itself. It is likely that the astonishment over Jesus' teaching is due to the fact that he fails to acknowledge his sources and authorities. This would have been seen as arrogance and, what was worse, as being destructive of the whole system of the authority of tradition, because the continuing line from authority to authority was being broken.

That there is a man with an **unclean spirit** in the synagogue is surprising, because being regarded as unclean would normally have prevented his being there. Perhaps Mark wishes to suggest that the synagogue is now also the place of the unclean spirit, an idea that is supported by the fact that the synagogue is referred to as **their** synagogue, which dissociates Mark, and presumably most of his audience, from it (see also v 39). An unclean spirit means a spirit which made the man ritually or cultically unclean. It is important to note that Mark always introduces evil spirits as being 'unclean', and only after that identity has been established is the spirit called a **demon** (see also 3:11,15,22; 5:2,8,13; 6:7, 13; 7:25,26,29,30; 9:25). It can also be noted that the literal translation is 'a man in an unclean spirit'. In other words, the man may not have constantly lived with the unclean spirit, but at that very moment, when Jesus was present, he was suddenly (**immediately**!) seized or possessed by it. The expression is comparable to that of the Christians at Corinth speaking 'in the Spirit' (1 Cor 14:2). At the moment of Jesus' presence in the synagogue, the unclean spirit possesses the man, and causes him to speak to the Clean One, who he knows threatens his authority and his claims to possession.

The unclean spirit knows Jesus. Jesus is the Clean One of God, but he has already been in unclean territory, and has associated with unclean spirits, so they know him! They know that Satan himself was not able to defile him. The naming of a person indicates power and possession. Crying out is characteristic of spirit-possession, a significant point to remember in relation to the crucifixion of Jesus (see commentary on 15:37). The fact that the demon uses the word **us** indicates that for Mark this story sets the agenda for the exercise by Jesus of his authority: it will be in strong opposition to everything demonic, everything that possesses people and dehumanises them. Mark's readers could well have understood this to mean not simply spirits as we understand them, but also political and social 'spirits' which dehumanise people and render them powerless. 'Demons' often means not much more than 'influences' or 'driving forces'. So it is possible to speak of the demon of the State. On an individual level, a person could be motivated or possessed by either a good spirit or an evil one. Some people saw demons as the spirits of the dead, either good or bad. Another view was that demons were the offspring resulting from copulation between angels and humans (see Gen 6:1-4).

Jesus rebukes the unclean spirit. 'Rebuke' is a strong word, which expresses the aggressive wresting away of power from the enemy. Mark's language, when referring to the saving actions of Jesus to make people clean, is very strong. The command, **Be silent**, is similar to that which Jesus later gives to the wind and the sea (4:39). In the Septuagint (the Greek translation of the Old Testament), the word that is used here is a technical term for the powerful divine word of rebuke and threat. Zechariah 3:2 is a good example of its use: 'The Lord rebuke you, O Satan! The Lord who has chosen Jerusalem rebuke you.' We have already noted the importance of Zechariah for Mark, and we will see further evidence of that later in the gospel. The powers of evil, the forces which are opposed to the Holy One of God, are commanded to be silent, and the only voice that is to be heard is the voice of God in Jesus Christ.

In Mark's story, the only one who has authority to rebuke is Jesus. True, there are occasions when others rebuke (8:32; 10:13,48), but Jesus at these times makes it very clear to them that they have acted without authority. Jesus alone can rebuke. Such power to rebuke was understood in the Old Testament to belong only to Yahweh. The point is now made: Jesus, the Son of God, has the authority of God. He has been declared clean, and has been given the Spirit of holiness, and so has authority over all that is unclean. Mark's community is told that authority does not come through tradition or human status, but through Jesus alone. In Jesus they stand under the authority of God himself, because all authority has been given to him.

When Jesus speaks – he who has come to break the powers which destroy and dehumanise – those powers must listen. However, they do not give up without a struggle and without a noise! But the kingdom of God is a rule of peace and justice, where the destructive powers of chaos and inhumanity are rebuked, and where the creation of God is restored to sanity. The unclean spirits cannot withstand the Son of God's authority. Their demonic screaming is the death-rattle of the old order.

Then comes the reaction and response to Jesus' authority: amazement and questioning. At this point the question is not, Who is this? but rather, **What is this?** What authority, what power, is being demonstrated here? What kingdom is this that so powerfully speaks against the demonic powers, that wrests power away through the word, that gives freedom and dignity to what was previously unclean and rejected? Jesus has taught, here in the synagogue, with an authority which has left people astonished. His teaching is not just words, but is power over the unclean and the demonic. **27, 28**

The portrayal of Jesus as a teacher is frequent in Mark, although little is given to enable us to determine the actual content of his teaching. For Mark, Jesus' teaching involves revelation of the will and authority of God, rather than instruction in moral or ethical matters.

## Cleaning the place up, 1:29-34

**29 And immediately he[e] left the synagogue, and entered the house of Simon and Andrew, with James and John. 30 Now Simon's mother-in-law lay sick with a fever, and immediately they told him of her. 31 And he came and took her by the hand and lifted her up, and the fever left her; and she served them. 32**

**That evening, at sundown, they brought to him all who were sick or possessed with demons. 33 And the whole city was gathered together about the door. 34 And he healed many who were sick with various diseases, and cast out many demons; and he would not permit the demons to speak, because they knew him.**

[e] Other ancient authorities read *they*

Jesus is on the move again, out of the synagogue, and into **the house of Simon and Andrew**. James and John, the only other disciples to have been called so far, go with him. **29**

Archaeologists claim to have excavated what was traditionally known as Peter's house.

It is quite likely that **house** here signifies more than a building. It may represent the church or, better, the Christian community. It is well known that the first Christians met in houses. Jesus moves away from the synagogue, which is the house of those who are unclean, into the house-church, where he is present with his cleansing authority.

In this house there is no ritual uncleanness; that belongs to the old order. However, there is still sickness, which does not spare those who are related to the church leaders: Peter's mother-in-law has a fever. But Jesus is present in **30** the house with his healing power. Fever was a far more serious sickness then than it is now; it could be fatal.

Jesus takes the hand of a woman, and a sick one at that! **31** He lifts her up, and she is healed. Jesus' action of taking her by the hand may seem to be insignificant, but it takes on much deeper significance when we understand the usual relationship between a holy man and a sick woman. There is little doubt that Jesus' attitude and behaviour toward women was quite shocking to people at that time. Sick women were regarded as unclean, and what made holy men holy was that they kept their distance. This is not to say that Jews regarded women as such as being unclean, but there were certain conditions peculiar to women which rendered them unclean. In this case the woman was sick, and sickness was seen as making a person unclean and therefore removed from what is holy. It should again be noted that holiness was not a moral or ethical condition, as we often understand it. It can often be observed in this gospel how physical Jesus is in the way he relates to people: he is not afraid to touch women or lepers; he picks children up in his arms; he takes the hand of a twelve-year-old girl; his head is anointed by a woman; his body is finally broken in agony on the cross, and laid as a corpse in the grave. Mark presents us with a very physical Jesus, a Jesus who is genuinely interested in the physical well-being of those with whom he comes in contact.

Mark continues to shock his readers by describing the woman's response: **and she served them**. Service here does not mean giving a cup of tea and biscuits. The word used here is the same as that used of the angels in 1:13, where it is translated 'ministered' (one wonders why the RSV translates it as **served** here). It is also the word used by Jesus, in 10:45, to describe his own purpose in coming. The woman responds to the humanising, healing touch of Jesus by acting in the way that he acts. What is said here of this woman is never said of any of the male disciples. She becomes a miniature model of discipleship, of following in the way of Jesus. It is still the sabbath, and by serving on the sabbath she also imitates Jesus, who sees the sabbath as a time for joyful and creative service to others.

Verses 32-34 portray, in summary form, the authority which Jesus demonstrated over the powers of sickness and over the demonic. The time is now **sundown**, which means that the sabbath is over. People can now legitimately carry their sick, and Jesus can legitimately exercise his healing authority. It is tempting to again see the house as a picture of the early Christian community, surrounded by the city, with its people who are sick or possessed with demons, crowding around its doors. It is evident that the power of the name of Jesus was one of the great attractions of the Christian message and witness. The powers of evil recognise Jesus as the stronger one (**they knew him**), but Jesus does **not permit the demons to speak**. He does not want his witnesses to be from the side of Satan or Beelzebul, but from his new cleansed community, who know that the powers of the unclean and demonic have been defeated. Satan is a liar, and his claim to be able to retain possession of human beings is a lie. As the prince of this world, he is constantly usurping the power which belongs legitimately and solely to God the King. Princes in biblical times were quite notorious for their usurping of power! But in the Christian church the authority of Jesus is present. In Jesus, the kingdom of God smashes the kingdoms of evil.

*A clean place to pray, 1:35-39*

**35 And in the morning, a great while before day, he rose and went out to a lonely place, and there he prayed. 36 And Simon and those who were with him pursued him, 37 and they found him and said to him, 'Every one is searching for you.' 38 And he said to them, 'Let us go on to the next towns, that I may preach there also; for that is why I came out.' 39 And he went throughout all Galilee, preaching in their synagogues and casting out demons.**

After defeating the powers of evil, Jesus rises early and **35** goes to **a lonely place** to pray. This is an interesting action on Jesus' part. Why does he not go to the synagogue, or to one of the other places of prayer, which certainly existed? It would appear that he regards such places as alien to God, places where the unclean spirit is present, and that this is why he goes into the deserted, lonely place, away from the appointed places of prayer. The irony is that deserted places were regarded as places of evil, the abode of the unclean forces! Irony is very much a feature of Mark's story-telling. Note that Mark again shows Jesus as being outside, finding his strength and renewing his relationship with his Father, out in the desert. It was in the desert that Jesus was announced by John, was declared Son of God and given the Spirit of holiness in his baptism, and began his mission against the powers of the unclean. It can be noted in passing that the Essenes and other groups went out into the desert to prepare for the coming kingdom when, as they hoped and expected, God would annihilate the unclean. However, instead of annihilating the unclean people, Jesus goes out to find them and to save them.

Simon and **those with him** follow Jesus. The disciples **36,** are those who are called to be *with* Jesus (see 3:14). Here **37** there are those who are **with** Simon. Mark says that they **followed** Jesus. This is not the word used in Mark for discipleship, but is a strong word which can include the meaning 'pursuing with hostile intent, persecuting'. **Simon** is called by the name that he had before he was called to be 'with Jesus'. The seeking for Jesus by the crowds is a mark of the world, which does not know Jesus. **Searching** is always the action of Jesus' opponents. So the language here, in relation to Simon and those who are with him, is very strong indeed. Is this sentence meant to be 'having a go' at a group calling themselves 'Simon's group'? It would seem to suggest that Simon's followers do not understand why Jesus rejects the traditional places of prayer. Maybe there was some conflict in Mark's community between those who no longer used Jewish places of prayer, and those who wanted such practices to continue. The incident does indicate a tension between Simon and Jesus: Simon wants Jesus' mission to be successful, but to be contained within the boundaries of the synagogues, and to be aimed at the 'clean'. Jesus, however, wants to include others. More importantly, the incident seems to indicate that Simon does not want to hear Jesus' call to return to the desert, to repent

(1:15), and to do battle with the evil powers. It is not the last time that Peter speaks this way (see 8:32). He does not want to go the way of the outsider, the way of the cross. The language here is very strong, and so it must be interpreted in a strong way.

Verse 39 is a summary statement of Jesus' mission: he moves around Galilee, preaching, and destroying the powers of evil and the dehumanising forces in society. He does this in **their** synagogues, which again suggests a distancing of Jesus, and the Christian community, from the synagogue. Jesus says of himself that he **came out**. There have been previous references to such movement by Jesus (1:29,35). He moved out into the deserted places, not into the synagogues and sacred places, so that he could pray (v 35), and now he moves out again in order to **preach**, to proclaim the message of God, in the areas outside.

38, 39

## Unclean meets clean, 1:40-45

**⁴⁰ And a leper came to him beseeching him, and kneeling said to him, 'If you will, you can make me clean.' ⁴¹ Moved with pity, he stretched out his hand and touched him, and said to him, 'I will; be clean.' ⁴² And immediately the leprosy left him, and he was made clean. ⁴³ And he sternly charged him, and sent him away at once, ⁴⁴ and said to him, 'See that you say nothing to any one; but go, show yourself to the priest, and offer for your cleansing what Moses commanded, for a proof to the people.'ᶠ ⁴⁵ But he went out and began to talk freely about it, and to spread the news, so that Jesusᵍ could no longer openly enter a town, but was out in the country; and people came to him from every quarter.**

ᶠ Greek *to them*
ᵍ Greek *he*

This section relates closely to the following chapters (chapters 2 and 3) with their major theme of Jesus, the Son of God, acknowledged by the unclean to be the Holy One, creating a new community from among the unclean, a community in which sins are forgiven in his name, table fellowship is open to those previously unworthy, and fasting and other prescribed traditions are no longer binding. Distinguishing between what was clean and what was unclean was crucial in many early Christian communities, just as it had been for earlier Jewish communities. For Christians, the temple was no longer the place of purity (it had possibly been destroyed by now anyway), and the synagogue had also lost its authority, so the house or church took their place and took over their role. However, many questions relating to clean and unclean remained or were even intensified.

Here, and in the next two chapters, Jesus associates with the sick, with sinners and with outcasts, that is, those who do not observe the rituals and customs which make a person pure. Naturally, this action of Jesus meets with opposition from those who feel that the very basis of their religion, and their authority as interpreters of that religion, are being undermined. Curiously, these opponents remain rather nebulous; they are not individually named, and so there is something impersonal about them. It is not so much that they are opponents of Jesus, but rather that they are outside the kingdom, and so do not have the ability to 'see' or 'hear' who Jesus is. The question about Jesus and his authority reaches a climax in chapter 3, where the question is asked: Is Jesus in league with Beelzebul, or is he against him? And if, as Jesus claims, he is acting in the name of God, and with his authority, what does this mean for Israel's understanding of itself as the people of God? (3:21-33). Mark's answer is clear: Jesus breaks down the barriers between what is clean and unclean, and creates a community not based on ritual or cultic purity, but consisting of those who do the will of God (3:35).

Here we have a powerful story which typifies the mission of Jesus among the unclean. The movement this time is that **40** of a leper who comes to Jesus. It is a move of desperation, a radical action on the part of an unclean person who is regarded as being outside, and who has to announce his unclean state to those around him. It involves the wresting of power from the unclean forces. As a good story-teller, Mark uses contrast: the one who has all authority to forgive sins, the Holy One of God, as even the demons acknowledge, now comes into contact with an unclean person. This man has broken the law simply by approaching Jesus. He has no doubt as to Jesus' ability or authority to heal him, but makes his request conditional on Jesus' will. Jesus is **moved with 41 pity** – or is it anger, as one manuscript tradition has it? If it is anger, this suggests a battle here between the liberating Jesus and the demonic power of society and church, which bind people with their purity laws. Jesus does not stand aloof as the Holy One of God, nor does he remind the man of his unclean state, and therefore the distance that exists between them. Instead, he reaches out to bridge the gulf, he crosses the sacred boundaries.

The stretching out of Jesus' hand might well recall similar actions by Moses and others in the Old Testament, who stretched out their hands in performing acts of salvation and liberation for the people of Israel. God's hand is often said to stretch out when he acts to save. It is a liberating and powerful action. No one can stand against God's outstretched hand. The touch of Jesus is his acceptance of the unclean, his breaking through the barriers separating clean from unclean. It is the touch of God creating a new community, a new society, where the oppressive barriers are breached. It is the gospel. Mark frequently portrays Jesus as being intensely interested in the physical well-being of people. He is not afraid to touch or to be touched. He recognises the importance of touch in all of human existence and in interpersonal relationships. Despite the fact that some touching contaminates, Jesus breaks these taboos, these limits, and reaches out to those whom others refuse to touch for fear of contamination. The gospel is the touch of God on the unclean, contaminated and contaminating areas of human existence, in society, church and nation.

42 There were magical chants which involved calling on the name of some power, with repeated demands that the power act immediately. What Jesus does is not like that. He acts on his own authority and with immediate effect. The leprosy leaves at Jesus' command. An interesting word occurs in verse 43. It is translated in the RSV as **he sternly charged** 43 **him**, but the verb really contains the idea of being angry, indignant, even of snorting!

The verb 'send away' has previously been used to mean 'exorcise' (1:34). The use of this word here suggests that Mark sees this healing also as a kind of exorcism. It suggests that there was a struggle going on here between Jesus and the unclean powers.

The unclean man who has been healed is now to go to the 44 priests, who are responsible for matters of purity, to prove to them that he is now pure, but he is not to tell others about it. Is there a bit of an 'in' joke involved with this command? Do the readers smile or laugh? It is generally understood as being part of the so-called messianic secret. The term 'secret' is misleading; it is not so much a secret as a mystery, something seen only by those who can 'see'. Nor is it the mystery of the Messiah, but of the Son of God, who is the Holy One, the Clean One, but who calls the unclean, the outsiders, the sinners to share in the new kingdom.

Jesus breaks down the barriers that have been built to separate what is profane from what is holy, what is unclean from what is clean. His community is called to follow in his steps, and to offer the cleansing touch of the Clean One to those who are, and who feel themselves to be, on the outside of society and church.

The healed man spreads **the news** (literally, 'the word'), **45** with the result that Jesus cannot go into the city, but instead goes outside to the deserted places (**country** is misleading). The chapter ends as it began, with Jesus in the desert. He has associated with outsiders, and outsiders have become proclaimers of his word. This makes Jesus himself an outsider. The contrast between inside and outside is a strong theme right through Mark's story. Jesus himself continually moves between being inside and outside. Already here there is provided a pointer to the outcome of the story: Jesus dies as the Outsider. The desert place was for the unclean. This is where Jesus is to be found and where people come to him. We have here a key to further developments in Mark's theme of Jesus as the Outsider.

## *Who actually is paralysed? 2:1-12*

**2:1 And when he returned to Capernaum after some days, it was reported that he was at home. ² And many were gathered together, so that there was no longer room for them, not even about the door; and he was preaching the word to them. ³ And they came, bringing to him a paralytic carried by four men. ⁴ And when they could not get near him because of the crowd, they removed the roof above him; and when they had made an opening, they let down the pallet on which the paralytic lay. ⁵ And when Jesus saw their faith, he said to the paralytic, 'My son, your sins are forgiven.' ⁶ Now some of the scribes were sitting there, questioning in their hearts, ⁷ 'Why does this man speak thus? It is blasphemy! Who can forgive sins but God alone?' ⁸ And immediately Jesus, perceiving in his spirit that they thus questioned within themselves, said to them, 'Why do you question thus in your hearts? ⁹ Which is easier, to say to the paralytic, "Your sins are forgiven," or to say, "Rise, take up your pallet and walk"? ¹⁰ But that you may know that the Son of man has author-**

**ity on earth to forgive sins' – he said to the paralytic –** [11] **'I say to you, rise, take up your pallet and go home.'** [12] **And he rose, and immediately took up the pallet and went out before them all; so that they were all amazed and glorified God, saying, 'We never saw anything like this!'**

In this chapter and the next we see Jesus associating with the sick, sinners, outcasts, and those who do not observe the sabbath, or the traditions of the elders regarding fasting, and are therefore ritually unclean. He is shown here as the law-less one, who pushes out the boundaries to include the unclean in the call of God. This reaches a climax at the end of chapter 3 with the question: Is Jesus in league with Beelzebul, or is he against him? Jesus' actions are also meant to answer such questions as: Who now belongs to the house (church) of God? Is fellowship within the community tied to physical, and therefore ethnic, roots? Jesus' answer, which is clearly Mark's answer, is at the heart of the gospel of the New Testament: In Jesus the barriers of family, race, and cultic origin are broken down, and the mercy of God and his covenant are extended and expanded so as to include even the outsiders. Anyone who does the will of God is a member of the new family created in and with Jesus (3:35).

'House' (translated here as **home**) occurs frequently, especially in the early part of the gospel (2:1,15; 3:19,31). It can signify a place of withdrawal (7:24); it is often a place which separates the disciples of Jesus from the crowds (3:20; 7:17; 9:28; 10:10); it can be a place of teaching or instruction for the disciples (3:20; 7:17; 9:28,33; 10:10); and it is sometimes used to refer to the Christian community (13:35), and also the temple (11:17). In many cases, especially those in which the house is seen as a place of special teaching and instruction, it stands in contrast to the synagogue or temple. What had once been the special place of God's revelation to Israel is now replaced by the revelation in Jesus Christ, who is present no longer in the temple or the synagogue, but in the communities of Christians wherever they may be. 'House', then, suggests the house-churches which came into use particularly after the Christians had been excluded from the synagogues, or had excluded themselves. It is quite likely that some within Mark's community were insisting that the traditional places of meeting and worship should be maintained, but

Mark comes down on the side of those who see the message of Jesus as liberating them from observance of such traditions.

The crowds of people who gather are those who do not accurately know the Torah (God's law), and therefore do not observe it fully. In Christian terms, they are the unevangelised, the great unwashed! Jerusalem Jews (and early Christians?) regard the crowds as being incapable of keeping God's law, and of piety in any form. They are, as the Pharisees say in John 7:49, the rabble who do not know the law and are therefore accursed. It is these outsiders who gather around the house to receive **the word** of Jesus. The crowds are more often than not *outside* either the house or the synagogue. They represent those who are to be reached with the word. Jesus speaks that word. **Preaching** should not be understood in terms of what this word means today. Jesus sat and spoke while the hearers milled around – no amplification, no pews, no soapbox, no pulpit! 2

The paralysed man is brought to Jesus, the speaker of the word. The unclean one comes into the presence of the Clean One. We see here again the typical Marcan miracle story construction: a person in need is brought to Jesus, who performs a saving action, which in turn evokes a response. The removal of the tiles of the roof (literally, 'unroofed the roof') suggests Roman rather than Palestinian architecture. Jesus sees their **faith**, that is, their trust and confidence in him to heal. Faith in Mark usually means 'courage' or 'daring', rather than individual, spiritual trust in the person of Jesus. There is often, as here, the idea of perseverance, of persistence against the odds. 3,4 5

Jesus surprises them by saying: **My son, your sins are forgiven**. This is not what the man himself, or his friends, would have expected. They expected and hoped for a physical healing, which Jesus is more than happy to give. But Jesus wishes to teach as well as to heal. He wants the man, and the bystanders, to know that there is more to what he has to offer than simply the healing of a sickness. In the first century, healers were very common. Someone has said that the market for miracles in the world of Christian antiquity was saturated. Jesus, the clean Son of God, is more than a wandering miracle-worker. So he addresses the man as his **son**, and thereby accepts him into that special relationship. This in itself is blasphemous, because in common thinking, sin and sickness were interrelated. Sickness was seen as the result of sinful action. By calling the man his son, Jesus is accepting the man's sinful condition as his own. Sonship also carried with it connotations of having the same characteristics as the father! To make matters worse, Jesus pronounces him forgiven, not in the name of God, but on his own authority. So it is possible to see the word of address, **My son**, when used in connection with the word of forgiveness, as placing Jesus in the position of *father* to this man. But only the Father can forgive! Such a way of talking and acting is bound to stir some people up!

The **scribes** are **sitting** there. Sitting was the position of **6** a teacher, of someone in authority (compare the phrase in the Apostles' Creed: 'and sits at the right hand of God'). The scribes represent the authority of Judaism. In their opinion, and according to their tradition, only God can forgive sin. The RSV here could be more accurate than it is. It suggests **7** that the emphasis is on **alone**, but if that is what the Greek had wanted to say, it could very simply have done so. Rather, what the scribes are saying is that God is one, that he is undivided, that he is unity itself, and that it is this One who forgives. Humanity, they say, can never be part of this unity or oneness which is the unique characteristic of God. **This man** (a phrase perhaps expressing contempt, but probably just making the point that forgiveness is the function of God, not man) cannot dare to claim the authority of the God who is one.

The scribes say this, questioning **within themselves**, in **8** their **hearts**. They are the guardians, not only of the tradition, but especially of certain secret knowledge. They know about the holy name and other mysteries of God. When speaking about such matters, they whisper, or speak in a very low voice. Since here they are talking about God and his authority to forgive, it may be that they talk in whispers or in low voices. Even if this is not the case, we can notice that the opposition to Jesus is not open and direct, but subdued and indirect. The scribes are not portrayed as being blatantly hostile opponents of Jesus.

Jesus, as a prophet of God, has the ability to read the hearts of his opponents, since it is God who knows the secrets of the heart. Mark's readers know that Jesus is the Son of God. Among other things, this title means that he has the authority of his Father. The readers also know that he has been given the Spirit of holiness in his baptism, and that he baptises with that same Spirit. This also means that Jesus has the right to draw the boundaries which determine what is holy and what is unclean. We have already seen, and will repeatedly see, that Jesus draws up different boundaries from those drawn up by the previous guardians of what is holy.

Jesus acknowledges the link between sin and sickness, and claims authority over both. He forgives and he also heals. The question about which is easier, is difficult! Most commentators take the simplest understanding: forgiveness cannot be proved, whereas healing is verifiable to the senses. However, this sounds very much like a Western, scientific approach. Jesus may rather be making the point that his authority extends over *both* sickness and sin; the one is not easier or more difficult than the other.

Here we have the first occasion on which Jesus uses the expression **Son of man**. It is important to have a closer look at this term which has greatly occupied the minds and pens of scholars. It is the only term that Jesus uses of himself. Many scholars have insisted that it is a title, but this is not likely, for the following reasons: No-one in Mark's gospel objects to it as they do to titles such as Son of God and Messiah, in fact, there is no reaction to it at all; it is never used in Christological confessions of faith; it is never used as a predicate, that is, it is never said: Jesus is the Son of man.

The traditional understanding is to associate the term with its use in Daniel 7:13,14, and to see it as a messianic title. Some see it as referring to a divine figure, in which case it is not very different from 'Son of God'. Many scholars today concede that it is not a title, but see it as a technical term. Maybe a closer connection could be made with 'son of man' in Ezekiel. In that book, the prophet himself is addressed by God as 'son of man', is given visions, and is asked to speak a message – usually a word of judgment – to Israel, and to Jerusalem in particular. There is a tendency in recent scholarship to understand the term more in the sense of 'this man here' (little more than a reference to Jesus himself) or 'this human being here' (this person in unique contrast to others).

There are a number of interrelated uses of 'Son of man' in Mark's gospel. First, the term can simply refer to a person's humanity. The phrase 'son of' means 'having all the characteristics of, belonging to, stemming from'. But it is not just any human being that is meant by this term, because it is used only by Jesus to refer exclusively to himself. It is Jesus who is *the* human. It is possible that Mark means his readers to see Jesus as the Adam. In Jewish tradition, some of it later than Jesus, Adam is regarded as a prophet with great wisdom and authority. His body is said to have filled the universe, until he was reduced in size by God. We will see later that many traditions about Adam appear to be paralleled at Jesus' crucifixion. Jesus, then, is the Man, the Human, Adam, who has the authority of God, and is in God's image. Could it be that 'Son of man' more often than not means 'Man'? If so, it would be better to capitalise 'Man' and leave 'son' in lower case, that is, the reverse of what is done in RSV and AV. TEV and NIV capitalise both words. As the Man, Jesus has come to oppose and bind all the demonic and unclean powers which dehumanise people, who are God's creation. By his authority to forgive, and his authority to heal, Jesus creates a new humanity, a new creation, restored to being in the image of God as originally intended. In Jesus, we see God's intention for humanity. Jesus is seen by Mark as the Symbol of God, that is, as the Man of God who has authority to pull things together (which is what the word 'symbol' literally means). As such, he is opposed by the diabolical, that is, by everything that seeks to pull God's creation apart (Greek: *diaballein*).

Secondly, Jesus uses 'Son of man' when speaking of himself as the one who goes to suffer, die, and rise again (8:31; 9:9,31; 10:33). As the Man, Jesus suffers at the hands of the diabolical powers which bring death and suffering to God's creatures, and so shares the lot of all humanity since the Great Seduction. At the same time, however, he offers that seduced humanity a new hope, a new existence, by becoming a new creation through the power of the Spirit of holiness.

Thirdly, Jesus speaks of himself as the Son of man who comes on the clouds of glory in judgment (14:62). Just as Adam, according to tradition, had been given wisdom and judgment, so the Man will finally come as the judge of all humanity. He will judge with wisdom and justice.

In conclusion, it must be said that the chief emphasis in Mark's use of the term 'Son of man' is on Jesus' authority. The Son of man has authority, an authority which breaks the power of all other authorities: sabbath, sin, uncleanness, and the ultimate uncleanness, death. All are broken by the Son of man. His authority is authenticated on the cross and through his resurrection. It is the authority of God himself.

As is always the case when the authority of Jesus is seen, **11,** the response of the people is one of amazement and wonder. **12** In this case, it leads to praise of God. The call to praise God is sometimes used in the New Testament to indicate acknowledgment of being in the wrong (see John 9:24). At other times, the response to a miracle performed by Jesus is that of plotting to kill him, or at least to destroy his reputation (see 3:6).

This passage indicates that within the Christian community, especially when it was still linked with the synagogue, the question of forgiveness was crucial. Can the Christian community really offer forgiveness in the name of Jesus, as it claims to be able to do? Mark writes to assure his community that the ability to offer forgiveness has been given by the authority of Jesus himself. And this Jesus has been given the stamp of approval from God. In this episode, as with many, the cross looms in the background. Jesus' death and resurrection are the guarantee of his authority over sin, and that authority has been given to the Christian community, which has Jesus going on before it. The Third Article of the Apostles' Creed catches the intention of Mark very well when it speaks of the forgiveness of sin in the context of the holy catholic church, the community of saints, and as the work of the Holy Spirit. Mark sees Jesus as the one on whom the Spirit of holiness has come, and who therefore has the Spirit's authority to declare clean what has been unclean when outside of his authority and presence. The authority to forgive in the name of Jesus Christ has been given to the Christian community: that is the clear message.

## *To eat or not to eat, 2:13-22*

¹³ **He went out again beside the sea; and all the crowd gathered about him, and he taught them.** ¹⁴ **And as he passed on, he saw Levi the son of Alphaeus sitting at the tax office, and he said to him, 'Follow me.' And he rose and followed him.**

¹⁵ **And as he sat at table in his house, many tax collectors and sinners were sitting with Jesus and his disciples; for there were many who followed him.** ¹⁶ **And the scribes of**ʰ **the Pharisees, when they saw that he was eating with sinners and tax collectors, said to his disciples, 'Why does he eat**ⁱ **with tax collectors and sinners?'** ¹⁷ **And when Jesus heard it, he said to them, 'Those who are well have no**

need of a physician, but those who are sick; I came not to call the righteous, but sinners.'

[18] Now John's disciples and the Pharisees were fasting; and people came and said to him, 'Why do John's disciples and the disciples of the Pharisees fast, but your disciples do not fast?' [19] And Jesus said to them, 'Can the wedding guests fast while the bridegroom is with them? As long as they have the bridegroom with them, they cannot fast. [20] The days will come, when the bridegroom is taken away from them, and then they will fast in that day. [21] No one sews a piece of unshrunk cloth on an old garment; if he does, the patch tears away from it, the new from the old, and a worse tear is made. [22] And no one puts new wine into old wineskins; if he does, the wine will burst the skins, and the wine is lost, and so are the skins; but new wine is for fresh skins.[j]

[h] Other ancient authorities read *and*
[i] Other ancient authorities add *and drink*
[j] Other ancient authorities omit *but new wine is for fresh skins*

Jesus is on the move again, this time out of the house and to the **sea**, that is, the Lake of Galilee. The lake has already been introduced into the story (1:16), to alert readers to its later significance. TEV and NIV lose the significance of Mark's use of 'sea' by using the word 'lake' instead (see the commentary at 1:16). The crowds follow Jesus, and he teaches them. The pattern is common in Mark's story-telling: Jesus moves from one place to another, people gather, and he teaches them. The content of the teaching is not given. It is enough that Jesus, the Son of God, should teach the crowds, who were regarded as being outside the grace and covenant of God, because they were ignorant of the Torah (God's law), the way and will of God. Teaching here is synonymous with revealing. That Jesus teaches means that he reveals the will of God to the masses, the outsiders. For many, the teaching of the will of God belonged exclusively to those who had authority, those who saw themselves as being God's chosen ones. This little verse, then, packs quite a punch! The Clean One of God reveals God's gracious will to those who are unclean in the opinion of the establishment. Jesus is seen to extend the boundaries, and even to cross over them. 13

The teaching takes place, not in the synagogue, but **beside the sea**. This also is remarkable, since the sea in Jewish mythology is far from being the idyllic, tranquil place that we might imagine here, but is rather the place of anti-God powers and chaotic forces. Jesus teaches on the edge, away from the safe places of tradition and regulated systems, out there where he is open to, and is threatened by, chaotic forces.

The radical grace of God to the outsider is further demonstrated as Jesus passes on, continuing a movement – the movement of God among people – which will reach its climax on the cross. While going on his way, Jesus calls outsiders to **follow** him. To follow Jesus does not mean to imitate him, but to fall into step behind him along the way which leads to the cross. We do not know who **Levi** was; he is not one of the twelve. Mark identifies him as the **son of Alphaeus**, and by doing so emphasises that he is a Jew, since Alphaeus, like Levi, is a distinctive Jewish name. The fact that he is a Jew stands in stark contrast to his job: that of collecting custom tax or, more accurately, the custom toll. This job meant, at least to the purists, that he had sold his soul to the oppressors, the Romans. It virtually excluded him from the people of God. He no longer had any claim to the covenant, and therefore none to the mercy of God. Tax collectors such as Levi had made a conscious decision: They knew that in choosing this occupation they were putting themselves outside the favour of God, outside God's covenant. There is no need to imagine that they were condemned only by the religious authorities; their own consciences also condemned them. **14**

Jesus, who has claimed to have the authority of God, the Holy One, associates again with one who is unclean, and calls him to join him along the way. Levi does just that. He hears the call, rises, and follows Jesus. There may have been people who listened to a reading or telling of this story, who at this point cheered and clapped as they saw themselves in Levi. They also had been outsiders who had heard the call of Jesus, had got up, and had followed him. They had made decisions which had put them outside, but now they knew that the kingdom of God extended also to them in their unclean state.

The call to follow Jesus is never a call to be alone. So Levi, having heard the call and having responded to it, is not left alone, but is immediately found to be in table-fellowship with others. Jesus goes into this outsider's house and eats with him – that is, if we understand the house as belonging to Levi. In Luke 5:29 it is made clear that it is Levi's house. Here, however, it is possible to understand the house as belonging to Jesus: Levi follows Jesus and shares in table- **15** fellowship in Jesus' house. In either case, it is hard to overestimate the significance of sharing food with another person. It has the effect of making people blood brothers or sisters. Who could eat with whom was not a matter of likes or dislikes, but something which was a direct expression of social and religious relationships. You could tell people by the company they kept at table, and by what they ate at their table. Dietary laws formed a large part of all Jewish laws. It is quite remarkable to what extent food and eating feature in the stories of Jesus, and in God's dealings with his people in general. It is not coincidental that the sharing of food has always been at the heart of the Christian community's gatherings and worship.

In addition, it can be noted that when a teacher, or rabbi, ate a meal with others, he would share with them not only food, but also a discussion on the Torah (God's law). Jesus not only shares food with Levi, and others who are outsiders and are unclean, but also shares a discussion of God's will with them. To many people this was a scandal.

There are **many** who follow Jesus. 'Many' occurs again in Jesus' words at the Last Supper: 'This is my blood of the covenant, which is poured out for many' (14:24). Is Mark here giving his readers a little clue or hint about that special meal in which Jesus binds himself as a blood brother with his people?

It may be that the house of Levi represents the houses of certain Christians which other Christians regarded as unworthy places in which to hold the communal meal. **Tax collectors and sinners** is a stock phrase identifying those who are outside the grace and covenant of God, because they are transgressors of his will. We need to be clear about these people: they are not to be pitied! They are rich. They lead comfortable lives, and their waistlines show it – they do not fast like the Pharisees. They are the successful business people around town. But from the religious and cultic point of view they are outsiders, because they themselves have chosen to live outside the law. They have a reputation for cheating, and for stealing from their own people. Faced with a choice between doing the will of God, as interpreted by the traditions of the elders, or not, they have chosen not to, for whatever reason. They know the consequences of making such a choice: prohibition from entering into the presence of God, an abandonment of their claim to belong to the covenant between God and Israel. The tax collector in Luke's parable (Luke 18:9-14) does not stand 'far off' simply out of humility and repentance; he is not allowed to go any further inside the temple, because he is a sinner. Sinners are a continual sore spot for Jesus' opponents, who cannot come to terms with the fact that his followers include those who come from that category! It is very likely that this also reflects the composition of the early Christian communities. It is those who are non-observers of the Torah (God's law) who find in Jesus' message the grace and mercy of God, and the call to belong to his new community. Strict observers of the purity laws must have found it unbearable that a man claiming to be holy, and to be doing and teaching God's will, should share food with the unclean.

It is possible, by a change of punctuation, to include **the scribes of the Pharisees** in the **many who followed** Jesus of verse 15. Many scholars have seen the scribes as people who were rejected by Jesus, and his greatest opponents, but there is a good case for seeing them as being close to the kingdom of God in their sincere desire to come to terms with what Jesus was saying and doing. They are not so much the opponents of Jesus, but those who simply *cannot* come to terms with him. In some manuscripts of this passage the scribes are spoken of as the scribes *of* the Pharisees (as RSV reads it), but in others they are mentioned as being *with* the Pharisees (so AV). Mention has already been made of the possible link between John the Baptist and the scribes and Pharisees (see commentary on 1:5). They apparently had quite a lot in common, a supposition which is supported by 2:18, where both John's disciples and the Pharisees are said to practise fasting. The scribes were highly respected members of their society. Some of them were priests, but the majority had other professions. Some were poor, some rich. There were even some who had pagan blood. What gave the scribes their power and status was their knowledge. They were men who were instructed in traditional and biblical knowledge, and were then ordained into the office of scribe. They made decisions on religious matters, and even arbitrated in criminal proceedings in courts of law. They could be addressed as Rabbi. Above all, they were the guardians of the secret, esoteric knowledge of Judaism, in regard to such things as the holy name of God and the mysteries of his creation. Such knowledge could not be divulged to ordinary people. A good description of a scribe is given in Ecclesiasticus, where it is said that he is one 'who devotes himself to the study of the law of the Most High. If the great Lord is willing, he will be filled with the spirit of understanding; he will pour forth words of wisdom and give thanks to the Lord in prayer. He will direct his counsel and knowledge aright, and meditate on his secrets. He will reveal instruction in his teaching, and will glory in the law of the Lord's covenant' (Ecclesiasticus 39:1,6-8). Knowledge, especially religious knowledge, is power, so the scribes were held in very high esteem in their society, in a similar way to the prophets.

The **Pharisees** were strict observers of the Torah (God's law) and the traditions of the elders. The name itself probably has the meaning of being separate. They saw themselves as those called to be apart from others in their intense desire to do God's will. But the name could also have the meaning of dividing or interpreting. They were the interpreters of the will of God. Their origins are somewhat hazy, but they certainly played a crucial role in the survival and revival of Judaism after the fall of Jerusalem in 70 AD. Unfortunately, their name is often seen as being synonymous with hypocrisy. This is an unjust perception. Their lifestyle reflected a sincere desire to do the will of God as given in the Torah and in the traditions of the elders. It heightens the irony of this episode that those so eager for purity cannot come to terms with a Jesus who associates with those who are impure. Jesus pushes out the boundaries far wider than they can accept. The one who has the Spirit of holiness, and who will baptise with fire, has become the one who now determines who and what is clean or unclean. He baptises with a fire that cleanses what others have regarded as unclean.

Verse 17 summarises the purpose for which Jesus has 17 come. **Those who are well** do not need a doctor. This is not a criticism of those who are well! Jesus (and possibly also the early Christians) is not rejecting those who desire to obey the will of God as given in the Torah; he is not being sarcastic about their righteousness. His mission, however, is to those who do *not* keep the Torah observances, the **sinners**, as they were called. The **righteous** are those who keep the Torah; **sinners** are those who do not. This takes us to the very heart of the gospel: God offers his grace, his solidarity, his table-fellowship, his protection, to those who have not kept his law, to those who have even made a conscious decision to live outside of it. It seems that the question of who could be admitted to table-fellowship in the Christian community was a burning issue (see Gal 2:11-21; Acts 10).

That God should go after the lost was not a new idea. Ezekiel had prophesied that God himself would search for his sheep, gather them together, seek the lost, bring back the strayed, bind up the crippled, and strengthen the weak (Ezek 34:11-16). But that was understood to mean that the lost would come back into the fold and participate in all the ritual and cultic holiness of the righteous ones. Jesus, however, and many of the Christian communities after him, does not make such demands on the strayed, or on those coming into the kingdom of God.

Mark, in his inimitable style, quickly moves from one controversial issue to another, that of **fasting**. This relates to the previous section, which spoke of eating, and which demonstrated Jesus' unorthodoxy in this matter. If Christians are unorthodox in their eating habits, what about fasting? Should Christians fast? From the Jewish viewpoint, fasting belonged more to the tradition of the elders than to the Torah itself. According to the first five books of the Old Testament, fasting was required on only one day of the year, the Day of Atonement (see Lev 16:29,31; 23:27). The second century Christian document, *The Didache*, indicates that the Jewish tradition was to fast on Monday and Thursday. Christians, however, chose to fast on Wednesday and Friday. In the modern, Western, Protestant tradition, fasting does not play an important role, but its significance in the early Christian communities cannot be overestimated. Among other things, it was seen as a way of preparing for the *parousia* (the return, or more correctly, the presence of Jesus Christ). Fasting before the Eucharistic meal had within it this expectation: when the kingdom finally comes, then the fast will be broken, and the banquet will commence. 18

John the Baptist continued to have a circle of followers even after Jesus' death and resurrection. **John's disciples** and **the Pharisees** both believed, as did many others, that one should prepare for the kingdom of God by fasting. Jesus' followers are distinguished from them in that they do not fast. The point that Jesus makes here is that the new and the old cannot be maintained together. Fasting is part of the old order, but now, in Jesus, the new order has come. The kingdom has come with the coming of Jesus. There is nothing more to expect or wait for. The bridegroom is here, and it is now the time of the messianic feasting and banqueting. 19

20-22

**In that day** does not refer to the time after Jesus' death, or the time of his return. It is most likely that it refers to one of the days of fasting observed by Christians, namely Friday, either the weekly Friday fast, or the annual fast of Good Friday. Fasting, ultimately, is related to Jesus' death. He goes to his death fasting. His fasting and his death are remembered by his followers, who are then fed from his cross. His cross and resurrection have become the food of Christians, who feast with him every first day of the week.

## *The sabbath, 2:23-3:6*

**²³ One sabbath he was going through the grainfields; and as they made their way his disciples began to pluck heads of grain. ²⁴ And the Pharisees said to him, 'Look, why are they doing what is not lawful on the sabbath?' ²⁵ And he said to them, 'Have you never read what David did, when he was in need and was hungry, he and those who were with him: ²⁶ how he entered the house of God, when Abiathar was high priest, and ate the bread of the Presence, which it is not lawful for any but the priests to eat, and also gave it to those who were with him?' ²⁷ And he said to them, 'The sabbath was made for man, not man for the sabbath; ²⁸ so the Son of man is lord even of the sabbath.'**

**³:¹ Again he entered the synagogue, and a man was there who had a withered hand. ² And they watched him, to see whether he would heal him on the sabbath, so that they might accuse him. ³ And he said to the man who had the withered hand, 'Come here.' ⁴ And he said to them, 'Is it lawful on the sabbath to do good or to do harm, to save life or to kill?' But they were silent. ⁵ And he looked around at them with anger, grieved at their hardness of heart, and said to the man, 'Stretch out your hand.' He stretched it out, and his hand was restored. ⁶ The Pharisees went out, and immediately held counsel with the Herodians against him, how to destroy him.**

Mark's account moves from the question of association with sinners, to the question of fasting, to the other great issue which the first Christian communities had to grapple with: the **sabbath** observance. This observance, like the practice of circumcision, was a badge of Judaism, one of the characteristic and distinctive features of the Jewish community in the non-Jewish world. It was laws such as these that made the Jewish nation different from others. This is very much the purpose of rules! Rules enable a group to demonstrate its distinctiveness in relation to others who do not follow those rules. They determine who is inside and who is outside. It is Israel's distinctiveness which constitutes its holiness. That it is holy means that it is set apart, as God's people, from the nations. It is the rules of circumcision, the sabbath, and the many dietary regulations that enable the distinction to be made between those who are God's people and those who are not. Here in this section, we again see that Jesus draws new lines, new boundaries.

The sabbath was the day of rest, since it was on the seventh day that God rested from his labours after creating the universe (Gen 2:2). In Jewish thought, the sabbath testified to the belief in God as creator and giver of life, and so the rabbis called it 'a memorial of creation'. According to their view, before God created the world, everything was in chaos, and matter was unformed and uncontrolled. So God said, Enough! and brought order and harmony into the world, and created life.

According to 1 Samuel 21:1-6, it was not **Abiathar** but Ahimelech (his father) who was high priest at the time David ate the consecrated bread. Jesus' reference to David's action deserves comment. First, it can be noted that it has nothing directly to do with the sabbath. What David did was to eat of the bread which was forbidden to him normally. In addition, he shared the bread with **those who were with him**. The question of eating is still being dealt with here, but is now seen in conjunction with the sabbath. Jesus eats with those who are **with him**, just as David did. For Jesus the sabbath is a memorial of creation, of joy and life. Hunger does not bring joy and life, but is the absence of the blessing of God. As will be seen later in the feeding stories (6:35-44; 8:1-10), to feed is to bless. Jesus here sees the action of David as one that befits the real point of the sabbath, even though no mention of the sabbath is made in the David story. The second point to notice is that Jesus does not argue from some principle or rule laid down in the Scriptures, but from the actions of an individual. This goes against traditional Jewish forms of authority, in which rules had to rest on actual precepts from Scripture. **25, 26**

Jesus says plainly that he, as the Son of man, brings in a new age, a new way. In this new era the Gentiles are included, even though they are people who do not observe the sabbath, and are not expected to. There is, then, no sabbath law for the Christian communities, at least the **27**

Gentile ones. It is possible that many Christian Jews maintained the observance, and did so with the support of many of the Christian leaders, even of Paul. Dissension came only when these Jewish Christians insisted that all Christians should observe the sabbath law. In opposition to them, Paul says that the sabbath, like other Jewish observances, is only a shadow of the reality to come (Col 2:16,17). The real **28** sabbath, the real rest, is Jesus, who invites all who are weary and heavy laden with the burden of the demands of the Torah (God's law) to come to him for rest (Matt 11:28-30). The sabbath exists for the good of God's people. The rabbis themselves acknowledged this when they said: 'The sabbath is delivered unto you and you are not delivered to the sabbath'.

Although there is a chapter break here, the sabbath theme continues into the third chapter. The question of the sabbath, and of their attitude to the Torah itself, must have been very important for the early Christians. When they were under pressure, as Mark's community appears to have been, they must sometimes have been tempted to think that God had abandoned them because they had abandoned his law. The destruction of Jerusalem and the temple would have aggravated such thinking.

Jesus enters the synagogue on the sabbath, at least in **1,2** this way observing the law. His opponents, who are wanting to **accuse** him, are not named (does Mark wish to avoid anchoring them in the past?). Verse 6 suggests that they are Pharisees. They watch Jesus, but this does not faze him. He takes the initiative and calls the man to come to him. **Here**, **3** in Jesus' command **Come here**, here is, literally, 'in the middle'. This phrase later had significance for certain Gnostics (unorthodox Christians) as referring to the place of authority.

Jesus' opponents are silent in response to his question, **4** because they know that he is right: the law exists for the good of people, to save and not to destroy. We can note that here, as often in Mark, the verb 'to save' has the idea of making someone well, of healing, of placing a person in a good situation. As noted earlier, the sabbath was a memorial of creation, the day to remember the creative power of God in bringing life and harmony into existence.

Jesus is angry. But what is he angry about? Interestingly, **5** the second verb, **grieved**, has the idea of Jesus feeling sympathy or grieving *with* his opponents. This suggests that Jesus' anger may not be directed against the people themselves, but against the existence of their **hardness of heart. Hardness of heart** is an expression used of Pharaoh in the Exodus story (see Exod 4-11). It is the inability to see the clear will of God in a certain situation. The expression is also used of the disciples (6:52), which shows that it is not a condition experienced only by the opponents of Jesus. It does not refer to some moral failure, but to the condition of a humanity which is blind to God and his will. It is this condition which angers Jesus, and which causes him to grieve with, or for, those who suffer from it.

Jesus has no hesitation in healing the man. He who himself is the sabbath brings rest, not a burden. The man had a **withered hand**. A person's hand is essential for work, for carrying things, for saving, and punishing. Jesus frees the man to use his hand, not simply to keep the laws of the sabbath (many of which involved the use of the hand), but also now for saving actions. The sabbath rule has been kept by Jesus: he has observed the day as a memorial of creation, by restoring a withered hand for use for its original created purpose.

The **Herodians** are mentioned only in the gospels. They 6 were probably supporters of Herod, who wanted to maintain good relations with Rome while holding on to power themselves. Jesus threatens this fragile peace, just as he threatens the authority of the Pharisees. Their plan is to **destroy** him. This probably means planning his death, but the verb can also mean ruining his reputation. For those who opposed Jesus, his eventual death was indeed the ruination of his reputation! This plan is, of course, highly ironical, in that the sabbath is meant to be for the creation of life, but the very sticklers for its observance use it in order to work out a plot to kill!

## *A pause for summary, 3:7-12*

⁷ **Jesus withdrew with his disciples to the sea, and a great multitude from Galilee followed; also from Judea ⁸ and Jerusalem and Idumea and from beyond the Jordan and from about Tyre and Sidon a great multitude, hearing all that he did, came to him. ⁹ And he told his disciples to have a boat ready for him because of the crowd, lest they should crush him; ¹⁰ for he had healed many, so that all who had diseases pressed upon him to touch him. ¹¹ And whenever the unclean spirits beheld him, they fell down before him and cried out, 'You are the**

**Son of God.' ¹² And he strictly ordered them not to make him known.**

Mark pauses here in his story to summarise things so far in Jesus' ministry. Jesus withdraws with his disciples, but the crowds still follow. Mark seems to wish to indicate the attraction that Jesus has for the crowds. The verb 'to follow' is so important in Mark's story that, whenever it appears, one is perhaps tempted to read more into it than is there. The Pharisees and the authoritative teachers of God's law do not follow Jesus, who teaches the will of God, but the ignorant masses do. They hear his word. They come to him.

The names of the various areas that are mentioned suggest that Mark means all Israel, the whole area of land inhabited by Jews. Samaria is not mentioned, or the Decapolis, because they were not inhabited by Jews.

Jesus is occasionally shown as being in a boat in order to withdraw from the crowds and to be with his disciples. In some ways, the boat serves a similar purpose in Mark's story as the house (see commentary on 1:29; 2:1).

The word **diseases** literally means 'scourges'. The diseases can be seen as whippings given by the unclean spirits or demons. No-one who is a victim of dehumanising systems or spirits comes away unmarked. The desire to touch Jesus probably has superstitious ideas associated with it. The thought would be that touching the healer imbues one with his power. The **many** are those for whom Jesus came to give his life (10:45), and to pour out his lifeblood (14:24). The many, who have been touched by the scourges of the unclean and demonic spirits, reach out to touch the one who has authority to make clean and whole. The **spirits** here are **unclean** rather than demonic. It is possible that what is meant is a spirit which makes a person ritually and cultically unclean. Spirits were commonly understood to be in the air that people breathed. One was possessed by, or in the possession of, either a good spirit or a bad one. The spirits here acknowledge the authority of Jesus and fall down before him. We are told that they **beheld** him, but theirs is not the vision of faith. A common characteristic of evil and unclean spirits is their loud crying out, something to be kept in mind in relation to Jesus' death (15:37)! They acknowledge him to be **Son of God**, that is, as having all the characteristics of God himself, especially the authority to rebuke. Those on the outside know who Jesus really is; those on the inside do not. They will come to know him only after he has become unclean in his death. That is Mark's secret or mystery.

Jesus 'strictly orders' them **not to make him known**. It **12** is a pity that the RSV does not translate here more literally and use the word 'rebuke'. Only Jesus can rebuke. Anyone else, in Mark's view, who tries to rebuke, does so without authority. Only Jesus, like Yahweh of old, has the authority to rebuke. It is interesting that it is the unclean spirits who know Jesus and who are commanded not to make him known. Does this mean that what we have here is some kind of spirit-to-spirit conversation between Jesus and the unclean spirits, which only they themselves understand? If so, Jesus is commanding that it stay that way, and that the hidden spirit-conversation not be made public. It is not the *people* 'in an unclean spirit' who are rebuked, but the spirits themselves.

Jesus does not wish to be acknowledged as a result of demonstrations of power, such as exorcisms. Rather, it is power that is exorcised by Jesus. There is a tendency in Mark to play down miracles as public evidence of Jesus' status as holy Son of God. The public sign of his status is the cross. This is where, paradoxically, the Son of God, the Holy One, is publicly revealed.

It is ironical – and this is the skill of Mark as a story-teller – that his readers already know who Jesus is! The frequently used term 'messianic secret' is therefore misleading. It is no secret for Mark's readers, but is simply used by him as a narrative device. In addition, it is not so much a *messianic* secret, although this is an aspect of it, but the riddle of Jesus as the holy Son of God. Who can see the Holy One in this Jesus of Nazareth who associates with the unholy? This is the riddle, this is the mystery of Jesus.


## *Who has authority to talk? 3:13-19*

[13] **And he went up on the mountain, and called to him those whom he desired; and they came to him.** [14] **And he appointed twelve,**[k] **to be with him, and to be sent out to preach** [15] **and have authority to cast out demons:** [16] **Simon whom he surnamed Peter;** [17] **James the son of Zebedee and John the brother of James, whom he surnamed Boanerges, that is, sons of thunder;** [18] **Andrew, and Philip, and Bartholomew, and Matthew, and Thomas, and James the son of Alphaeus, and Thaddaeus, and Simon the Cananaean,** [19] **and Judas Iscariot, who betrayed him.**

[k] Other ancient authorities add *whom also he named apostles*

Jesus goes to **the mountain** and calls those whom he wishes, and they come to him. The call of Jesus has that creative power to change the direction of people's lives. The mountain here is not just any mountain but, as often in Mark, *the* mountain. The mountain represents the presence of God. Jesus finds the presence of God, not in the synagogue or temple, but on the mountain. The readers know that it is on the mountain that God's answer to the question of who Jesus is will be answered (9:2-8). 13

The mountain in Mark serves much the same purpose as the sea and the desert: it is the place where Jesus goes to be alone, or with only a few of his disciples. It is the place of withdrawal, the place where Jesus finds his identity as Son of God. In the case of Moses and Elijah, mountain and desert are tightly linked, because the mountain involved is in the desert. Sinai/Horeb is the mountain of God, and it is here that God calls his prophet, and also calls his people to be his son. The verb 'call to' is common in Mark (see 3:23; 6:7; 7:14; 8:1,34; 10:42; 12:43). Jesus calls people to himself to walk along his way, and thus to do the will of God.

The same creative word which expels all that is dehumanising and unclean, and rebukes the demons, commanding them to be silent, is now spoken again to create a new community, whose ministry is the same as that of Jesus: to preach, and to cast out the demons which oppress, dehumanise and make unclean. He chooses **twelve** (some manuscripts add: **whom also he named apostles**) to be **with him**. This is a signal for readers in relation to Jesus' last week, when those whom he has called and wants to be with him in fact leave him, deny him, betray him. Once again, irony features strongly. 14

Jesus chooses the twelve for the purpose of sending them out to preach, or proclaim, and to have authority over the demons. Even though they will be sent out on their own, they have been chosen to be with Jesus. The community of Mark is conscious of Jesus' abiding presence. It is somewhat strange that Mark makes no mention of the kingdom of God, or of the gospel, in relation to the mission of the twelve. Is this because these can be understood only *after* the Easter experience? 15

At certain turning points in people's lives, it can happen that they take on a new name. It signifies a change of direction. The fact that it is Jesus who gives a new name to some of the twelve indicates his total authority over them, because being able to name means being in a position of 16 authority. **Simon** is now known as **Peter**, a name which means something like 'rock'. Some scholars think that there may be a reference to the 'rocky ground' of the parable about the seeds (4:5), and that Peter therefore represents those followers who have heard the call of Jesus but in whom his word has not taken deep root. **James** and **John** are called **Boanerges**, **sons of thunder**. It is difficult to know what is meant by this name. Some have understood it to refer to their temper, but it almost certainly has deeper significance than that. The thunder of water is often used in relation to God (see for example, Ps 29:3; Rev 14:2). Clouds, and the ability to make rain, are also associated with God and his prophets, especially Elijah (see, for example, 1 Kgs 18:41-45). Rain was understood as an end-time gift but, rather curiously, Jesus is never portrayed as the bringer of rain. It may be that **sons of thunder** is a name reflecting the hopes and expectations of James and John in relation to the end-time. Note that in 10:35-45 it is James and John who want to hold positions of power in the end-time kingdom of Jesus.

As is usual in listings of the disciples, Peter, James and John are to the fore. The name of **Simon the Cananaean** is interesting, inasmuch as the word **Cananaean** appears to be a misunderstanding of the Aramaic word which really means 'Zealot' (the name of a group of radical Jewish nationalists). Does Mark wish to play down the fact that Jesus had a politically radical disciple? Is he perhaps even embarrassed by this? Some scholars have argued that Mark writes immediately after the destruction of Jerusalem by the Roman general Titus (70 AD), and that he writes in Rome for the Christian community there, and for this reason can ill afford to give credence to any suggestion that the new Christian Way is anti-Roman, or that it stands in the tradition of the Zealots or other Jewish nationalist groups. Mark normally translates Aramaic terms so that his readers can understand them, and in fact this is what he does with the name Boanerges (v 17). It is possible that he does not do that here with Simon's nickname because he knows that it means Zealot.

**Judas** is invariably portrayed as the betrayer. It is clear that the Christian communities knew only too well the story of Judas, and were aware of the danger of going that same way themselves. His act of betrayal is the great unclean action, because it involves handing the Clean One over to death, the ultimate unclean power.

The fact that the twelve are listed here suggests that Mark's readers may not have known all of them by name.

## The crucial question: By what authority? 3:20-30

Then he went home; [20] **and the crowd came together again, so that they could not even eat.** [21] **And when his family heard it, they went out to seize him, for people were saying, 'He is beside himself.'** [22] **And the scribes who came down from Jerusalem said, 'He is possessed by Beelzebul, and by the prince of demons he casts out the demons.'** [23] **And he called them to him, and said to them in parables, 'How can Satan cast out Satan?** [24] **If a kingdom is divided against itself, that kingdom cannot stand.** [25] **And if a house is divided against itself, that house will not be able to stand.** [26] **And if Satan has risen up against himself and is divided, he cannot stand, but is coming to an end.** [27] **But no one can enter a strong man's house and plunder his goods, unless he first binds the strong man; then indeed he may plunder his house.** [28] **' Truly, I say to you, all sins will be forgiven the sons of men, and whatever blasphemies they utter;** [29] **but whoever blasphemes against the Holy Spirit never has forgiveness, but is guilty of an eternal sin'** — [30] **for they had said, 'He has an unclean spirit.'**

Jesus returns **home** (literally, 'he comes to a house'), a typical Marcan technique to keep the story moving. The inevitable **crowd** is there again. It is difficult to know what is meant by the statement that the crowd was so great **that they could not even eat**. Who is it who could not eat? It could be either Jesus and his disciples, or Jesus and the crowd. The NIV thinks it refers to Jesus and his disciples. The eating of bread is a central theme later in the gospel (6:35-44; 8:1-10; 14:22). Is Mark simply alerting his readers, here in advance, to this important theme? However, the verses that follow indicate that there is some significance right here in the fact that Jesus does not eat. His not eating seems to be linked somehow with the claim that he is mad. It has been suggested that times of eating were also the time when serious debate and discussion about the Torah (God's law) took place, especially if rabbis or scribes were present. There were also particular rituals of blessing and thanksgiving in connection with meals, and it may be that the presence of the crowds prevented these, causing some to think that Jesus must be mad. (See the similar situation at 6:31, and the comments there.)

**21** Jesus' **family** seek to **seize** or arrest him, because people are saying that he is out of his mind. 'Family' is translated 'friends' by AV. Literally, it is 'those from his side, those emanating from him'. It is unclear who is really meant. Some manuscripts have 'the scribes and the others' instead of 'family'. Mark has already indicated, by the way he begins his story, that he is not interested in Jesus' birth or his genealogy. Family purity was very important for many Jews, especially those in Palestine, and Jerusalem in particular, but for Jesus and Mark it is of no importance. **22** The authorities from Jerusalem agree with the view that Jesus is out of his mind (note once again the implication that Jesus is *outside*), but describe Jesus' condition in 'spiritual' terms: he is **possessed by Beelzebul,** and **casts out the demons** by the power of **the prince of demons.** Jesus gives a very logical answer: 'If I am casting out demons, how can you say that I am on their side?'

**23** Here we have the first mention of **parables** by Mark. It comes in the context of Jesus calling his disciples to him. There is always a particular purpose in such calling by Jesus. Parables are more than stories; they are riddles or mysteries which are only revealed to those on the inside, who even then often do not understand. There is always something quite enigmatic about Jesus' parables. The opposite to speaking in parables is to speak plainly or openly (see 8:32).

**24 26** Very early in Christian thought, Jesus is known as the Stronger One. In order to free people from the power of Satan, Jesus must first of all tie him up and so reduce his power. Only then can Satan's house be plundered, that is, people can be freed from his power. However, there is also another way of understanding verse 27. The **strong man 27** could refer to Jesus. Satan cannot enter Jesus' house unless he is first bound, and only then can the house be plundered. It is when Jesus is actually bound (see 15:1) that those of his house flee for their lives and deny him.

**28** What is characteristic of the **sons of men** (the plural form of 'Son of man' as used by Jesus) is their sin. Sin **will be forgiven**, even the sin of blasphemy, but the sin which consists of rejection of the Spirit of holiness, and the accu- **29** sation that it is in league with the spirit of uncleanness, will not be forgiven. Were there people within the synagogues where Christians also worshipped, who claimed that Jesus was not Lord, but that he should be cursed (see 1 Cor 12:3)? Did some believe that Jesus was a magician working with the name and power of Satan rather than that of God? One of the common accusations made against Jesus in later Jewish writings is that of being a deceiver.

## *Insiders and outsiders, 3:31-35*

**³¹ And his mother and his brothers came; and standing outside they sent to him and called him. ³² And a crowd was sitting about him; and they said to him, 'Your mother and your brothers!¹ are outside, asking for you.' ³³ And he replied, 'Who are my mother and my brothers?' ³⁴ And looking around on those who sat about him, he said, 'Here are my mother and my brothers! ³⁵ Whoever does the will of God is my brother, and sister, and mother.'**

¹ Other early authorities add *and your sisters*

In the context of the preceding passage, with its serious message, Jesus speaks harsh words about his family and their claims on him. It can be said with some justification that, next to wealth, Jesus saw the family as the biggest obstacle to discipleship. There is no reference here to Jesus' father. This is due more to the importance for Christians of seeing Jesus as Son of God, than to the death of Joseph or any other explanation for his absence. Jesus' family is **outside** the house when they send to him and call him. His own family is not counted among the insiders. Does this reflect the position of some Christians, who were in the 'house' (church), and were asked for by their families who had not followed them into the Christian community? It may also be a rejection of some in the Christian community who claimed authority because they were blood relatives of Jesus. The crowds are closer to Jesus than his family. They are his family because they do the **will of God**. They are insiders, those who sit in the circle around Jesus. Blood ties and family relationships mean nothing in the kingdom of God, where disciples are called to leave family, and to do their Father's will, as they fall in step behind their brother. What Jesus says here must have hit the Pharisees and others from Jerusalem very hard, since in Jewish society, especially in Jerusalem, purity of descent was important. Only families of pure ancestry, as traced through the genealogies of Ezra, Nehemiah and Chronicles, were assured of the messianic salvation. Others would have to rely on their own merit. Jesus, however, totally rejects any such claims. The salvation which he brings does not come through purity of descent, but through doing the will of God. This means hearing the call of Jesus to walk his way, and rising to follow him within his new community.

The warning is clear: just as those who ought to have been inside – the family of Jesus and the scribes – are in fact outside, so also in the Christian community, those who ought to be inside – the disciples and the first-generation Christians – may also be outside.

The division between those who are 'inside' and those who are 'outside' is further emphasised in the following chapter.

## *The riddle of the kingdom, 4:1-34*

**4:1 Again he began to teach beside the sea. And a very large crowd gathered about him, so that he got into a boat and sat in it on the sea; and the whole crowd was beside the sea on the land. ² And he taught them many things in parables, and in his teaching he said to them: ³ 'Listen! A sower went out to sow. ⁴ And as he sowed, some seed fell along the path, and the birds came and devoured it. ⁵ Other seed fell on rocky ground, where it had not much soil, and immediately it sprang up, since it had no depth of soil; ⁶ and when the sun rose it was scorched, and since it had no root it withered away. ⁷ Other seed fell among thorns and the thorns grew up and choked it, and it yielded no grain. ⁸ And other seeds fell into good soil and brought forth grain, growing up and increasing and yielding thirtyfold and sixtyfold and a hundredfold.' ⁹ And he said, 'He who has ears to hear, let him hear.'**

**¹⁰ And when he was alone, those who were about him with the twelve asked him concerning the parables. ¹¹ And he said to them, 'To you has been given the secret of the kingdom of God, but for those outside everything is in parables; ¹² so that they may indeed see but not perceive, and may indeed hear but not understand; lest they should turn again, and be forgiven.' ¹³ And he said to them, 'Do you not understand this parable? How then will you understand all the parables? ¹⁴ The sower sows the word. ¹⁵ And these are the ones along the path, where the word is sown; when they hear, Satan immediately comes and takes away the word which is sown in them. ¹⁶ And these in like manner are the ones sown upon rocky**

ground, who, when they hear the word, immediately receive it with joy; [17] and they have no root in themselves, but endure for a while; then, when tribulation or persecution arises on account of the word, immediately they fall away.[m] [18] And others are the ones sown among thorns; they are those who hear the word, [19] but the cares of the world, and the delight in riches, and the desire for other things, enter in and choke the word, and it proves unfruitful. [20] But those that were sown upon the good soil are the ones who hear the word and accept it and bear fruit, thirtyfold and sixtyfold and a hundredfold.'

[21] And he said to them, 'Is a lamp brought in to be put under a bushel, or under a bed, and not on a stand? [22] For there is nothing hid, except to be made manifest; nor is anything secret, except to come to light. [23] If any man has ears to hear, let him hear.' [24] And he said to them, 'Take heed what you hear; the measure you give will be the measure you get, and still more will be given you. [25] For to him who has will more be given; and from him who has not, even what he has will be taken away.'

[26] And he said, 'The kingdom of God is as if a man should scatter seed upon the ground, [27] and should sleep and rise night and day, and the seed should sprout and grow, he knows not how. [28] The earth produces of itself, first the blade, then the ear, then the full grain in the ear. [29] But when the grain is ripe, at once he puts in the sickle, because the harvest has come.'

[30] And he said, 'With what can we compare the kingdom of God, or what parable shall we use for it? [31] It is like a grain of mustard seed, which, when sown upon the ground, is the smallest of all the seeds on earth; [32] yet when it is sown it grows up and becomes the greatest of all shrubs, and puts forth large branches, so that the birds of the air can make nests in its shade.'

[33] With many such parables he spoke the word to them, as they were able to hear it; [34] he did not speak to them without a parable, but privately to his own disciples he explained everything.

[m] Or *stumble*

Using his by now familiar technique of frequent changes of scene, Mark moves his story along by now placing Jesus at the sea, where he is teaching. Once again, **a very large crowd** is there. When Jesus performs a miracle, we are usually told about the response of those who are there, but we rarely hear of people's response to his teaching. Also, Mark tells us little about the content of Jesus' teaching. Jesus teaches here, in parables, from a **boat**. In Mark's gospel the boat, rather like the house, is a place where revelation occurs. The boat is an early symbol for the church, but whether the symbol existed as early as Mark's time of writing is difficult to determine. For Mark the boat serves rather as a symbol of transition. Mark seems to place emphasis on the fact that Jesus is in a boat, and that the boat is on the sea. The sea also is a symbol of transition, but also of uncertainty, and even distress and fear. Jesus' teaching, then, in this situation, is for those who are in transition. The crowds, however, are **on the land**. Mark seems to be making a deliberate point here: the crowds are never quite inside; they do not get into the boat! For Jews, the land meant promise; the sea meant chaos and threat. Jesus again and again calls his followers to leave the land and to cross the sea.

Jesus' use of parables fits Mark's story about him as the one who is only recognised and understood by those 'within', that is, by those who see and hear with the eyes and ears of faith (v 9).    2

Jesus' command: **Listen**! may reflect the great command of God in the revelation of his will to Israel: 'Hear, O Israel' (Deut 6:4). Hearing, which is central to this section (4:9,12,15,16,18, 20,23,24,33) means more than use of the ears; it means understanding. Jesus' command suggests that what he is about to say is very important, and it is. In a way, it is the whole point of Mark's story! It is quite legitimate to see the whole gospel in terms of this parable of the seed and the ground into which it falls. Mark's readers are constantly asked, 'Which soil are you?' as they hear the stories about Peter, about various women, about the disciples, about those who are healed, and so on.    3

The sower goes **out**. The sowing of the gospel is for those outside. In Palestine, sowing took place before ploughing. There is no need to understand the sower as being careless! The rocky ground of verse 5, for example, would be limestone with only a thin layer of topsoil. The story, as it is told by Jesus, is clear and simple: the seed is sown, but the fruit that it produces varies from nothing at all to a full crop. Something very ordinary can yield surprising results.    4

   5-8

In verse 9 Jesus challenges his hearers: 'Do you understand what I have said?' When he says: **He who has ears to hear, let him hear**, this is like saying: 'If you are "inside", you will understand'. Rather than explain the    9 parable – which, like explaining a joke, could ruin the story – Jesus allows his listeners to participate in discovering its meaning. His concluding words also highlight the effect of his teaching on people: the insiders can hear, the outsiders cannot.

The discussion that follows takes place when Jesus is **alone**. There are other occasions when he is alone with his close followers (4:34; 6:31,47; 9:2). We have already seen that to find and know Jesus, one needs to go outside, out into the desert, where Jesus is alone (see commentary on 1:3,14,37). It is there that Jesus explains the parables to those around him. The secret is not given to everyone, but to the twelve, who in the early Christian communities must have carried a great deal of authority in their interpretation of Jesus, his message and his ministry. Jesus says as much: **To you has been given the secret**. Others have only the parables. The phrase **those who were about him with the twelve** is difficult. Are we meant to understand two groups: the twelve and others? Or does **those who were about him** refer to the inner group of Peter, James and John? 10

Here Jesus speaks of the **kingdom of God** for the first time since the announcement of his message in 1:15. It is clear from the gospels that Jesus frequently used parables in his teaching of the kingdom. The kingdom is a **secret**; its existence is not clear. It is seen and perceived only by those who have been given the secret, that is, those whom Jesus has called and chosen. But even they need to have the enigma explained and revealed to them, because their call by Jesus is not sufficient in itself for them to be able to understand. This is not to say that Jesus deliberately spoke in riddles to outsiders (or insiders for that matter), but that everything is a riddle to those who do not see or hear. It is to those who are around Jesus that the secret is given. Those **outside** see only the riddle. Jesus' words in verse 12 echo Isaiah 6:9. Luke (8:10) and Matthew (13:13) appear to soften these words a little in comparison to Mark. The words are probably best understood as being consistent with Mark's view of Jesus as the one whose true nature is hidden from all except those who believe. Mark's use of the text differs from the original form in Isaiah, and also from its use in Matthew (13:13) and Acts (28:26), in that he reverses 11 12 the order of hearing and seeing, and makes no reference to the hearts of the people being 'fat' (Isa 6:10). Mark's emphasis is not on the hardening of the people's hearts, but on Jesus and his words as riddles to those outside.

It is clear that Jesus' parables are more than just stories. They are riddles. In Mark's view everything that Jesus says and does is a parable, a mystery to those outside. This is exactly what he says in verse 11: **for those outside everything is in parables**. 'Everything' means everything, not just the immediate words of Jesus. The whole gospel of Jesus is a riddle. The parables in Mark can be defined as riddles. When revelation is not received by people, it remains a riddle to them. It is like seed which falls onto hard and rocky ground and does not bear fruit.

Jesus rarely explained his parables. The fact that he does so here means that Mark sees it as being crucial to his readers' understanding. If they do not understand this **13** parable, they will not understand the gospel story as a whole (this is exactly what Jesus says in verse 13). The emphasis in Jesus' explanation is on *hearing*. The word of **14-** the kingdom meets with varying responses. Some hear, but are like plants with shallow roots, and when a time of **16** testing comes, they **fall away**. The verb that occurs here is **17,** the same as that used by Jesus in warning his disciples that **18** they will all fall away (14:27,29), and its occurrence here is no doubt meant to point ahead to what comes later. Others hear, but the alluring voice of wealth – the great obstacle to true hearing/following (see 10:22) – blocks out the voice of **19** Jesus. Finally, there are those who hear, and their hearing produces much fruit, in varying amounts, in their lives. What begins in weakness, and in quite ordinary fashion, **20** ends with the abundant blessing of God. The cross once again is there in the background. He who is shamefully executed on a cross, and is buried in the ground, produces an amazing harvest. The fruit of this harvest is found not so much in the disciples, but in those who are unclean: women, those who are healed, Gentiles.

The next section, verses 21-25, contains a short parable which again emphasises the importance of hearing. Those who hear will let their hearing produce actions that are compatible with it. Just as a lamp is not put under a cover, **21-** but in a place where it can give light, so the one who hears **23** will understand. Jesus' words in verse 25 mean that the one **24,** who hears well will follow Jesus' way, and will come to know **25** more. Those, however, who in their hearing are like the seed falling on hard ground, will lose what they first had, little as it was.

The short parable in verses 26-29 demonstrates that the kingdom of God comes **of itself**, as Luther also says in his explanation of the second petition of the Lord's Prayer. The kingdom is hidden, it is secret, and is not at all dependent on human activity, or measurable by human standards.

The words, **he puts in the sickle, because the harvest has come**, echo Joel 3:13. The harvest here is a picture of judgment. Only at the time of harvest can judgment be made, not before.

Verses 30-32 are another short parable, which stresses the hiddenness or, in this case, the smallness, of the kingdom to human observation. The small **mustard seed** grows into a large bush, in which the birds can rest and shelter. The kingdom of God may look small, but it provides a nesting place and shelter for many, including outsiders, the unclean and Gentiles. In all these parables, the cross of Jesus is foreshadowed. The cross looks weak, small, insignificant. But it is this cross that produces much fruit, gives light, brings judgment, and provides rest and a nesting place for those outside. The Marcan community faces defeat and division, but the sowing that has taken place gives promise of a great harvest still to come. The present situation does not yet show what the kingdom promised to bring. But it will come. At present it is in prenatal darkness, like seed in the dark ground, like a lamp under a bushel. But the time of birth will come, the time when the seed will bear fruit and the lamp will give light.

Verses 33 and 34 are a summary statement. Jesus teaches the people in parables, explaining their meaning only to those who have been called to learn from him. To those outside the parables remain unexplained. The section that follows does not at first appear to be related to what has come before. However, it demonstrates the point that the disciples have not heard and do not understand. The present passage says that Jesus **explained everything** to his disciples, but in the passage that follows they are shown, on that same day, to be ignorant, fearful and doubting, as they ask of Jesus: 'Who then is this?' (v 41).

## PART II : 4:35 – 8:21

*Transitions are rough, 4:35-41*

<sup>35</sup> **On that day, when evening had come, he said to them, 'Let us go across to the other side.'** <sup>36</sup> **And leaving the crowd, they took him with them, just as he was, in the boat. And other boats were with him.** <sup>37</sup> **And a great storm of wind arose, and the waves beat into the boat, so that the boat was already filling.** <sup>38</sup> **But he was in the stern, asleep on the cushion; and they woke him and said to him, 'Teacher, do you not care if we perish?'** <sup>39</sup> **And he awoke and rebuked the wind, and said to the sea, 'Peace! Be still!' And the wind ceased, and there was a great calm.** <sup>40</sup> **He said to them, 'Why are you afraid? Have you no faith?'** <sup>41</sup> **And they were filled with awe, and said to one another, 'Who then is this, that even wind and sea obey him?'**

**35, 36** Verse 35 introduces the first of six crossings of the Sea of Galilee that Jesus makes. The lake was a barrier between Galilee, which was Jewish territory, and the Decapolis, which was Gentile country. Christians in Mark's community are in transition from the old ways of Judaism to the new Christian ways, which involve the inclusion of the previously unclean Gentiles. It is not surprising that this transition is stormy and evokes fear in many Christians. Here again the boat is the place for a revelation of Jesus (see commentary on 4:1), in this case of his power and authority over the chaotic forces which threaten the disciples. Mark's story moves from the previous section, with the parable of sowing and of seeds growing quietly and indiscernibly, to this scene with its wild storm. The 'hearers' of the previous section are now put to the test! This episode takes place **on that day**, 'it being late' (to translate verse 35 more literally). **On that day** is the phrase used in the Old Testament to refer to the so-called day of the Lord, on which God would act in a decisive way. It was seen as the day when the evil powers would be broken, the authority of God would be seen, and his people would be rescued.

**37, 38** Sudden storms on Lake Galilee still occur today. What Jesus sleeps on is not so much a **cushion** as a small leather or wooden seat used by a rower or the helmsman. The disciples call out to Jesus, addressing him as **teacher**. This title means more than it normally does to us. Jesus as teacher is the revealer of God, and of the wisdom of God.

Nevertheless, it is not the title that Mark wishes the followers of Jesus to give him. It indicates a failure to 'see' on the part of the disciples. We see here a reticence by Mark to call Jesus 'Lord' (compare Matt 8:25). Does the title carry political overtones for Mark that he wishes to avoid?

There are echoes of various parts of this story in the Psalms. Psalm 35:23, 44:23, and 59:4 all call on God to wake up and come to the help of his righteous people. In Psalm 69 (vv 1,2,14,15) the seas are portrayed as the great waters of chaos, the evil forces that threaten to overwhelm and destroy (according to Revelation 21:1 there will be no sea in the new creation!). Psalm 89:9, 93:4, 106:9 and Isaiah 51:10 all speak of God as the one who controls the sea and the tempests. Sleep is often seen in the Bible as a sign of trust (Prov 3:24; Pss 3:5; 4:8; Job 11:18; Lev 26:6).

**39** Jesus rebukes the wind. In Mark's gospel only Jesus has authority to rebuke. Whenever other people rebuke, they do so without authority, and are rebuked in turn by Jesus. Yahweh alone rebukes the powers of evil. Among humans only Jesus has that authority. The word used by Jesus to calm the storm (translated here as **Be still**), is a word that could be used in relation to a wild and ferocious animal: 'Be muzzled!' This command the powers of chaos must obey. Jesus' word has the same power as that first word, spoken by God, that overcame chaos at creation. His word has that same authority to create peace out of chaos. There had been a **great storm** (v 37), but now, at his word, there is a **great calm** (v 39). The transition is rough, but the word of Jesus brings peace and reconciliation in the face of the chaotic powers which threaten to destroy the Christian community.

Where Jesus is present the kingdom of God is present, and in his presence all other claims to authority must give way and be obedient. The Christian community may be fearful in the transition between the old and the new, but Jesus is present. In the early Christian communities there was a struggle between some who wanted to go forward, pouring the new wine into new skins, and others who wanted to hang on to the old and familiar, the promises of the God of their ancestors, and their traditions. Like the disciples crossing the lake, they encountered the storm and were afraid of going under. But Jesus has authority. He is present. He creates calm. The transition will succeed, because Jesus is there with them in the storm.

**40** Jesus' words in verse 40 would be better translated: 'Why are you cowardly? Don't you have faith yet?' The 'yet' is significant, and parallels Jesus' rebuke in 8:17,21. The disciples are slow to understand, to see, to have courage. But in the presence of Jesus' authority there is no room for cowardice. Faith trusts that word which is spoken into all situations of chaos – where the evil powers are active – and which creates peace. Faith is not a possession, but the response to the call to walk a certain way, the call to make crossings or transitions. It involves the call to leave the things that have given security in the past, and to live with hope. Faith calls for courage in times of pressure. It is no wonder that this story was a favourite among early Christian groups, which found themselves under great pressure as they made their transitions, and which felt that God needed to be roused from sleep to rescue his people.

The disciples respond with **awe** (literally, 'they were afraid with a great fear'). They wonder who this is who has such authority over the forces of chaos. Fear, as a response to the one who makes transitions possible in situations of chaos, is also the response to his final great transition, the one from death to life (see 16:8). **41**

*There is uncleanness on the other side of the lake too, 5:1-20*

**¹ They came to the other side of the sea, to the country of the Gerasenes[n]. ² And when he had come out of the boat, there met him out of the tombs a man with an unclean spirit, ³ who lived among the tombs; and no one could bind him any more, even with a chain; ⁴ for he had often been bound with fetters and chains, but the chains he wrenched apart, and the fetters he broke in pieces; and no one had the strength to subdue him. ⁵ Night and day among the tombs and on the mountains he was always crying out, and bruising himself with stones. ⁶ And when he saw Jesus from afar, he ran and worshipped him; ⁷ and crying out with a loud voice, he said, 'What have you to do with me, Jesus, Son of the Most High God? I adjure you by God, do not torment me.' ⁸ For he had said to him, 'Come out of the man, you unclean spirit!' ⁹ And Jesus[o] asked him, 'What is your name?' He replied, 'My name is Legion; for we are many.' ¹⁰ And he begged him eagerly not to send them out of the country. ¹¹ Now a great herd of swine was feeding there on the hillside; ¹² and they**

begged him, 'Send us to the swine, let us enter them.'¹³ So he gave them leave. **And the unclean spirits came out, and entered the swine; and the herd, numbering about two thousand, rushed down the steep bank into the sea, and were drowned in the sea.**

¹⁴ **The herdsmen fled, and told it in the city and in the country. And people came to see what it was that had happened.** ¹⁵ **And they came to Jesus, and saw the demoniac sitting there, clothed and in his right mind, the man who had had the legion; and they were afraid.** ¹⁶ **And those who had seen it told what had happened to the demoniac and to the swine.** ¹⁷ **And they began to beg Jesusᵖ to depart from their neighbourhood.** ¹⁸ **And as he was getting into the boat, the man who had been possessed with demons begged him that he might be with him.** ¹⁹ **But he refused, and said to him, 'Go home to your friends, and tell them how much the Lord has done for you, and how he has had mercy on you.'** ²⁰ **And he went away and began to proclaim in the Decapolis how much Jesus had done for him; and all men marvelled.**

ⁿ Other ancient authorities read *Gergesenes*, some *Gadarenes*
º Greek *he*
ᵖ Greek *him*

Mark introduces this important episode with a sentence linking it to the previous one. In travelling across the lake, Jesus had to overcome the powers of evil. Now, when he reaches the other side, he comes into 'unclean' territory. The **country of the Gerasenes** is a Gentile area. The exact form of the name is uncertain. Gerasa was a place about 60 kilometres inland from the lake. Gadara and Gergesa, which are other possibilities suggested by some manuscripts, were places that were closer to the lake. Because this is unclean territory, it is not surprising that the first person to meet Jesus as soon as he sets foot on shore is **unclean** (literally, 'a man in an unclean spirit'). Just as Jesus' first action in Galilee was an exorcism, so his first action among the Gentiles is to exorcise one who is unclean. As usual, Mark calls the spirit an **unclean spirit** rather than a demon. Not only is the man 'in an unclean spirit', but he also lives among the unclean. Dead bodies and cemeteries were considered by Jews to be particularly unclean. It is not unknown for possessed people to exhibit superhuman strength. However, the point here of the description of the man's strength is to show that no human being can subdue the strong one, the devil. That can be done only by the

Stronger One: Jesus (3:27). Just as Jesus rebuked the storm on the lake, so he now rebukes the forces of chaos which have made this man unclean.

**Crying out** is a sign of a demon or unclean spirit. This man cries out **with a loud voice**. He bruises himself with stones. He is dehumanised. All powers in social, religious, and political structures which dehumanise are evil, and must be exorcised by the power, and in the name of, the Stronger One, Jesus Christ.  5

The man runs to Jesus and worships him (the word that is used means 'to go down on one's knees'). As on previous occasions (1:24,34), the unclean spirit knows who Jesus is. In response to the command of Jesus for the unclean spirit to come out, the man acknowledges that Jesus, as the **Son of the Most High God**, can have nothing to do with him, since he has an unclean spirit. It is a frequent part of Marcan irony that the disciples have to ask, 'Who is this?' whereas those who are unclean know! Jesus has been declared the clean Son of God out in the desert, and he will be declared Son of God again in the loneliness of the mountain top (9:7), and in the desert/mountain of the cross (15:39). From Jesus' brief exchange with this man, it appears that this story is part of the continuing theme in Mark about what is clean and what is unclean. This question was obviously crucial in the thinking and practice of the Christian community. As a non-Jew, the man in this story was unclean. Even if he had been a Jew, he would still have been unclean, and therefore, to all intents and purposes, a Gentile. When Jesus asks him his **name** (an action that shows Jesus' authority) he says, '**My name is Legion for we are many**'. This man is really unclean! Some have suggested that the name Legion would have made Mark's reader's think immediately of the legions of the Roman army. In this case, the man represents those living under the rule of the Romans, who were an unclean power opposed to the claims of Jesus as Lord. It is well known that some Roman emperors, either in their own lifetime or after they had died, were proclaimed to be a god and were honoured as lord. Mark uses this story as an indirect way of opposing Rome. Its point would have been clear to his readers, but would not have been so easily understood by the Roman authorities.  6   7,8   9, 10

That the motif of clean/unclean is at the heart of this story is further evidenced by the reference to the **swine**. Pigs are unclean in Jewish thinking. The unclean spirits are transferred to the unclean animals, who then rush headlong over  11, 12 the cliff and are drowned. Mark mentions that there were about 2000 swine. A Roman legion normally numbered 6000. A battalion consisted of 2048. If Mark was thinking along these lines at all, he may have been aware of this number. It is possible that Mark intends his readers to notice that the **sea**, which in 4:35-41 threatened to become the grave of Jesus and his flock, actually does become the burial place of the demons. It is as though, at Jesus' command, the forces of death devour each other, since they are powerless when facing the Son of God. Or, to put it another way, the unclean powers devour each other at the command of the Clean One.

Some have suggested that the behaviour of the pigs in this episode is highly unpiglike! Apparently pigs do not move around in herds, and do not stampede as horses or cattle sometimes do. If this is the case, the rushing of 2000 pigs in formation could well support the idea that Mark has Roman legions in mind.

The locals hear what has happened, and so come to have a look. They see that, in the presence of Jesus, the one who was once unclean and beyond human acceptance is now clean. Their response is predictable: they are **afraid**. It is not clear from verse 17 whether the locals want Jesus or the healed man to leave their area. Most translations suggest the former, and, in the light of verse 18, this makes the best sense. The man asks to **be with** Jesus (compare 3:14, where the disciples are chosen to 'be with' Jesus), but Jesus refuses, and tells him to go home (literally, to his house. Does this mean the local church?), and tell people how much the Lord has done for him, and how God offers mercy also to those who are unclean. The **Lord** here probably means God, especially since Mark is very reticent to have Jesus addressed as Lord. However, if this episode is an attack against the unclean power of the Roman military and political system, then the command to speak of what the Lord (meaning Jesus) has done, would be a deliberate smack in the eye for the Roman claim that Caesar is lord. The man goes and proclaims in his local area, known as **the Decapolis**, a confederation of ten cities east of the Jordan, what Jesus has done for him. There is no record of Christian communities in that area. But Mark is saying to his readers: Do not cross back over to Judaism, but stay where you are in Gentile territory, which has now been made clean.

This episode demonstrates the authority of Jesus over all unclean powers, even on their home ground. At the same time, it shows that the mercy of the Lord extends to all who are unclean, ritually, cultically, or in any other way. What God has called clean let no-one call unclean (Acts 10:15). Both sides of the lake are made clean by Jesus!

## *The faith that makes clean, 5:21-43*

[21] **And when Jesus had crossed again in the boat to the other side, a great crowd gathered about him; and he was beside the sea.** [22] **Then came one of the rulers of the synagogue, Jairus by name; and seeing him, he fell at his feet,** [23] **and besought him, saying, 'My little daughter is at the point of death. Come and lay your hands on her, so that she may be made well, and live.'** [24] **And he went with him.**

**And a great crowd followed him and thronged about him.** [25] **And there was a woman who had had a flow of blood for twelve years,** [26] **and who had suffered much under many physicians, and had spent all that she had, and was no better but rather grew worse.** [27] **She had heard the reports about Jesus, and came up behind him in the crowd and touched his garment.** [28] **For she said, 'If I touch even his garments, I shall be made well.'** [29] **And immediately the hemorrhage ceased; and she felt in her body that she was healed of her disease.** [30] **And Jesus, perceiving in himself that power had gone forth from him, immediately turned about in the crowd, and said, 'Who touched my garments?'** [31] **And his disciples said to him, 'You see the crowd pressing around you, and yet you say, "Who touched me?"'** [32] **And he looked around to see who had done it.** [33] **But the woman, knowing what had been done to her, came in fear and trembling and fell down before him, and told him the whole truth.** [34] **And he said to her, 'Daughter, your faith has made you well; go in peace, and be healed of your disease.'**

[35] **While he was still speaking, there came from the ruler's house some who said, 'Your daughter is dead. Why trouble the Teacher any further?'** [36] **But ignoring**[q] **what they said, Jesus said to the ruler of the synagogue, 'Do not fear, only believe.'** [37] **And he allowed no one to follow him except Peter and James and John the brother of James.** [38] **When they came to the house of the ruler of the synagogue, he saw a tumult, and people weeping and wailing loudly.** [39] **And when he had entered, he said to them, 'Why do you make a tumult and weep? The child is not dead but sleeping.'** [40] **And they laughed at him. But he**

**put them all outside, and took the child's father and mother and those who were with him, and went in where the child was. [41] Taking her by the hand he said to her, 'Talitha cumi'; which means, 'Little girl, I say to you, arise.' [42] And immediately the girl got up and walked (she was twelve years of age), and they were immediately overcome with amazement. [43] And he strictly charged them that no one should know this, and told them to give her something to eat.**

[q] Or *overhearing*. Other ancient authorities read *hearing*

Jesus has moved back **to the other side**, that is, the 21
Jewish side of the lake. We are back on familiar ground
and, as usual, there is a **great crowd** of people around
him. Among the Gentiles, on the other side of the lake, the
unclean spirits had been 'many' (5:9). Now again, on the
Jewish side, Jesus is crowded by many people, among whom
also there are unclean spirits.
**Jairus** is one of the leaders in the local synagogue, some 22
of whom later belonged to the Christian community. He falls 23
at Jesus' feet, and begs him to come and lay his hands on
his young daughter, who is **at the point of death**. He
believes that Jesus can make her well, so that she will live.
The short sentence, **And he went with him**, is poignant. 24
Jesus listens to the man's plea, and goes with him. This
story was meant to give courage and hope to Christians who
experienced sickness and death in their families. The message is that Jesus goes with them.
But this is not the end of the story. While Jesus is on the
way to Jairus's place, **a great crowd** follows. We can
imagine Jairus's anxiety increasing as Jesus' progress becomes slower and slower. To make things worse, their
progress is interrupted by a woman, and an unclean woman 25
at that! She takes centre stage, while Jairus must wait in
the wings. For **twelve years** she has been suffering from what appears to have been a menstrual problem. Women's menstrual blood made them doubly unclean, since it not only affected the women themselves, but was seen as having power to make others unclean as well. Numbers 5:1-4 gives the command that lepers, those who had a discharge, and those who were unclean through contact with a dead body, were to be sent out of the camp so that they would not defile it. Leviticus 12 and 15:19-33 explain the rituals involved in the purification of 'unclean' women. It can be noted that the concern, in relation to menstruating women, was not so

much for the purity of the women as for the purity of males, who would be made unclean by contact with such women!

The doctors have not been able to help this woman. Her situation parallels that of the Gerasene man, who also was beyond help, because he could not be bound or clothed by anyone. Debilitating powers, physical or otherwise, cannot be overcome except by the Stronger One, who has come to heal and to liberate (3:27).

The woman has **heard** about Jesus. The parable about the seeds (4:1-9) demonstrated how central hearing is for Mark. Faith and hearing are inseparable. The woman's touching of Jesus' garment indicates that in early Christian communities there may sometimes have been elements of superstition in people's faith. Faith is the courage to break through the boundaries. The power of Christ and his followers was a strong attraction for many people to believe 'in the name of Jesus'. This woman believes that simply by her touching Jesus' clothes, his power will be transferred to her, and she will be healed. And sure enough, this is exactly what happens! Jesus realises that **power** has gone out of him. Mark here is not afraid to use the language of magic, but the expression may also reflect the common opinion that a menstruating woman drained a man of power. Jesus asks: **who touched my garments?** In the gospels, Jesus is often shown as wanting to make personal contact with the people who come to him. He is not a magician. What heals the woman is not simply her touching of his garment, but his word personally addressed to her. As usually happens, the disciples cannot understand Jesus' question about who touched him. We see here again how much the crowds are involved in Jesus' ministry.

The woman comes **in fear and trembling** and falls down before Jesus. She is afraid, because she knows that in touching Jesus she was contaminating him. She was breaking all the rules of the Torah (God's law) and the traditions regarding clean and unclean. What is more, Jesus is now asking her to *publicly* acknowledge her illness, her uncleanness, her shame, her transgression of the law. She may well have talked about her problem with her mother, or with other women in small groups and in their homes, but now she is called upon to acknowledge her uncleanness in front of all these men, including the leader of her local synagogue, the disciples (some of whom were locals, and fishermen at that), and this stranger from Nazareth. She is asked to make a courageous but humiliating step. She is asked to make a transition, something which the disciples made only in great fear and doubt (see 4:35-41). She is asked to have faith. But Jesus speaks to her a word of **peace**. The Clean One has power to release the one who is unclean. Touching is clearly significant in this story. Jesus is not concerned here about becoming ceremonially unclean. In fact, the contagion is reversed: the unclean person who touches Jesus becomes clean! Here again the cross is not far away. Mark's readers understand that Jesus is the Clean One, whose life is given for the sake of the unclean who confess him as Son of God.

The woman, in some respects, stands in contrast to Jairus. Unlike him, she is not named, but is identified only by her unclean illness. Like Jairus, she approaches Jesus, but not from in front, falling at his feet in traditional worship style, but from behind, furtively, with somewhat superstitious thoughts. What they have in common is that both have faith, that is, both take risks and are courageous. Both of them are also temporarily diverted from obtaining their request, Jairus by the woman, the woman by the disciples.

Jesus assures the woman that her faith has been rewarded. Now the account turns back to Jairus. How will his faith stand up? He has been anxiously waiting. Jesus had gone with him, but now there has been this delay! This reflects the experience of the early Christians, as also of us today: Jesus delays. And then comes the fateful word: 'It is too late. Don't bother the teacher any longer. **Your daughter is dead.**' **34, 35**

The first Christians, living in the knowledge of Jesus' resurrection, and expecting the *parousia* (return or presence) of Jesus at any time, must have found it hard to come to terms with death within their community. Jesus delays his coming. If someone has died before Jesus' return, what then?

Jesus ignores (the word can also mean 'overhears') them, and says to Jairus: **Do not fear**. It has been said that whenever God says, 'Don't be afraid', it is time to start worrying, because God is about to ask you to do the impossible (think of Abraham or Mary)! Jesus adds: **Only believe!** For Jairus that must have been a hard word to hear. He *had* believed. He had come to Jesus in front of the crowd, but now, because of the delay, it is too late to believe. Will Jairus learn from the perseverance of the woman? Can a ruler of the synagogue learn something from an unclean woman? **36**

They come to the house, Jesus taking Peter, James, and 37
John with him, as he did at times of revelation, or on other
special occasions. The people are weeping. Death has 38
struck. Jesus goes inside, even though some would say that
it is not right for the Clean One to go into the presence of
one who is dead and therefore unclean. The girl is most 39
certainly dead, despite Jesus' assurance that she is only
**sleeping** (the idea that death is a sleep was common among
early Christians). The people laugh at Jesus' suggestion
that the girl is sleeping, just as some of the people of Athens
later laughed at Paul when he spoke of the resurrection 40
from the dead (Acts 17:32).

The people are sent outside by Jesus. We again see the
outside/inside theme that Mark has previously developed.
Those who are **with him** (an echo of 3:14 again) go with
Jesus into the child's room. While those outside laugh, those
inside see the power of the life-giving Jesus. The high priest
was strictly forbidden to enter a house where people were
mourning (priestly ideas about Jesus are near the surface
in Mark's thinking). Jesus does what was unthinkable for 41
anyone who obeyed the Torah and the traditions of the
elders: he touches the dead girl. Touching the dead defiled
a person (see Num 5:2). Jesus speaks to the girl and restores
her to life. His words are recorded in Aramaic, which was
his mother tongue. It is possible that Mark retains Jesus'
words in Aramaic here because of the common idea that
foreign languages have a certain magical power. But he
gives a translation of the words to indicate that this is not
a magician who is performing here, but the one whose word
gives life, and who himself is life. It may be that Christian
wonder-workers later used Jesus' words as a formula for
raising the dead.

The girl immediately gets up and walks. This is resurrec- 42
tion language. There is no doubt that she is alive. Why is it
mentioned that she was twelve years old? One plausible
suggestion is that it again highlights the meeting of the
Clean One with what is unclean. Twelve years was the age
of puberty, the age at which a girl became marriageable, the
age of fertility. In touching this girl, Jesus was touching
someone who was regarded by men as being socially and
culturally unclean. This heightens the irony of the story,
and emphasises the power of Jesus. Here is a twelve-year-
old girl, on the verge of producing and bearing life – but she
is dead. The true giver of life comes and creates life in her.
Just as the woman in the previous story had been suffering

for twelve years from a flow of blood which made her unclean, this girl had lived for only the same period of time, and had become unclean because of death. It is the living word of Jesus which renders both of them clean.

The response of those who saw what happened is one of **amazement** (literally, 'they were outside of themselves with great ecstasy'). Jesus' command that they keep silent about what happened is ironical, because Mark's readers already know the story and revel in its retelling! It is part of the mystery that the resurrection that is to be talked about is actually that of Jesus himself.

## *A sharpening of the question: Who is this Jesus? 6:1-6a*

**¹ He went away from there and came to his own country; and his disciples followed him. ² And on the sabbath he began to teach in the synagogue; and many who heard him were astonished, saying, 'Where did this man get all this? What is the wisdom given to him? What mighty works are wrought by his hands! ³ Is not this the carpenter, the son of Mary and brother of James and Joseph and Judas and Simon, and are not his sisters here with us?' And they took offence<sup>r</sup> at him. ⁴ And Jesus said to them, 'A prophet is not without honour, except in his own country, and among his own kin, and in his own house.' ⁵ And he could do no mighty work there, except that he laid his hands upon a few sick people and healed them. ⁶ And he marvelled because of their unbelief.**

ʳ Or *stumbled*

This new episode begins in the usual way, with Jesus moving to a different locality in the company of others, this time the disciples. Where are the crowds that usually accompany him? In his home town they are conspicuous by their absence. Jesus has been rejected by his own family (see 3:31-35); now he comes **to his own country**. His disciples follow him. He teaches in the synagogue, and astonishes his hearers, so that they ask what is increasingly becoming the crucial question of Mark's story: 'Who is this man? From where does he have this teaching/revelation?' They ask: **What is the wisdom given to him? Wisdom** and power are often linked in Jewish thought (see Rev 5:12; 7:12). Solomon was regarded as being not only wise, but also powerful. It is ironical that Jesus comes from Nazareth, and yet the people there are the very ones who ask, in effect: 'Where does he come from?' Jesus is not at home in Nazareth.

Jesus here is called a **carpenter**. Some manuscripts, (but 3 not the better ones), read 'son of the carpenter', but this may reflect a Semitic way of simply saying 'carpenter'. There is possibly a kind of insult intended by calling Jesus **son of Mary**, since men were always referred to in relation to their father, not their mother. The point of their questions is: 'How can this man, whose origins we know, have such wisdom and power?' They are scandalised. Of course, the first readers and hearers of this gospel would have smiled, might have laughed out loud, at the irony of these people not knowing Jesus' origins at all. They already know, from Mark's account so far, that this Jesus is the Son of God!

Jesus comes to his own, and his own do not receive him 4 (see John 1:11). Jesus here refers to himself as a **prophet**. His role as prophet is apparent throughout the gospel, sometimes obviously, sometimes less so. Christian tradition often highlighted the rejection of the prophets by Israel. Just as the prophets were rejected, so is Jesus, and so is the Christian community as a whole.

One of the marks of a prophet is the ability to do great 5 works or signs. However, Jesus is limited in this aspect of his role as a prophet by the obstinacy and dullness of perception of the people of his home country. The usual situation is that the crowds marvel at the faith of Jesus which can produce such powerful works of healing. Here, 6 however, it is Jesus' turn to marvel at the lack of faith of the people of his own homeland. Instead of staying in his home town, he goes out to the villages in the neighbourhood, literally, 'the villages in a circle'. The 'circle' around Jesus was mentioned in 3:34, where those who were in the circle, close to Jesus, stood in contrast to Jesus' own family. Here, those in the circle of villages stand in contrast to those in Jesus' home town.

## *The mission of the twelve, 6:6b-13*

**And he went about among the villages teaching.**

**⁷ And he called to him the twelve, and began to send them out two by two, and gave them authority over the unclean spirits. ⁸ He charged them to take nothing for their journey except a staff; no bread, no bag, no money in their belts; ⁹ but to wear sandals and not put on two**

tunics. ¹⁰ And he said to them, 'Where you enter a house, stay there until you leave the place. ¹¹ And if any place will not receive you and they refuse to hear you, when you leave, shake off the dust that is on your feet for a testimony against them.' ¹² **So they went out and preached that men should repent.** ¹³ **And they cast out many demons, and anointed with oil many that were sick and healed them.**

In a situation far removed from the religious centre, Jesus calls to himself the twelve, and then sends them out on their mission. That they go **two by two** suggests that this may have been the practice of early wandering charismatic preachers. They go out with the **authority** of Jesus **over the unclean spirits**, that is, the spirits which cause people to be regarded as ritually, socially and religiously unclean. Mark is not referring here to demon-possessed people. Here in Mark the disciples are allowed to wear sandals, whereas in Luke 10:4 and Matthew 10:10 sandals are prohibited. The sparse possessions parallel the attire of John the Baptist, but also correspond to the garb of wandering Cynic philosophers, whose message had many points of similarity with the ethical standards of early Christian preachers. Some have suggested that there is an echo of the Exodus here (see Exod 12:11). The disciples are called to leave the temple and the synagogues, and to go out into the countryside, into the villages. Their mission is to go beyond the boundaries of Judea, out into the 'desert' of Galilee, Samaria and beyond, because it is in the desert that God makes his covenant with his people, and calls Israel his son.  [7]  [8,9]

The immediate background to Jesus' words in verses 10 and 11 is Jesus' own rejection in his home region. The pupil is not greater than the Master!  [10, 11]

The twelve preach that people **should repent**. This had been the message of John the Baptist, and the call to repent was also central to Jesus' message (see 1:15). They also **cast out many demons**, and anoint people with **oil** (which was commonly used to treat wounds; see Luke 10:34) in healing them of their sickness (compare Jas 5:14). The sick here are literally 'the powerless'. Demons deprive human beings of their dignity and their social, political and human status. The gospel of the kingdom, which comes in Jesus Christ, restores those who are powerless. Note that the disciples go **out**, and that their message and work is effective. This  [12]  [13] contrasts with Jesus who went in to his home town, but was unable to have any effect (6:1-6). The disciples, like Jesus, are effective in their mission when they are outside, across the boundaries, in the desert.

## *What can the disciples expect? 6:14-29*

**¹⁴ King Herod heard of it; for Jesus'ˢ name had become known. Some**ᵗ **said, 'John the baptizer has been raised from the dead; that is why these powers are at work in him.' ¹⁵ But others said, 'It is Elijah.' And others said, 'It is a prophet, like one of the prophets of old.' ¹⁶ But when Herod heard of it he said, 'John, whom I beheaded, has been raised.' ¹⁷ For Herod had sent and seized John, and bound him in prison for the sake of Herodias, his brother Philip's wife; because he had married her. ¹⁸ For John said to Herod, 'It is not lawful for you to have your brother's wife.' ¹⁹ And Herodias had a grudge against him, and wanted to kill him. But she could not, ²⁰ for Herod feared John, knowing that he was a righteous and holy man, and kept him safe. When he heard him, he was much perplexed; and yet he heard him gladly. ²¹ But an opportunity came when Herod on his birthday gave a banquet for his courtiers and officers and the leading men of Galilee. ²² For when Herodias' daughter came in and danced, she pleased Herod and his guests; and the king said to the girl, 'Ask me for whatever you wish, and I will grant it.' ²³ And he vowed to her, 'Whatever you ask me, I will give you, even half of my kingdom.' ²⁴ And she went out, and said to her mother, 'What shall I ask?' And she said, 'The head of John the baptizer.' ²⁵ And she came in immediately with haste to the king, and asked, saying, 'I want you to give me at once the head of John the Baptist on a platter.' ²⁶ And the king was exceedingly sorry; but because of his oaths and his guests he did not want to break his word to her. ²⁷ And immediately the king sent a soldier of the guard and gave orders to bring his head. He went and beheaded him in the prison, ²⁸ and brought his head on a platter, and gave it to the girl; and the girl gave it to her mother. ²⁹ When his disciples heard of it, they came and took his body, and laid it in a tomb.**

ˢ Greek *his*
ᵗ Other ancient authorities read *he*

The account of the unjust and cruel death of the Baptist is given here in the context of the mission of the twelve in order to show the fate that might well befall those who go out with the message of Jesus. It also prepares readers of the gospel for the ultimate fate of Jesus himself. So although this appears to be the only passage in Mark's gospel which does not relate directly to Jesus, indirectly it still does! The fate of John is a warning and anticipation of Jesus' fate, and that of his followers. The gospel of the kingdom offers life, hope and freedom to the powerless, but threatens and exposes the powerful and politically corrupt.

Herod is called a **king** which, strictly speaking, he was not. He was a tetrach (see Matt 14:1; Luke 3:1; 9:7). He had divorced his first wife, the daughter of the Nabatean king, Aretas, in order to marry his sister-in-law Herodias, who was the wife of his half-brother Philip. Herodias had a daughter from her first marriage, whose name was Salome, according to the Jewish historian Josephus. **14**

Three ideas about Jesus are mentioned here (as also in 8:28): first, that Jesus is John resurrected; second, that Jesus is Elijah returned (see Mal 3:23 for this expectation); and third, that Jesus is a prophet. Again, it is ironical that the opponents of Jesus should have such a discussion. Herod is one of several political authorities who do not know or understand who Jesus is. In this respect he foreshadows the Roman authority figure, Pilate, who likewise does not understand Jesus, and who, like Herod, condemns the one who is holy and just. Mark's readers have already been told who Jesus is: he is the Son of God, the Christ, the Son of man with authority. **15, 16**

Jewish law prohibited the marrying of one's sister-in-law (see Lev 18:16), but this was not against Roman or Greek custom. Herod is shown here as being unfaithful to Jewish law, and therefore discredited as a Jewish king. **17, 18**

Stories of women having an evil influence on the actions of evil men are not uncommon, but this story is more about the abuse of political power. The leading men of Galilee are invited to the feast, but no mention is made of Perea, which was also under Herod's jurisdiction. Josephus records that it was actually in Perea that John was imprisoned, in the Machaerus fortress. John, like Jesus after him, was **righteous and holy**, two adjectives often used to describe God's prophets. Jesus is the Holy One and the Righteous One. There were also certain priestly groups who called them- **19 20** selves the Righteous Ones and the Holy Ones. Did John belong to such a priestly group?

**Herodias' daughter** dances at the banquet. Instead of **Herodias' daughter** some manuscripts have 'his daughter Herodias', suggesting that the girl was the daughter of Herod and Herodias, and that she had the same name as her mother. The word that is used to refer to her in verse 22 suggests that she may have been a rather young girl.    21, 22

Herod's vow is remarkably similar to the promise made to Esther (Esth 5:3; 7:2). The king keeps his vow, and so John is executed. There is no trial, although the Jewish legal system demanded one before any execution. The abuse of political power cannot stand exposure to what is clean and just.    23 28

John's **disciples** (such followers are mentioned also in Acts 18:25 and 19:3,4) take away John's **body** (literally, his 'corpse'). For Jews a corpse was more contaminating and profane than anything else. The holy and righteous John is rendered unclean and profane. The language that is used here is similar to that used to describe Jesus' death. This indicates that the fate of John foreshadows that of Jesus. There is some irony in the fact that John is buried by his disciples. When Jesus is buried, his disciples are nowhere to be seen (15:42-47).    29

## *Twelve baskets full, 6:30-44*

**30 The apostles returned to Jesus, and told him all that they had done and taught. 31 And he said to them, 'Come away by yourselves to a lonely place, and rest a while.' For many were coming and going, and they had no leisure even to eat. 32 And they went away in the boat to a lonely place by themselves. 33 Now many saw them going, and knew them, and they ran there on foot from all the towns, and got there ahead of them. 34 As he went ashore he saw a great throng, and he had compassion on them, because they were like sheep without a shepherd; and he began to teach them many things. 35 And when it grew late, his disciples came to him and said, 'This is a lonely place, and the hour is now late; 36 send them away, to go into the country and villages round about and buy themselves something to eat.' 37 But he answered them, 'You**

give them something to eat.' And they said to him, 'Shall we go and buy two hundred denarii[u] worth of bread, and give it to them to eat?' ³⁸ And he said to them, 'How many loaves have you? Go and see.' And when they had found out, they said, 'Five, and two fish.' ³⁹ Then he commanded them all to sit down by companies upon the green grass. ⁴⁰ So they sat down in groups, by hundreds and by fifties. ⁴¹ And taking the five loaves and the two fish he looked up to heaven, and blessed, and broke the loaves, and gave them to the disciples to set before the people; and he divided the two fish among them all. ⁴² And they all ate and were satisfied. ⁴³ And they took up twelve baskets full of broken pieces and of the fish. ⁴⁴ And those who ate the loaves were five thousand men.

[u] The denarius was a day's wage for a labourer

Here the twelve are called **apostles** for the first time. An apostle acts with the authority of the one who sends. It is because Jesus had sent them that they can now report success in their teaching and proclamation. The authority to teach, that is, to expound and interpret the will of God, was given to them by Jesus.

Jesus says to them: **Come away by yourselves to a lonely place.** Mark has previously recorded how Jesus liked to go into the desert to be alone (1:35; 4:10). (**Lonely place** should probably be translated 'desert'.) They have been so busy that they have not been able **to eat** (compare 3:20). It is not entirely clear who could not eat: Jesus and his disciples or those who were **coming and going**. The reference to eating serves as an introduction to the feeding that is about to take place. The impression is given that things are not normal here. Normally, meals had an air of sacredness about them. They were eaten at leisure, and were not rushed. It was good to have quietness and serenity as the Blessing and Thanksgiving were said. Meals were also times for contemplation and discussion. A present-day rabbi has suggested that the words of Rabbi Simeon in the Mishna (the collection of the Jewish Oral Law) are relevant here. Rabbi Simeon said that if three had eaten at a table and had spoken there no words of Torah (God's law), it is as if they had eaten of sacrifices to dead idols. But if three had eaten at a table, and had spoken there words of Torah, it is as if they had eaten at the table of the All-Present. This suggests that having no time to eat may not simply mean being too busy to put food into one's mouth, but may also mean being too busy to eat of God's food in the Torah. Such an understanding makes sense in the context of what happens next.

The going away of Jesus to the desert to be alone with his disciples brings to mind 4:10,11, where parables are explained to the disciples when they are alone with Jesus. This suggests that the feeding that is about to take place should be seen as a parable, that is, a mystery. The feeding miracles performed by Jesus are also parables, mysteries, riddles. This is supported by verse 52 in this chapter which says that the disciples did not understand about the loaves.

32 Jesus and his disciples get away by going in a boat, the place of previous intimate experiences and revelations of Jesus to his disciples (see 4:1,36). There is no mention here of a crossing of the lake, and so there is no point being made about transition, as there is with the actual crossing episodes (4:35; 5:21; 6:45; 8:10,13). Once more the crowds 33 follow. The enthusiasm of the people of Galilee might suggest a pro-Galilean bias by Mark. This enthusiasm is not shared by those in Jerusalem. Jerusalem is usually represented rather by the scribes and Pharisees, and those who wish Jesus out of the way. Jesus has compassion for the outsiders, for the Galileans who are enthusiastic toward him, but who know little of the Jewish law and the will of God. Once again, he teaches them. The compassion of Jesus 34 motivates him to teach. To teach people is also to feed them.

35 The miracle story that begins at verse 35 has Mark's typical construction: there is a situation of need; a request is made to Jesus; he provides for the need through a miracle; there is a response.

36 The disciples wish to send the crowd away, but Jesus challenges them to feed the people instead. Maybe Jesus' sending out of the disciples (vv 7-13) is meant to still be in the minds of Mark's readers. At that time they were given authority by Jesus, and they preached to people and healed those who were sick. Now, however, they seem to have forgotten that experience, and so their dullness (a common feature of Mark's picture of the disciples) stands out. They have forgotten Jesus' authority. Their response to Jesus' challenge that they feed the people is that they would need a lot of money to feed a crowd of this size. Jesus asks them to go and see what food they have between them. The 37, insignificant amount that is discovered is now taken by 38 Jesus, who previously has created life out of death, cleanli-

ness where there was uncleanliness. The disciples think that what they have is not enough, that their meagre contributions can do nothing to satisfy the hunger of the starving thousands around them. They are too dull to see that Jesus is the one who feeds his people, and that he can take their small contributions and bless them to satisfy the needs of others.

Jesus commands the people to sit in groups, and they do so in groups of fifty and a hundred. There may be a reference here to Exodus 18:21, but it is difficult to find any significance in these numbers. The **green grass** is mentioned, not so much to indicate the time of year, as to suggest that when Jesus is present, and when he feeds his people, the desert is turned into a place of fertility and rest. 39, 40

According to Jewish custom before a meal, Jesus takes the bread and the fish, says the blessing, breaks the bread, and then has the food distributed. Everyone eats and is satisfied. There is more than enough, so much so that plenty is left over. For Jewish readers, and also for non-Jews acquainted with the Septuagint (the Greek translation of the Old Testament), abundance of food was strongly associated with the promised kingdom of the Messiah. 41, 42, 43

**Five thousand men** ate the loaves. There is some doubt about whether 'the loaves' is part of the original text. The phrase **those who ate** again highlights the centrality of eating in this story. The feeding takes place in the desert, the place where God is to be found, and where he chooses his Son. It takes place, not within the boundaries, not within the sacred places, but in the desert, in the area outside. 44

To feed people is to bless them. God blesses his creatures and his people by feeding them. Feeding and blessing are the hallmarks of God's relationship with his people and his creation. Here Jesus blesses his new community by feeding them. Where there is hunger, and where that hunger is brought about by greed and the abuse of political and military power, the blessing of God is not and cannot be present. It is the will of God that his people be fed, that they receive their daily bread. His concern is not merely with spiritual feeding. There is no suggestion in the message of Jesus that he is concerned only with people's souls or their spiritual life. He commands his disciples to feed his people with actual food that has been blessed by him.

*Making the transition with or without Jesus, 6:45-52*

**⁴⁵ Immediately he made his disciples get into the boat and go before him to the other side, to Bethsaida, while**

he dismissed the crowd. ⁴⁶ **And after he had taken leave of them, he went up on the mountain to pray.** ⁴⁷ **And when evening came, the boat was out on the sea, and he was alone on the land.** ⁴⁸ **And he saw that they were making headway painfully, for the wind was against them. And about the fourth watch of the night he came to them, walking on the sea. He meant to pass by them,** ⁴⁹ **but when they saw him walking on the sea they thought it was a ghost, and cried out;** ⁵⁰ **for they all saw him, and were terrified. But immediately he spoke to them and said, 'Take heart, it is I; have no fear.'** ⁵¹ **And he got into the boat with them and the wind ceased. And they were utterly astounded,** ⁵² **for they did not understand about the loaves, but their hearts were hardened.**

Jesus **made his disciples get into the boat**. Why the compulsion? Is Jesus making arrangements for performing his next miracle? Or does it indicate his desire that his disciples follow his example and go to the unclean Gentile area of Bethsaida. The account that follows highlights the failure of the disciples, who have difficulty making headway in the crossing. Jesus dismisses the crowd. What is about to happen is only for those who are 'inside'. The transition from Judaism to a Christianity in which Gentiles were accepted into full table-fellowship, without adherence to all the demands of the Jewish law, was made only painfully by many followers of Christ. But the transition *must* be made. This may be the point of Jesus *making* his disciples get into the boat.  45

The disciples intend to cross over to Bethsaida, but they land, in fact, at Gennesaret (v 53). Bethsaida was a village on the north coast of the lake. According to John 1:44 Peter and Andrew, as well as Philip, came from there. It was razed by Vespasian and his troops in the rebellion of 66-70 AD.  46

Jesus goes to the mountain **to pray**. Once again Mark shows Jesus alternating between being with the disciples, being with the crowds, and being alone. Why does Jesus not go to the regular houses or places of prayer? It is because they are rejected. Jesus goes instead **into the hills**. The noun here is actually singular, suggesting that he went to a particular hill or mountain, perhaps the same one on which he was later shown and declared to be Son of God (9:2). The mountain, in the Bible, often represents the presence of God, as is the case in many other religions. The mountain, in Mark, often has the same significance as the desert: only those who are inside, only those who are called to be with Jesus, are with him in the desert or on the mountain.

Like Moses, Jesus goes up the mountain to be in the presence of God while his people stay below. Verse 47 sets the scene: it is evening time, the boat is out on the sea, and Jesus is alone on the land. Even the time of day suggests transition, as the old day comes to an end, and the new day, according to Jewish reckoning, begins. Mark shows Jesus here as being absent from his disciples, who are making a transition and are not coping well. How does the Christian community fare when Jesus is absent? For the community the experience of strong winds and difficulty in making progress in the transition was only too real. Members of Christian communities were battling with the question of who was inside and who was outside, who was clean and who was unclean, what of the old was to be retained and what it meant to be new people. The struggle to cross over from the old way to the new was a very painful one. The word **distressed** here is the same word translated as 'torment' in 5:7. Without Jesus the transition is torment.

The division of the night into four watches, between 6 pm and 6 am, was the Roman practice. The Jews divided the night into three watches. The **fourth watch** would have been between three and six o'clock in the morning. There is something mysterious about this appearance of Jesus. It is similar to the resurrection appearances, which Mark does not include in his gospel. Jesus comes walking on the water toward the tormented disciples. He walks across water as if it were land. For him the sea, which was something threatening for the Jews, becomes like land, which was the place of promise for them. Jesus means **to pass by them**. The significance of this has baffled scholars. It would seem best to understand the verb as it is used in Exodus 33:19,22. Here Moses asks to see the glory of God. God says that his glory will 'pass by' him, but he will not see the face of God, only his back. So the idea of revelation may be contained in Jesus' 'passing by'. In certain other passages, the same verb is related to God's saving action. For example, in Amos 7:8 and 8:2 God promises never again to 'pass by' his people, but to save them.

Jesus comes to his disciples, who are making heavy weather of the crossing, in order to save them by his presence with them. The disciples think that he is a ghost, and they cry out. Verse 50 emphasises that **all** the disciples see him and are terrified. Jesus speaks to them (literally, 'with' them). The word **spoke**, which is the same word that is translated as 'preach' in 2:2, means more than ordinary conversation. **Take heart** is not quite the same as the more common, 'Do not be afraid'. It is a call for faith, which Mark often understands in the sense of having courage. The words, **It is I**, are the same two Greek words used by Jesus in his well-known 'I am' statements in John's gospel (for example, John 8:58). There they are words of epiphany, or revelation, referring to God's Old Testament name (see Exod 3:14), and indicating that Jesus is God himself.

In early Christian communities this story must have been told to very hushed and enthralled audiences. You would have been able to hear a pin drop. There would have been no laughing or clapping in connection with this story. The people would have had the feeling that they were on holy ground, and that this was the time for silence in the presence of God. They would have loved to hear it. It was a sacred story, with special language used to create a special, sacred atmosphere.

Jesus gets into the boat with his disciples, and the wind ceases. When Jesus is present there is peace. His presence, like his word, is able to muzzle the evil powers which threaten people. It is tempting to see the ceasing of the wind as referring also to the storm of fear which the disciples, and also the Marcan Christian community, had been experiencing. The disciples respond, as usual, with wonder and astonishment. Their response is not so much to the drop in the wind as Jesus joins them in the boat, but rather to the mysterious appearance of Jesus as they were making their transition. **51**

Verse 52 is difficult to interpret. Bread/loaves is a significant motif in Mark, especially here in relation to the preceding section. The statement that the disciples **did not understand about the loaves** suggests that the understanding of the miracle of the feeding of the five thousand was important. The story of Jesus feeding the crowds must have been one of the most well-known traditions. It is reported in all four gospels, and was probably seen as being linked with the Passover meal, and so also with the Eucharistic meal of the Christian community. **52**

The incomprehension of the disciples is not due to some moral weakness on their part, but to the fact that **their hearts were hardened**. Mark is probably saying that the mystery of Jesus cannot be comprehended in normal human ways, but is made clear only through divine assistance. So the incomprehension of the disciples (sometimes called 'discipleship failure') actually says more about Jesus than about the disciples. Hardening of the heart is not the response of an individual who is antagonistic to God, but is the action of God himself. Just as it was God who hardened the heart of Pharaoh (see, for example, Exod 9:12), so it is God who hardens the disciples' hearts, so that they cannot understand unless the Spirit of the Clean One empowers them to do so.

The feeding miracles (6:35-44; 8:1-10) appear to be decisive for Mark's understanding of the question: Who is Jesus? There is a strong link here between the feeding of the five thousand and the crossing of the lake. When the Christian community goes through the torment of making transitions, Jesus is present as the one who feeds his community in that special meal which is the assurance of the new covenant. It is this feeding that gives them the courage to make the transition.

## A pause in the story, 6:53-56

**[53] And when they had crossed over, they came to land at Gennesaret, and moored to the shore. [54] And when they got out of the boat, immediately the people recognised him, [55] and ran about the whole neighbourhood and began to bring sick people on their pallets to any place where they heard he was. [56] And wherever he came, in villages, cities, or country, they laid the sick in the market places, and besought him that they might touch even the fringe of his garment; and as many as touched it were made well.**

This passage appears to be a general summary of Jesus' ministry, marking the end of a section. This suggests that the feeding miracle (6:35-44) and the epiphany on the water (6:45-52) are the climax to the story so far. The ultimate climax of Mark's gospel – Jesus' death – can also be seen as a kind of feeding miracle and an epiphany. This is another example of Mark's story-line not proceeding in a straight line, but in circles which are linked together, and which lead the reader to look ahead to what is still coming. So the stories of the feeding and the transition, while significant in themselves, and of immense value to the readers, are also loops in the story linked to that climactic feeding that Jesus performs on the cross, and his transition from death to life through his resurrection. It is there, in Jesus' death and resurrection, that the great feeding and the great transition occur.

When Jesus and his disciples have crossed the lake, the crowds appear again. Significantly, they recognise Jesus, whereas the disciples out on the lake had not (6:49). But the people's recognition of him is very much determined by his miracles. It is the desire for healing, for a miracle, that drives them to Jesus. And it happens that through the simple touch of his clothes they are healed (literally, as often in the New Testament, 'are saved'). Salvation involves the whole person and is not simply a spiritual gift. Mark constantly shows Jesus as someone who was deeply concerned also about the physical needs of people, and who was willing to extend his healing touch to people. **53, 54, 55, 56**

## *Cleanliness and the traditions, 7:1-23*

**¹ Now when the Pharisees gathered together to him, with some of the scribes, who had come from Jerusalem, ² they saw that some of his disciples ate with hands defiled, that is, unwashed. ³ (For the Pharisees, and all the Jews, do not eat unless they wash their hands,ᵛ observing the tradition of the elders; ⁴ and when they come from the market place, they do not eat unless they purifyʷ themselves; and there are many other traditions which they observe, the washing of cups and pots and vessels of bronze.ˣ) ⁵ And the Pharisees and the scribes asked him, 'Why do your disciples not liveʸ according to the tradition of the elders, but eat with hands defiled?' ⁶ And he said to them, 'Well did Isaiah prophesy of you hypocrites, as it is written,**

"This people honours me with their lips,
  but their heart is far from me;
⁷ in vain do they worship me,
  teaching as doctrines the precepts of men.'
**⁸ You leave the commandment of God, and hold fast the tradition of men.'**

**⁹ And he said to them, 'You have a fine way of rejecting the commandment of God, in order to keep your tradition! ¹⁰ For Moses said, "Honour your father and your mother"; and, "He who speaks evil of father or mother, let him surely die"; ¹¹ but you say, "If a man tells his father or his mother, What you would have gained from me is**

Corban" (that is, given to God)[z] – [12] then you no longer permit him to do anything for his father or mother, [13] thus making void the word of God through your tradition which you hand on. And many such things you do.'
[14] And he called the people to him again, and said to them, 'Hear me, all of you, and understand: [15] there is nothing outside a man which by going into him can defile him; but the things which come out of a man are what defile him.'[a] [17] And when he had entered the house, and left the people, his disciples asked him about the parable. [18] And he said to them, 'Then are you also without understanding? Do you not see that whatever goes into a man from outside cannot defile him, [19] since it enters, not his heart but his stomach, and so passes on?'[b] (Thus he declared all foods clean.) [20] And he said, 'What comes out of a man is what defiles a man. [21] For from within, out of the heart of man, come evil thoughts, fornication, theft, murder, adultery, [22] coveting, wickedness, deceit, licentiousness, envy, slander, pride, foolishness. [23] All these evil things come from within, and they defile a man.'

[v] One Greek word is of uncertain meaning and is not translated
[w] Other ancient authorities read *baptize*
[x] Other ancient authorities add *and beds*
[y] Greek *walk*
[z] Or *an offering*
[a] Other ancient authorities add verse 16, 'If any man has ears to hear, let him hear'
[b] Or *is evacuated*

This chapter is not a radical break from what has gone before it. The previous section, in which the healing activity of Jesus took place among the Gentiles on the 'other side' of the lake, leads directly into this chapter, which deals with the problems associated with Gentile membership in the new community.

The tension rebuilds as Jesus faces the Jewish authorities on the question of what is clean and unclean. This is a crucial chapter in Mark's gospel, which tells the story of the Clean One who expands the borders of the community of God to include those who do not observe the traditions of the past. It has been previously noted that Mark seems to show Jerusalem as being in conflict with Jesus, while the Galileans flock to him and are the ones whom he teaches and heals, and to whom he preaches the good news of the kingdom. This conflict can be seen again here as the Pharisees question Jesus on the matter of what is clean and unclean. The scribes, who some scholars believe formed the strongest opposition to Jesus, come, significantly, **from**

**Jerusalem**. Jerusalem was the centre of Judaism, mainly because the temple was there. The temple was accessible only to Jews, as the special place of God's revelation to them and his presence among them. Outsiders were unclean, and were therefore prohibited from entering the temple under penalty of death. Clean and unclean cannot meet. When the temple was destroyed in 70 AD, and when Christians were ostracised from the Jewish cultic community, substitutes for the temple had to be found. For Christians the substitute was Christ's body, both in its individual physical sense, and in the corporate sense of the church. Since there were strong rules, in relation to the temple, about what was clean and unclean, it was natural that some Christians wanted to maintain these rules in a Christian environment. The issue was a real one also for Gentiles who, in their religious ceremonies, also had clear laws and practices regarding what was clean and unclean.

Some of Jesus' disciples are eating with unclean hands. There is the possibility that other disciples (also, later, certain Christians) still observed the practice of washing hands ritually before the sacred act of eating. This practice was based on tradition rather than the written law. Ritual washings were a strong feature of purity laws, especially in relation to such things as leprosy, sexual emissions, sexual relations, and the handling of corpses.

The explanation given in verses 3 and 4 indicates that Mark's readers were not Jews, or at least not all Jews, otherwise such an explanation would not have been necessary. In verse 3 an unusual word meaning, literally, 'with the fist', whose meaning is obscure, may refer to a special Jewish custom in relation to the washing of hands. Verse 4 indicates how thorough the practice of washing was: it included not just the body, but vessels as well (some manuscripts add beds). The eating of food was regarded as a sacred act, and therefore ritual purification was essential before eating. Which of the disciples were not following this custom? Maybe those from Galilee were the ones who were not so strict in this observance, although the expression **all the Jews** in verse 3 is comprehensive. Maybe Philip – it's a Greek name – represents those Greek-loving Jews who did not observe this tradition.

The accusation of the Pharisees and scribes in verse 5 lumps all the disciples together – generalisations are often made in connection with accusations! The language here is traditional: to **live according to the tradition** is, literally, to 'walk' according to it. The tradition was seen as a way, a path, a walking. Jesus calls people to follow a new way, one not based on traditions.

Jesus' response to the Pharisees and scribes is to call them **hypocrites**. He cites Isaiah 29:13 which, interestingly, is spoken in the context of God's promise to 'do marvellous things with these people ... and the wisdom of their wise men shall perish, and the discernment of their discerning men shall be hid'. Hypocrisy is pretending – in this case, pretending that there is a limit to the mercy of God. It also means putting on a mask – pretending to be someone you are not, putting on a face to cover the reality. For these Jewish leaders the traditions have become a mask. The traditions cover the reality. They involve the pretence that God accepts only those who live by these traditions.

It is **the commandment of God**, not **the tradition of men**, that is essential to living God's way. The Christian community was often torn by controversy over this matter, some insisting that such traditions be maintained (the line taken by the Jerusalem Christians), while others claimed that such traditions were not binding, especially for Gentile Christians (this was Paul's line).

Jesus takes the commandment about honouring one's parents as an example of how God's commands have been corrupted. The honouring of parents is being neglected by the Jewish leaders on the pretext of a greater honour being given to God through **Corban**. **Corban** is a transliteration of a Hebrew word meaning 'gift' or 'offering to God'. It was used in making an oath to God which was regarded as binding. God's command is avoided on the basis of a human command claiming to give honour to God!

Jesus calls the people to him – once again the unclean crowd is **called** into his presence – and he gives them God's new 'Hear!' (see Deut 6:4). What is from the outside of a person does not make him or her unclean, but the things which come out of a person make that person common or unclean. Similarly, what comes from outside the Christian community is not what defiles, but what comes from within the community. Verse 16, which appears in a footnote in RSV, is not in the best manuscripts, although the western texts do include it.

Jesus goes into **the house**, which seems here to be a means of separation between Jesus and the crowd, or between the crowd and his disciples. The house, in other places in Mark, is a special place of revelation (3:19; 7:17; 9:28,33; 10:10), and probably also refers to the meeting place of Christians. The disciples ask Jesus to explain what his teaching means. His words, **Then are you also without understanding**? suggest that some Christians also were not clear about the matter dealt with here. Questions about eating food do not deal with the heart, but with the stomach. God, however, is not so much interested in what people do with their stomach as where their heart is. People can observe all the dietary laws they like, but if their heart is far from God (v 6), their worship is vain. For the Christian, then, all foods are clean – a point made in other places in the New Testament (Acts 10:9-16; 1 Cor 8:7,8; Col 2:16, 20-23; 1 Tim 4:3-5). **18, 19**

Jesus says that it is what comes out of people which makes them unclean. The unclean actions that are listed are nearly all ones that are directed toward another person. What makes a person clean is love that is directed toward the neighbour. We become defiled when our neighbour is the victim of our schemes and actions. **20-23**

In the section that follows, this teaching of Jesus is put into practice by him who is the Clean One – clean not by his dietary or religious observances, but by his obedience to the second great commandment, that of love to the neighbour no matter how unclean that neighbour may be.

### The case of the Syrophoenician woman, 7:24-30

[24] **And from there he arose and went away to the region of Tyre and Sidon.**[c] **And he entered a house, and would not have any one know it; yet he could not be hid.** [25] **But immediately a woman, whose little daughter was possessed by an unclean spirit, heard of him, and came and fell down at his feet.** [26] **Now the woman was a Greek, a Syrophoenician by birth. And she begged him to cast the demon out of her daughter.** [27] **And he said to her, 'Let the children first be fed, for it is not right to take the children's bread and throw it to the dogs.'** [28] **But she answered him, 'Yes, Lord; yet even the dogs under the table eat the children's crumbs.'** [29] **And he said to her, 'For this saying you may go your way; the demon has left your daughter.'** [30] **And she went home, and found the child lying in bed, and the demon had gone.**

c Other ancient authorities omit *and Sidon*

The region of **Tyre and Sidon** (some manuscripts have 24
only Tyre) is an area of people who are unclean. Both towns
lie some distance to the north-west of the Lake of Galilee,
Sidon being the further north. Elijah, who is a significant
figure in this gospel, also went to this region, where a
non-Jewish woman and her son provided food for him during a famine (1 Kings 17:8-16), so it is likely that Mark and
some of his readers would have thought of Elijah in connection with this story. Jesus deliberately goes to this place
beyond the boundaries of Israel, into the land of the Gentiles, of those who are unclean. To make matters worse, at
least from his critics' viewpoint, he actually enters the house
of an unclean person! He tries to do it secretly, but it is not
possible for him to do so – the unclean people recognise him!
Jesus is present in the houses of Gentile Christians and, for
the Marcan community, this is impossible to hide. It is well
known that Christians opened their houses to those who
were unclean.

By Jewish standards, how unclean can Jesus get! Not
only does he enter the house, accepting hospitality and
protection from a Gentile, but he allows a woman – a woman 25
whose daughter is unclean – to come to him and fall at his
feet in homage and respect. Verse 26 makes the point clear: 26
the woman is Greek, not a Jew. As always, the outsider
stands in strong and ironical contrast to those claiming to
be 'inside'. Where this story was read or told to groups of
Christians, Gentiles in the audience, and particularly
women, might have clapped at this point. They would have
known what was coming. They would have seen themselves
in this woman!

The woman asks Jesus to cast the demon out of her
daughter. This is one of very few cases in Mark where a
woman speaks. The position and status of women in Christian communities, especially Gentile women, was obviously
crucial. The dialogue here between Jesus and the woman is
fundamental to Mark's understanding of the gospel in the
church. Jesus responds to her with the standard Jewish 27
reply, which may have been the way that some of Mark's
readers also would have argued: **Let the children first be
fed, for it is not right to take the children's bread and
throw it to the dogs**. The 'children' are Israel. This woman
is a non-Israelite. Only Israel can expect to sit at table with
the Lord. This is part of the great Jewish hope – to take part
in the messianic banquet, the feast of the new kingdom of
God. Others will share in it, but they will not sit in the places

of honour at the table. Jesus speaks of the children's bread. Bread is the source of life. In John's gospel, Jesus calls himself 'the bread of life' (John 6:35). Mark does not use the expression, but has the same understanding of Jesus. Bread is also a symbol of the feast that is to come (in the Lord's Prayer, 'Give us this day our daily bread' may mean, 'Give us the bread of tomorrow – the bread of the kingdom – today'). Such bread belongs only to the children, and is not to be given to the dogs, which are unclean animals (see also Luke 16:21). The idea that Israel has not lost her special status as God's chosen people is also the view of Paul, who speaks of the Gentiles as being grafted on to Israel (Rom 11:17-24).

**28** The woman acknowledges her position as an unclean person and a non-Jew. This must have been very hard for her to do. She was a Greek, and the Greeks regarded themselves as culturally and socially civilised and sophisticated, and the Jews as barbarians. And yet she accepts being called a bitch by this Jew! Most Greek women would have slapped him in the face. But, instead, she says to Jesus, 'Kyrie', that is, she addresses him as **Lord**, which is more than the Jewish critics, and even the disciples, are prepared to do. She may well have been using this word as a common form of respectful address, but the irony would not have been lost on Mark's readers. She then humbly asks Jesus for the crumbs.

**29, 30** The demon is sent out of the girl by Jesus. Because of the word spoken by this woman, the word of humility and confidence in the Lord who accepts the unclean, the unclean demon is gone from her house. Gentile Christian houses (churches) are clean, and no longer under the power of any unclean spirit or demon. The gospel of the authority of Jesus over all that is unclean and demonic is true, not just for the first generation of Gentiles who belong to the Christian community, but also for their children. There may be some significance in the fact that it is the woman's **daughter** who is healed. For Jews, one's ancestry was always worked out through the male line – one was a son of Abraham or Israel. In the Christian community, also women are given a place in the genealogy of the new Israel, the new people of God.

## *The case of the deaf man, 7:31-37*

**31 Then he returned from the region of Tyre, and went through Sidon to the Sea of Galilee, through the region of the Decapolis. 32 And they brought to him a man who**

was deaf and had an impediment in his speech; and they besought him to lay his hand upon him. ³³ **And taking him aside from the multitude privately, he put his fingers into his ears, and he spat and touched his tongue;** ³⁴ **and looking up to heaven, he sighed, and said to him, 'Ephphatha,' that is, 'Be opened.'** ³⁵ **And his ears were opened, his tongue was released, and he spoke plainly.** ³⁶ **And he charged them to tell no one; but the more he charged them, the more zealously they proclaimed it.** ³⁷ **And they were astonished beyond measure, saying, 'He has done all things well; he even makes the deaf hear and the dumb speak.'**

In this section Jesus continues to move in the area of the unclean. He has been in the Decapolis area before, where he healed a possessed man (5:1-20). Now a **deaf** man is brought to him. Like most deaf people, he has a speech impediment as well. The inevitable crowd is there, but Jesus takes the man aside from the crowd and deals with him **privately**. The expression is the same as that used in 4:34 (see the commentary at that point) and suggests, as it did there, that one hears and obeys the call of Jesus only when one is called apart, called to be inside – which from others' perspective always means being outside! The crowds, while often being around Jesus, are never seen as belonging to the inside. Certain things they can hear, certain things are taught them, but the ability to hear the truth of who Jesus is, is given only to those who are on the inside.

Jesus goes through what appears to be a standard healing ritual: touching the affected spots, spitting (spittle was believed to contain the power of the person), and sighing. Sighing was probably an indication that a person was about to release power, or was trying to make contact with a particular power; exorcisms were often conducted in a whisper. Mark records Jesus' word, **Ephphatha**, in the original Aramaic, a foreign language for many of his readers. Many miracle-workers used foreign language words in performing their miracles. The language of the Jews, especially God's holy name Yahweh, or forms of the same, was believed to have special magical power. Mark's readers already know that Jesus' touch will effect a cure (see 1:31,41; 5:23,41; 6:2,5). Verse 35 consists of the kind of terminology used to describe the success of a magic spell. As in an earlier account (5:41), Mark prevents Jesus' word being seen as a magic formula by giving a translation of it. The word of Jesus has immediate effect, and the man hears. His tongue is **released**. This is the language of exorcism, since spirits or demons were thought to bind people. In this case, the man's tongue had been bound, but Jesus, the Stronger One, breaks the bondage. Those who are deaf to the word of God, and to his call, are unclean, and can only be freed from that state when the word of Jesus, with its power and authority, is spoken to them in their deafness.

Again, the command not to tell anyone is ineffectual. Here the command is given not to the one who is healed but to the bystanders. And, as usual, the response of people to the miracle is one of amazement. Their exclamation, **He has done all things well**, echoes the statement in Genesis 1:31, that 'God saw everything that he had made, and behold, it was very good'. The healing of the deaf and dumb was seen by Isaiah as a sign of the new era that God would bring into existence for his people (Isa 35:5,6). For the person who is deaf and dumb communication with other people is cut off, and he or she is left isolated. Loneliness and aloneness are demonic, and are not part of God's intention for humanity. Jesus breaks through the barriers erected by the demonic powers, who do not want to have anything to do with the one who restores humanity (see 1:24; 5:7).

**He has done all things well** can be seen as a summary statement about the mission of Jesus to the Gentiles. It refers to the whole chapter, which begins with the question of ritual washing and the observation of the traditions, and then has Jesus moving into the area of those who are unclean, where such washings and such traditions are not observed. But the authoritative word of Jesus makes all things clean. Previously, the Gentiles were unclean – deaf and dumb. They had not heard the call of God to hear – that is, to obey and to walk in his paths – and they could not speak the words of God. They were outside of the creative and healing influence of the word of God. But now Jesus has extended the boundaries to include them also. **All things** should be seen as referring to the whole ministry of Jesus.

## *Seven baskets full, 8:1-13*

¹ **In those days, when again a great crowd had gathered, and they had nothing to eat, he called his disciples to him, and said to them,** ² **'I have compassion on the**

crowd, because they have been with me now three days, and have nothing to eat; ³ and if I send them away hungry to their homes, they will faint on the way; and some of them have come a long way.' ⁴ And his disciples answered him, 'How can one feed these men with bread here in the desert?' ⁵ And he asked them, 'How many loaves have you?' They said, 'Seven.' ⁶ And he commanded the crowd to sit down on the ground; and he took the seven loaves, and having given thanks he broke them and gave them to his disciples to set before the people; and they set them before the crowd. ⁷ And they had a few small fish; and having blessed them, he commanded that these also should be set before them. ⁸ And they ate, and were satisfied; and they took up the broken pieces left over, seven baskets full. ⁹ And there were about four thousand people. ¹⁰ And he sent them away; and immediately he got into the boat with his disciples, and went to the district of Dalmanutha.ᵈ

¹¹ The Pharisees came and began to argue with him, seeking from him a sign from heaven, to test him. ¹² And he sighed deeply in his spirit, and said, 'Why does this generation seek a sign? Truly, I say to you, no sign shall be given to this generation.' ¹³ And he left them, and getting into the boat again he departed to the other side.

ᵈ Other ancient authorities read *Magadan* or *Magdala*

This story parallels that of 6:34-44 quite closely. Some have suggested that the earlier feeding was for Jews and that this one is for Gentiles. Since this story accentuates the people's hunger, the desert location, and the distress of the crowds, it is reasonable to suppose that it depicts the condition of the Gentiles from a Jewish perspective. The Jews know that God will feed *them* in the desert (the desert is not mentioned in chapter 6), but what about the Gentiles? Is the Bread of Life, the manna that God provides, also for the Gentiles? And if the answer is yes, does this mean that Gentiles and Jews now share together the common Bread, the common Host, at the common table? The answer given by this story is an emphatic yes.

In those days may simply be Mark's loose way of linking 1 episodes in the story, but the words were also used frequently by the prophets when speaking of the great saving acts of God among his people in the days when God would act in a final way (see, for example, Jer 33:15,16). The feeding by God of his people was always seen as a sign of his blessing. It was also seen as pointing ahead to the great final act of God for his people gathered together from all over the earth.

The word **again** reminds readers of something that has happened before. Jesus has already fed a large crowd (6:34-44). What will happen this time? Will the disciples be any clearer in their understanding of who Jesus is?

The **three days** that the people spend in the desert, and their being hungry and without food, refer to the time when the Gentiles were 'outside' the people of God. That the people have come **a long way** could also be a reference to Gentiles, who once 'were far off' (Eph 2:13,17). Jesus has **compassion on the crowd** who have been **with** him in the desert. Jesus is with those who have been 'far off', and who have been treated accordingly. He is with them in the desert, the place where he himself went, in solidarity with his people, to be baptised, and where he heard the call to be the Son of God. Jesus shares with them the experience of being outside. This presence of Jesus with his people is important in Mark's message.  **2**

Jesus has compassion on the people, and is concerned that they might faint **on the way**. This significant phrase appears in certain important passages referring to Jesus' death and resurrection (see 8:27; 9:33; 10:52). Jesus' way leads to the cross. He has compassion on those who wish to follow on this way, but who will not have the strength to do so unless he feeds them. He does not want to send them away hungry **to their homes**. It has been previously noted that the house/home in Mark commonly represents the Christian community, and this may well be the case also here. There are those who are new to the Christian community, who have come from a long way, and Jesus does not want to send them back to their community hungry, but fed and sustained by him, so that they are able to walk along his way.  **3**

It is ironic that the disciples, who were present at the first feeding, seem to have forgotten what Jesus did on that occasion! Mark's readers, of course, know what is going to happen. Maybe they laugh at the dullness of the disciples. In doing so, they also laugh at themselves! The question, **How many loaves have you**?– the same one that was asked on the previous occasion (6:38) – heightens the irony. The failure of the disciples to understand is just as important in this story as it was in the first feeding story.  **4**

**5**

The parallels between this account and the one of the first feeding in 6:34-44 are very close indeed, and the commen-  **6-9** tary at that point can be read in relation to this passage. Once again we see how Jesus takes such a small amount which seems so inadequate, but, through his blessing of it, provides more than enough for everyone. It may happen that the Christian community is faced with what appears to be an impossible task, but Jesus blesses what is there in the community, and it turns out to be enough for the task. When faced with the feeding of those who are beyond the boundaries of what is traditionally regarded as clean and holy, what the Christian church has to offer seems so inadequate. Faith involves having the courage and daring to believe that Jesus will bless and feed. The point is similar to that of the parable of the sower: what seems to be so ordinary, so weak, turns out to be surprisingly fruitful. The crucified Jesus appears in weakness and shame, but he is the one who provides food for his people precisely through that act of weakness and shame on the cross.

**Dalmanutha** is unknown to us, and the alternative place names that exist in some manuscripts suggest that there were copyists who were not familiar with the place either. 10

The Pharisees seek from Jesus **a sign from heaven**, testing him. The sign of the presence of God with his people in the desert was his feeding of them, something that remained central in the tradition of Israel. Now Jesus has fed the people in the desert, and still the Pharisees ask for a sign, that is, an indication that Jesus is from heaven, from God. This demand clearly upsets Jesus, who sighs or groans deeply within his spirit; the Spirit of God has been grieved. (The verb translated 'sighed deeply' is basically the same as that used at 7:34). It is quite likely that the same demand was made of Christian communities by the Jews: What is the sign that this Jesus you preach is in fact from God? Mark's response in this gospel, like Paul's, is to point to the cross as *the* sign of God. Jesus' answer here could well be translated: 'God will not give a sign to this generation'. **Generation** is often used in a negative and condemning sense in the New Testament (see, for example, 8:38; 9:19; Matt 11:16; 12:42). 'This generation' is blind and deaf, and cannot understand the riddle. For Mark, signs do not constitute the legitimisation of Jesus' ministry as the prophet, or the one who comes from God (see 13:22). The sign-from-heaven demand highlights the ignorance of those who make it. Mark's readers know that the sign has already been given at Jesus' baptism: 'Thou art my beloved Son' (1:11). *God* vindicates Jesus. And the ultimate sign of God's feeding of his community is the cross. 11 12

Jesus boards a boat, which serves again as a means of separating him from others. The Pharisees do not get into the boat with him! He leaves them. They never share that crossing, that transition, nor do they participate in the secret revelation that Jesus gives his disciples in the boat.

## *How many baskets full? 8:14-21*

**¹⁴ Now they had forgotten to bring bread; and they had only one loaf with them in the boat. ¹⁵ And he cautioned them, saying, 'Take heed, beware of the leaven of the Pharisees and the leaven of Herod.ᵉ ¹⁶ And they discussed it with one another, saying, 'We have no bread.' ¹⁷ And being aware of it, Jesus said to them, 'Why do you discuss the fact that you have no bread? Do you not yet perceive or understand? Are your hearts hardened? ¹⁸ Having eyes do you not see, and having ears do you not hear? And do you not remember? ¹⁹ When I broke the five loaves for the five thousand, how many baskets full of broken pieces did you take up?' They said to him, 'Twelve.' ²⁰ 'And the seven for the four thousand, how many baskets full of broken pieces did you take up?' And they said to him, 'Seven.' ²¹ And he said to them, 'Do you not yet understand?'**

ᵉ Other ancient authorities read *the Herodians*

This is a very interesting section. We notice that the question of having something to eat crops up again, as it seems to quite frequently in this section of the gospel. Jesus, the feeder of his community, is central. The disciples have **only one loaf**. They are in the same boat (pardon the expression!) as the four and five thousand before them. Before, there were seven loaves for the 4000 and five for the 5000, so why shouldn't one be enough for twelve? It is interesting that once again the dullness of the disciples is seen while they are crossing the lake, while they are in transition (see 6:52). Jesus gives a warning to his disciples not to think along the same lines as his opponents, who do not understand who he is. **Leaven** was regarded as the unclean element in bread, hence its omission from the Passover when everything had to be ritually clean. It is therefore here a reference to the corruption, the impurity, of the **Pharisees** and **Herod**, which is ironical, since the Pharisees were sticklers for purity. The disciples are told to

**beware**. The same danger exists for the disciples as for the Pharisees – the danger of thinking themselves to be the guardians of purity, of the traditions, and of the will of God. Impurity is just as likely to be found among the disciples, as later events show to be the case.

The disciples are as blind and deaf as the Pharisees. Once again, they are depicted in a light not very different from that of the opponents of Jesus. Weakness, and inability to believe and understand, are potentially there in the followers of Jesus.

Jesus' words, **Are your hearts hardened**? call to mind the hardening of their hearts by the people of Israel against Moses and against God in the desert. Also after the first feeding, Jesus spoke of a hardening of the heart (6:52). The point is that there were many in the Christian community for whom Mark was writing who could not see that Jesus was offering his food and his table-fellowship also to the unclean. The hardening of their heart was their stubborn inability to see or understand Jesus' attitude and action toward those who were unclean.

Jesus speaks as if there was an obvious significance in the gathering of the twelve baskets at the first feeding and seven at the second. Our understanding of what he means supports the view that the first feeding miracle refers to the feeding by God of the Jews, and the second to that of the Gentiles. The twelve baskets indicate the feeding of the people of Israel, since twelve was a significant number in Palestinian Judaism. (The word used for 'baskets' in the first feeding (6:43) is apparently a word used only of Jewish baskets, and is different from the word used in the second feeding.) Because there were twelve sons of Jacob, the number twelve was used to symbolise Israel, the people of God. It is possible that the number **seven** had particular significance for the Christians, both Jews and Gentiles, living outside the boundaries of Israel. The book of Revelation, written from Asia Minor, has seven letters to the churches. The number seven here could represent all the people of God in the diaspora. Seven was a significant symbolical number in Jewish thought. The menorah, or lampstand, had seven arms, and was a common symbol of Judaism, especially in the diaspora.

So Jesus is saying to his disciples: 'Don't you understand that I am the Bread of Life for both clean and unclean, not just for the Palestinian Christians, but for those in the diaspora as well, also those who come from a non-Jewish background? Don't you understand that you do not have any bread of yourselves, that what you have to offer will not suffice? Don't you remember that I fed thousands with so little? The feeding is my action, not yours. The blessing is mine, not yours. On this basis I call you to go and feed my people, whoever and wherever they may be. The seed may be small, but the branches will provide shelter enough (4:30-32). The sowing may seem haphazard and ineffective, but the harvest will produce surprising fruit' (4:1-8).

In recording Jesus' question and comments to his disciples, Mark directs them also to his readers. He is saying to them: 'Do *you* understand any more than the disciples did? Will you make the transition, and feed the unclean, with any more daring and courage than they did?'

There is probably a Eucharistic significance to this discussion. The question of whether the feeding by Jesus in the Eucharist was for all Christians or not was a real one in many communities. Can so insignificant a meal be sufficient for so many? Can those from across the boundaries truly share the same meal with those of us who regard ourselves as being inside?

## PART III : 8:22 – 10:52

*Do you see now? 8:22-26*

²² **And they came to Bethsaida. And some people brought to him a blind man, and begged him to touch him. ²³ And he took the blind man by the hand, and led him out of the village; and when he had spit on his eyes and laid his hands upon him, he asked him, 'Do you see anything?' ²⁴ And he looked up and said, 'I see men; but they look like trees, walking.' ²⁵ Then again he laid his hands upon his eyes; and he looked intently and was restored, and saw everything clearly. ²⁶ And he sent him away to his home, saying, 'Do not even enter the village.'**

This section begins with the usual Marcan narrative link – a movement of Jesus from one place to another. The story serves to illustrate the lack of vision/perception on the part of the disciples. Jesus' words in the previous section, 'Having eyes do you not see', have a connection with this episode. **Bethsaida** is on the north coast of the lake. According to John 1:44, it was the city of Peter, Andrew and Philip. Would Mark's readers have known that it was Peter's home town? If they did, it would have been a clue for them to expect a prominent role for Peter in coming episodes. The question of blindness in this section is related to the blindness of Peter later in the chapter in verses 32 and 33.

The episode has some of the common features of miracle stories: there is a need, which is brought to Jesus' attention, and he heals the person involved. This is a central episode in Mark's cycle of stories.

It is not clear why Jesus leads the man **out of the village**. Maybe it is a form of identifying with him. Jesus is the outsider, and those who follow him are called to leave the security of home and village. One 'sees' only when one stands 'outside'. Something similar occurs in 7:33. As in that healing episode, spit is used here, indicating that the power of the person himself, Jesus, is involved in the healing. In this healing, however, the cure is not instant! The man at first sees only opaquely. Jesus lays his hands on his eyes a second time, and his sight is fully restored: he sees **everything clearly** (or, more accurately, 'very clearly').

This healing is a kind of parable for the disciples. Like the blind man, they do not understand, they do not see at all clearly. They need a further 'touch' from Jesus for proper sight to be obtained. That 'touch' is the cross of Jesus. From this point on, the cross comes more and more clearly into view, both for Jesus himself, and also for the readers of this gospel. It is through the cross that the disciples are given the gift of sight, so that they can see clearly who Jesus is and what he came to do, namely, that he is the Clean One from God, who has come to make clean what has previously been regarded as unclean. This story may also indicate that within Mark's community there are those who are seeing this only opaquely, and who need to have their eyes fully opened so that they too can see clearly.

In the light of the fact that **home** (or 'house') in Mark's gospel may refer to the house churches of the early Christians, it would seem that Jesus commands the man to return to his Christian community (**his home**), and not to the wider community (**the village**). It is essential for the Christian community first of all to see very clearly, before it begins its mission of proclaiming the power of Jesus to heal. There can be no real mission, no true preaching of Jesus, no spreading abroad of his actions, until he is more clearly and more fully understood by those who are his, and that can only take place after Easter. Again and again the point is being made: Jesus can be known as the Christ, who is Son of God, only in the light of his cross and resurrection. And it is this Jesus alone who is to be proclaimed. **26**

What is central to this story is not the restoration of physical sight to a man previously blind, but the miracle of the follower of Jesus 'seeing' him for who and what he really is, instead of seeing him opaquely merely as rabbi or teacher, wonder-worker, or even Messiah.

## Who is he? 8:27-30

[27] **And Jesus went on with his disciples, to the villages of Caesarea Philippi; and on the way he asked his disciples, 'Who do men say that I am?'** [28] **And they told him, 'John the Baptist; and others say, Elijah; and others one of the prophets.'** [29] **And he asked them, 'But who do you say that I am?' Peter answered him, 'You are the Christ.'** [30] **And he charged them to tell no one about him.**

Jesus is on his way. **The way** inevitably leads him toward Jerusalem. **Went on** could be better translated 'went out', which expresses a typical movement of Jesus in Mark. Caesarea Philippi (some 40 kilometres north of Lake Galilee) is the destination of Jesus and the disciples, but the central question is raised by Jesus while they are **on the** **27**

**way**. Jesus is on the way to Jerusalem and the cross, as he will shortly make plain to his followers (v 31). Which way are the disciples going? That is the question, and Peter's answer will show that their way is not the way of Jesus. The Christian community also is on the way, and the question also for them is whether or not it is the way of Jesus.

The miracles of Jesus are usually followed by a response from the crowds. Following the healing of the blind man, Jesus himself now asks his disciples for a response. He asks them: **Who do men say that I am?** Mark's readers already know what the crowds have said. But now Jesus is asking his disciples, not the crowds, not the unevangelised, but the evangelists themselves. For the unevangelised, Jesus is a great prophet, and his authority as a prophet has been demonstrated by his power to do miracles. The crowds' response is partly right; they see, but what they see are only shadows of the reality. Mark has already made the point that John the Baptist and Elijah are key figures in contributing to an understanding of who Jesus is, but they are only his servants, pointing to him and preparing the way for him. But through his healing of the blind man, Jesus has made it clear that he expects his disciples to see more clearly than the crowds. So Peter states what Mark's readers already know: **You are the Christ**.

The proclamation of Jesus as the Christ was seen by many New Testament writers as being central to the Christian message (see the preaching in Acts). But if Peter has answered correctly, why does Jesus command the disciples to be silent about this? The verb translated here as **charged**, is the same as that used in relation to Jesus' stilling of the storm when he 'rebuked' the wind (4:39), and his ordering of the evil spirits, who have called him 'Son of God', not to make him known (3:12). It is a verb full of authority. According to Mark, Peter's confession of Jesus as the Christ is not what Jesus himself understands as being central to his person and work. As in the case of the blind man who at first did not see clearly, Peter's confession is that of one who sees only opaquely. Scholars have frequently seen this confession as the apex of the gospel, as if the question of who Jesus is has now finally been answered clearly and unequivocally: Jesus is the Christ. At last the messianic secret is no longer a secret. Now we all know the answer. But such an interpretation completely misses the point: Peter has yet to see clearly who Jesus is! It must have been quite a shock to Mark's readers to be told that Peter, a leading authority in some Christian communities (but not all?), has only partial sight when it comes to seeing the real Jesus. To call Jesus 'the Christ' is only half the truth. It is seeing Jesus opaquely. That this is the very point that Mark is making is evident from what now follows.

### *Where is he going? 8:31-9:1*

**[31] And he began to teach them that the Son of man must suffer many things, and be rejected by the elders and the chief priests and the scribes, and be killed, and after three days rise again. [32] And he said this plainly. And Peter took him, and began to rebuke him. [33] But turning and seeing his disciples, he rebuked Peter, and said, 'Get behind me, Satan! For you are not on the side of God, but of men.'**

**[34] And he called to him the multitude with his disciples, and said to them, 'If any man would come after me, let him deny himself and take up his cross and follow me. [35] For whoever would save his life will lose it; and whoever loses his life for my sake and the gospel's will save it. [36] For what does it profit a man, to gain the whole world and forfeit his life? [37] For what can a man give in return for his life? [38] For whoever is ashamed of me and of my words in this adulterous and sinful generation, of him will the Son of man also be ashamed, when he comes in the glory of his Father with the holy angels.'**

**[9:1] And he said to them, 'Truly, I say to you, there are some standing here who will not taste death before they see that the kingdom of God has come with power.'**

The title 'Christ' appears very suddenly in the gospel with Peter's confession, but it disappears just as quickly. Jesus now begins to teach his disciples – that is, to reveal to them by opening their eyes – his true mission. He quite deliberately ignores the title 'Christ', and chooses instead the term **Son of man**. And now, for the first time, the very crux of Mark's story is introduced, to be emphasised and to reach its graphic climax in the chapters that follow as Jesus goes on his way to the cross, to death – the ultimate uncleanness!

The term **Son of man** is used in three ways by Mark (see the commentary on 2:10), and all three ways are highlighted in the climax to the gospel. Here in this section Jesus speaks of the Son of man suffering, dying and rising again. Mark's readers so far have known the Son of man only as a person having authority – authority to forgive sins, authority as lord of the sabbath. Now he is introduced as the suffering, dying one, who is raised to life on the third day. This is not to present a different Son of man. The Jesus who forgives, heals, and sets aside the sabbath observance, has authority to do that on the basis of his death and resurrection, which is God's validation of his claims.

Verse 32 is important. Jesus speaks **plainly** to them, not in parables or riddles as previously. There could be no misunderstanding now, surely! But there is. Peter, later to become the pillar of the church, does not see clearly. What is revealed is that his confession of Jesus as the Christ involves only partial sight at best. He turns on Jesus and begins to **rebuke** him. **Rebuke** is the same word used earlier in the gospel in connection with Jesus' exorcisms (see, for example, 1:25). With all the authority that he can muster, Peter rejects the Son of man who must suffer and die. This has important implications in relation to discipleship. Peter, the disciple chosen first by Jesus, and listed first among his disciples, uses his authority to reject the cross, to refuse to walk along Jesus' way. He refuses to step over the boundaries with Jesus, to face the ultimate profanity: death on a cross. 32

Jesus, in the presence of all the disciples, rebukes Peter in the strongest possible terms. The language he uses is that of exorcism. He names the demon: **Satan**, who is the chief accuser and attacker. He rebukes him with the same authority with which he rebuked all the other unclean and evil spirits and demons. He commands him, not simply to leave Peter, but to get behind him (Jesus). **Get behind me** can be a call to discipleship (see 1:17)! Satan himself is called on to leave Peter and fall in line behind Jesus! **You are not on the side of God, but of men** is, more literally, 'You do not think the things of God but of humans'. The things of God can be learnt only when one falls in behind Jesus and walks along his way, the way that leads to suffering, death, and the rising to life. Any other way is not God's way. The mind of God is spelled out similarly in Philippians 2:5-9. 33

Jesus calls to himself both the crowds and the disciples, as he often does when he has something to teach that is particularly important, and speaks to them plainly. Following Jesus means, first of all, denial of oneself. Denial in this context is significant, because Mark's readers know that Peter will feature again in the story with his denial of Jesus. It is not Jesus who is to be denied, but oneself. Such denial of self must be accompanied by a following of Jesus, and that 34 means taking up one's cross – not Jesus' cross, but one's own. That is what discipleship is. It does not rest on authority – Peter's authority is rejected. It does not rest on power or status, but involves suffering, dying, and experiencing the resurrection to life by the power of God. As will be noted later, the cross was a political form of punishment, reserved mainly for revolutionaries and political upstarts. The disciples are commanded to take seriously the political consequences of following Jesus. He himself was rejected by the political powers, and his followers can expect to be treated in a similar way. Such is the way that Jesus goes, and that his followers travel with him.

When Jesus speaks of losing or saving one's **life**, this 35 refers to more than the biological and physiological body with its beating heart. It includes also one's spirit or mind or, to reproduce the Greek word, the psyche. Meaning and wholeness of mind and life are found in losing one's own psyche for the sake of the gospel, that is, for the sake of the freedom which the kingdom of God brings in Jesus Christ, the Son of God (see 1:1,15). The search for meaning is concluded when one falls into step behind the one who goes the way of suffering political and religious injustice, and who gives his life as a ransom for the many (10:45). Such a life has the benediction of God. A person does not make any 36 profit by gaining possession of the whole world at the cost of his or her psyche. What exchange can be made for whole- 37 ness of mind and life? Such life is found in Jesus and the 38 **words** which he speaks. The truth of this has been well-attested for Mark's readers, as they have seen how Jesus restored life where there was death, made clean what was unclean, brought mercy where there was hopelessness.

Jesus speaks of how the Son of man will be **ashamed** of those who are ashamed of him. Shame is the loss of face experienced when one is accused by an outsider. The follower of Jesus can expect rejection and loss of face at the hands of the opponents of Jesus. When Jesus speaks of this generation being an **adulterous and sinful** one, this is not meant in some moralistic sense, but in a deeply relational sense. Adultery by God's people always means walking along the paths of another god, making covenants with other gods, and such breaking of the covenant with God invariably leads to injustices, involving especially the powerful against the weak, the rich against the poor. When Christians, collectively or individually, choose to walk along a way other than the way of the cross, they are being adulterous and sinful, as evidenced by their acts of injustice.

The final judgment, the final word spoken over the life of the follower of Jesus, is not that of any political or church court, but the word of that Son of man who will come finally in glory with the angels of God. Jesus will be vindicated, and his vindication will be ultimately revealed when he comes as judge of all humanity. He has been given authority over sin and death by his own resurrection from the dead, by the holy power of the God who has declared him to be his Son. He has been given authority to have the last word.

Here Mark uses the term **Son of man** in its meaning of final judge. But the Son of man who will come as judge is the same one who suffered, died, and was raised to life. So also those who walk the way of Jesus will suffer and die, but will be raised to life, which will be God's vindication of their suffering and death. There is no other way of discipleship. Those who claim the name Christian are called to walk this way and this way alone. It is the way of the cross, of death and suffering. This is a strong smack in the face for those wishing to travel the glory road, the road of success and triumph. On Jesus' way there is no promise of wealth, success, power, or status. Instead, there is the call to leave everything that gives security, and to have the courage to follow the way of the Master. This call is given to all, not just to individuals, not just to the disciples, but to the crowds as well. Even those who are not yet fully 'in' must understand what they are getting 'in' to! Jesus' call, therefore, is a call to the church as church, as a community in the society in which it lives. He gives no choice in the matter. He has gone ahead, and he calls us to follow.

**9:1** The first verse of chapter 9 is difficult to interpret. In some ways it fits in with the story of the transfiguration that follows, the linking word being **see**. On the mountain the disciples see Jesus in all his power and glory. But they are there asked to hear rather than see (v 7). It is more likely that this verse links with what has preceded it. What is expressed here is the strong early Christian hope that Jesus would establish his kingdom on earth in power, and that he would do it soon. It is quite likely that Jesus shared that hope.

Jesus speaks of some who are **standing** here. **Standing** is often the posture of worshippers as they appear in visions of the end-times, but whether this is what is referred to here is difficult to determine. The language of the verse is that of the end-times. On the basis of one manuscript (one of the most reliable), it has been suggested that Elijah and Moses are the ones 'standing here'. This suggestion has some merit in view of the significance of 'standing' in the Old Testament and other ancient literature. In these writings, 'to stand' often represents stability, and is a characteristic of God, who is sometimes depicted as the standing one. Plato refers to souls as 'standing' when they have become immortal by reaching the upper regions, and now gaze upon the realities there. Elijah and Moses to some extent fit this understanding: they represent those who *stand* in the presence of God. They have not tasted death, and they **see the kingdom of God**, something which mortals cannot do because it is hidden from them and is a riddle to them. Standing before the Lord is a common Old Testament thought, which is often used in the context of the covenant between God and his people (see, for example, Lev 9:5; Deut 5:31; 29:10). Psalm 24:3-6 could well be in Mark's mind here: 'Who shall ascend the hill of the Lord? And who shall stand in his holy place?' (v 3).

## *Would the real Jesus stand up! 9:2-13*

² **And after six days Jesus took with him Peter and James and John, and led them up a high mountain apart by themselves; and he was transfigured before them,** ³ **and his garments became glistening, intensely white, as no fuller on earth could bleach them.** ⁴ **And there appeared to them Elijah with Moses; and they were talking to Jesus.** ⁵ **And Peter said to Jesus, 'Master,**ᶠ **it is well that we are here; let us make three booths, one for you and one for Moses and one for Elijah.'** ⁶ **For he did not know what to say, for they were exceedingly afraid.** ⁷ **And a cloud overshadowed them, and a voice came out of the cloud, 'This is my beloved Son;**ᵍ **listen to him.'** ⁸ **And suddenly looking around they no longer saw any one with them but Jesus only.**

⁹ **And as they were coming down the mountain, he charged them to tell no one what they had seen, until the Son of man should have risen from the dead.** ¹⁰ **So they kept the matter to themselves, questioning what the rising from the dead meant.** ¹¹ **And they asked him, 'Why do the scribes say that first Elijah must come?'**¹² **And he said to them, 'Elijah does come first to restore all things; and how is it written of the Son of man, that he should**

**suffer many things and be treated with contempt?** [13] **But I tell you that Elijah has come, and they did to him whatever they pleased, as it is written of him.'**

[f] Or *Rabbi*
[g] Or *my Son, my* (or *the*) *Beloved*

**And after six days** seems at first to provide only a loose 2 connection between this section and the preceding one. However, a deeper significance in the words is suggested by Exodus 24:16: 'The glory of the Lord settled on Mount Sinai, and the cloud covered it six days; and on the seventh day he called to Moses out of the midst of the cloud'. In Mark's episode it is Jesus who is revealed as the glory of God on the mountain. This also is a seventh day revelation.

The mountain is described as being **high**. The Jews believed that the temple mountain was the highest hill in the world. It was there that God was present and could be heard (see Mic 4). The purpose of this story is to show that there is a higher mountain, where the true glory of God is revealed, and where the voice of God is heard declaring Jesus to be his Son. God speaks only twice in the whole of the gospel, so each occasion must certainly be important, particularly when he says the same thing both times! So we can be sure that this event is very important to Mark. In fact, it is the climax of his story so far. It is here that the real Jesus is identified and the secret uncovered. Peter's confession (8:29) was incomplete. Jesus is not only the Christ; he is, more importantly, the Son of God.

Familiar motifs from earlier parts of the gospel are present here: the mountain (3:13; 6:46); the same three disciples are taken aside (5:37); Peter is the spokesperson (8:29); and Jesus is pronounced Son of God (1:11; 3:11; 5:7). The episode is full of the language of revelation: the mountain, Moses and Elijah, the cloud, the tents, the overshadowing.

The whiteness of Jesus' garments as he is transfigured 3 stresses his cleanliness. He is shown to be what Mark's readers already know him to be: the Holy One of God. Bleaches that claim to make whiter than white do not compare with the cleanliness of the Jesus revealed here! Reference has previously been made to Jewish traditions about Adam and their similarity with the picture of Jesus in Mark's tradition. We have those traditions reflected here. Jewish tradition has Adam wearing a 'garment of light' before the Fall. Were Mark's readers aware of this tradition, and were they meant to see Jesus as the Adam here?

Elijah and Moses are the two great prophets of Jewish tradition. They are also prophets of the mountain, Mount Horeb/Sinai. It was there at that mountain that God was with his servants, and established his relationship with his people through those prophets. In Mark's gospel, the mountain is the place where Jesus goes to be alone, where he calls those who are to be with him, and where he removes the mystery of his person and identity as Son of God. The mountain can be seen as being outside, in the desert, and this thought points forward to Jesus' ascension to the mountain of his crucifixion, where he dies as the outsider – in the desert, as it were.

According to Old Testament traditions, neither Moses nor Elijah was contaminated by death in leaving this life and going to God (see the tradition based on Deut 34:5; 2 Kgs 2:1-11). It is tempting to see Jesus as the new Joshua (the name Jesus is a form of Joshua) and the new Elisha, that is, as the 'successor' to both Moses and Elijah. Moses and Elijah were also regarded as revealers of God's will, and here they are seen **talking** with Jesus. The word used here for 'talk' can also have the idea of 'proclaiming'; it certainly expresses more than just having a conversation. But Jesus is more than the successor of Moses and Elijah; he is the 'successor' to God himself! He is declared to be the Son of God. This declaration from God echoes the word spoken over Jesus at his baptism (1:11), and looks forward to the confession by the centurion at the end of the gospel (15:39).

It can be noted that Mark, in his gospel, seems to give greater emphasis to Elijah than to Moses. Even here, in the phrase **Elijah with Moses**, Elijah seems to be presented as the dominant figure, with Moses tagging along. Peter, however, refers to them in the usual order: Moses and Elijah. Is this another small example of Peter's inability to understand correctly, in this case that Jesus is to be seen more in the light of Elijah than of Moses? Jesus, like Elijah (see Mal 4:5,6), is the bringer of the new covenant which is not based on Mosaic purity laws.

Peter speaks, and it is clear that his thinking has not changed since his rebuke from Jesus (8:32,33); he still hankers for security and the glory experience, not the cross. The word he uses to address Jesus – **Master**, or **Rabbi** – is rather surprising in this context. One might have expected 'Lord', but Mark's extreme, and rather surprising, reticence to use this title in relation to Jesus has previously been noted. On the other hand, Peter's use of 'Rabbi' suggests that he is aware that here a great revelation is taking place, since it was the role of the rabbi to expound the revelation of God. Rabbi literally means 'my great one'. Peter's use of the term also suggests that he sees Jesus more in the light of Moses, in his role as a teacher, as the one who received the law from God, and the one who was the supreme arbiter on matters of what was clean and unclean. Elijah, on the other hand, who appears to be the more important person for Mark, is the forerunner of the one who brings in the new aeon of God, in which the lines between what is clean and unclean are drastically altered or removed.

Peter's response to what he saw is rejected by Mark (**he did not know what to say**), and is attributed to an overwhelming awe (**for they were exceedingly afraid**). It indicates again the lack of perception on the part of the chief disciple. It can be noted that the final great revelation of Jesus, his resurrection, also evokes the response of fear in his followers (16:8).

Verse 7 is the key to the episode. The language that is used here is full of revelatory terms which are found in the book of Exodus. In Exodus 40, for example, Moses erects the tabernacle of the tent of meeting (is this what Peter has in mind also?), and the cloud covers the tent and the glory of the Lord fills the tabernacle (Exod 40:34). In that account, the cloud is the sign of the presence of God, as it is elsewhere in the Scriptures. In a sense, the **cloud** itself is the 'voice' expressing God's approval. But here, in the story of the transfiguration, it is not simply the cloud which is present at this holy meeting place, but the **voice** of God also speaks from that cloud: **This is my beloved Son; listen to him**. Israel claimed to be, and was called, God's son (see Hos 11:1). Moses and Elijah, as representatives of God, called Israel to hear the revelatory will of God spoken through them. But here is one who is greater than Moses and Elijah. Israel's sonship is now determined, not by ethnic ties or by 'hearing' the will of God through Moses and the prophets, but by ties with Jesus, the holy Son of God. It is by hearing him that one hears the will of God. And hearing Jesus means nothing less than obeying him, that is, walking his way, the way of the cross, the way that rejects power and status, and that opposes all powers and systems which oppress and alienate. Hearing, in Mark, is also closely associated with understanding; it is in hearing Jesus that one understands who he is.

If that is true, then it is not surprising that Moses and Elijah should suddenly be gone, and that the disciples see no-one but Jesus alone. Mark says that they no longer saw anyone **with them**. Jesus calls his disciples to be 'with him' (3:14). That is the mark of a disciple, to be 'with' Jesus, something that Peter later denies having done (14:67). The only one who is left with the disciples is Jesus. Peter's hankering for the other glory-figures, Moses and Elijah, is not granted him or any follower of Jesus. For the disciple now the only one to hear is Jesus, and he alone is the revealer of God's will. A person can come to a true understanding only by being with Jesus. His way is the only way to walk. The way of Moses and Elijah was good, it was God's way, but now God calls his community to walk in the way of his own true successor. The verb **saw** cannot go unnoticed either, especially since this revelation of Jesus as Son of God follows closely on the heels of the story of the blind man and all that that 'parable' was saying (8:22-26). The disciples saw Moses and Elijah, but in the end they are left with no-one to see but Jesus. Hearing and seeing – key themes in Mark – find their object in Jesus alone.

The disciples have had a revelation of Jesus as a result of their ascension with him up the high mountain. But now they descend. As they are coming down, Jesus commands them to be silent about what they have **seen**. Only after the Son of man has risen from the dead can the silence be broken. Only then will they see clearly. In 16:7, on Easter morning, the women are commanded to go and tell. The resurrection breaks the silence. Here again, when Jesus speaks of his death and resurrection, he refuses to use the title Christ or Messiah, and speaks of the **Son of man** instead.

Verse 10 is one of the tantalising asides that Mark throws into his story from time to time. The first part might be translated, more literally, 'They seized on the saying among themselves'. Questions concerning the resurrection were keenly debated among the Jews (such questions divided the Pharisees and the Sadducees, for example) but also caused problems among Christian communities (see 1 Cor 15; 2 Tim 2:18).

The disciples ask Jesus about the teaching of the scribes that **first Elijah must come**. The **scribes**, as noted earlier, were more than secretaries. They had influence and authority in interpreting the Scriptures. Malachi 4:5,6 speaks of **Elijah** appearing before the new age begins. The resurrection of the dead was understood to be one of the signs of the coming kingdom of God and the new age. The disciples keep this particular question of the resurrection to themselves. They do not ask Jesus about it. In later Gnostic (unorthodox

Christian) writings, revelation follows a common pattern: the disciples ask questions, usually about the future, and Jesus, the revealer, answers. Not surprisingly, questions about the resurrection also figure prominently in such Gnostic revelations, which are always post-Easter. Possibly Mark is affected, to some extent, by this kind of thinking: questions concerning the resurrection of the dead can be asked only after Jesus' resurrection. Jesus can be fully understood only in the light of his resurrection.

Jesus tells his disciples that **Elijah does come first to restore all things**. The verb **restore** is the same as that used by the disciples after the resurrection when they ask Jesus: 'Will you at this time restore the kingdom to Israel?' (Acts 1:6). This was the Malachi hope. For some, it meant that Elijah would remove all impurity from Israel, which would include purifying those people who had been wrongly declared impure in their genealogy. The Son of man, too, was a figure of national hope (see Dan 7), but one which Jesus tied to suffering and rejection. It seems that Jesus sees John the Baptist as the promised Elijah who has indeed come, but who has been prevented, by the nation's rejection of him, from doing what was said of him in prophecy. 12

**As it is written of him** is difficult to understand, because there is no Old Testament suggestion that when Elijah returns he will be rejected. It probably refers to some other writing, once regarded as having some authority, which is now lost to us. 13

## The unclean spirit returns 9:14-29

**[14] And when they came to the disciples, they saw a great crowd about them, and scribes arguing with them. [15] And immediately all the crowd, when they saw him, were greatly amazed, and ran up to him and greeted him. [16] And he asked them, 'What are you discussing with them?' [17] And one of the crowd answered him, 'Teacher, I brought my son to you, for he has a dumb spirit; [18] and wherever it seizes him, it dashes him down; and he foams and grinds his teeth and becomes rigid; and I asked your disciples to cast it out, and they were not able.' [19] And he answered them, 'O faithless generation, how long am I to be with you? How long am I to bear with you? Bring him to me.' [20] And they brought the boy to him; and when the spirit saw him, immediately it convulsed the boy, and he**

fell on the ground and rolled about, foaming at the mouth. ²¹ And Jesus[h] asked his father, 'How long has he had this?' And he said, 'From childhood. ²² And it has often cast him into the fire and into the water, to destroy him; but if you can do anything, have pity on us and help us.' ²³ And Jesus said to him, 'If you can! All things are possible to him who believes.' ²⁴ Immediately the father of the child cried out[i] and said, 'I believe; help my unbelief!' ²⁵ And when Jesus saw that a crowd came running together, he rebuked the unclean spirit, saying to it, 'You dumb and deaf spirit, I command you, come out of him, and never enter him again.' ²⁶ And after crying out and convulsing him terribly, it came out, and the boy was like a corpse; so that most of them said, 'He is dead.' ²⁷ But Jesus took him by the hand and lifted him up, and he arose. ²⁸ And when he had entered the house, his disciples asked him privately, 'Why could we not cast it out?' ²⁹ And he said to them, 'This kind cannot be driven out by anything but prayer.'[j]

[h] Greek *he*
[i] Other ancient authorities add *with tears*
[j] Other ancient authorities add *and fasting*

**14** The revelation of Jesus' glory on the mountain was given only to Peter, James and John, and now they join the other disciples who are dealing with the crowds and the scribes. The crowds again represent the masses of unevangelised people, while, the scribes represent the opposition. The scribes are **arguing** with the disciples. The verb translated **arguing** is the same one that was used of the three disciples in verse 10, where it was translated 'questioning'. Maybe the disciples too were debating or arguing!

**15** The reaction of the crowd to Jesus' arrival is unusual: they are **greatly amazed**, and they run up to him to greet him. They were not present at the revelation on the mountain, and yet they respond as if they had been. In their eagerness to welcome Jesus, the Clean One who has been declared the holy Son of God, they stand in contrast to the traditionalists and the disciples. There appear to be some parallels with Exodus 32 and 33, where Moses comes down from the mountain and finds Aaron and the people in rebellious debate. Maybe the crowd's exuberant welcome of Jesus as he comes down from the mountain of revelation is meant to be seen as a contrast to Israel's rebellious welcome of Moses.

The question under discussion has been why Jesus' disci- 16-
ples have not been able to cast a **dumb spirit** out of a boy. 18
We see here again how Mark's story moves in cycles. In his
baptism Jesus was declared to be Son of God, and was then
immediately sent out into the desert, the region of the
unclean. This was followed by a confrontation with an
unclean spirit in the synagogue in Capernaum (1:9-27).
Now, here in this episode, Jesus is once more back in the
realm of the unclean: a man in the crowd has a son with a
**dumb spirit**. There has just been the story of the Father
acknowledging Jesus as his Son, and giving authority to his
word, which must be listened to because he has the Holy
Spirit. Jesus does not have a dumb spirit, but a Spirit which
speaks a word of life and salvation.

Jesus addresses the people as a **faithless generation**. 19
Earlier, Mark has indicated that where there is no faith,
Jesus is unable to do any mighty work (6:5,6a). Since the
disciples have not seen clearly who Jesus is, they cannot
exorcise the unclean spirit.

In the presence of the one who speaks the word and will 20
of God, the dumb spirit struggles to maintain its authority.
Only the Holy Spirit produces clean speech; the dumb spirit
allows no speech. Dumbness means no communication,
which in turn means aloneness, which is characteristic of
the demonic. An illness from birth or, as in this case, **from
childhood**, was commonly regarded as incurable, and John
9 suggests that it was thought to be the result of parental
sin. This is why the father begs Jesus to help him as well as 21,
his Son: **Have pity on us and help us**. Jesus picks up the 22
man's expression of faithlessness: **If you can! All things** 23
**are possible to him who believes**. The man cries out,
something that often happens when a spirit is exorcised.
The spirit of unfaith in this man is exorcised, and the spirit 24,
of faith now speaks the confession: **I believe**. 25

Jesus sees a crowd beginning to form – they have learnt
what to expect from Jesus! – and so rebukes (that same
strong word again) the **unclean spirit**. Notice that it is
called an unclean spirit now, not a dumb spirit and never,
in this episode, a demon. Jesus names the spirit (**You dumb
and deaf spirit**) in order to demonstrate his authority over
it, and emphatically commands it to come out and leave the
child alone. After crying out and convulsing the child, the 26
unclean spirit obeys the one who has authority to speak, and
who must be listened to (9:7). The spirit is dumb, but Jesus
speaks.

As if to emphasise the unclean nature of this dumb spirit, the child appears to be a **corpse**, something totally unclean. Jesus seizes him by the hand and raises him up – the language is that of resurrection. The Clean One speaks the word of life.

Jesus enters **the house**, where he converses with his disciples privately. Here again the house is the location of secret or special revelation from Jesus to his disciples while they are alone together. Jesus' reference to prayer (**This kind cannot be driven out by anything but prayer**) comes out of the blue, and many commentators suggest that it is a later addition to the text. When Mark pictures Jesus praying, he is often shown being alone, and as being in the presence of God. Prayer involves being in the presence of the God whose word heals and cleans. When Jesus is absent, the disciples have no authority, and their faith weakens. This story suggests that there was a difference between the authority of Jesus over such unclean spirits and that of the disciples, that is, the Christian community. That is why the discussion takes place in the house, that is, the church. Mark's community knows the tradition of Jesus' healing authority, and wonders why it is not sharing in that authority. The section that follows (vv 30-32) can also be seen as Jesus' answer to their questioning. The desire to have authority over unclean spirits is good, but first the community must learn to walk the way of the cross. Only then will they, like Jesus, have God's approval, and only then can they share in Jesus' authority.

## *Jesus tells them again, 9:30-32*

**[30] They went on from there and passed through Galilee. And he would not have any one know it; [31] for he was teaching his disciples, saying to them, 'The Son of man will be delivered into the hands of men, and they will kill him; and when he is killed, after three days he will rise.' [32] But they did not understand the saying, and they were afraid to ask him.**

This short section echoes that of 8:31. It reinforces in the minds of the readers the way along which Jesus is walking. It is the way to the cross. It also reinforces the motif of the disciples' dullness and fear.

Jesus passes **through Galilee**, wishing to do so incognito. There is something mysterious about the statement that **he would not have anyone know it**. What was it that he did not want anyone to know? It would appear that the revelation that he gives about his future is meant only for the disciples, and that this is why he travels incognito. Revelation, which is the purpose of Jesus' teaching, can be perceived only where the Spirit is present, and not by human flesh and blood. The secret of the Christian church is that its God and Saviour is one who suffers, dies and rises again. The violence of Jesus' death is a scandal.

The disciples do not know what Jesus is talking about. Jesus teaches them, but they are slow to learn. Fear again characterises them, just as it does many others. They are **afraid to ask him**. Asking is part of the revelation process, but they are afraid to have any further revelation. The disciples react with fear to Jesus' words about his death and resurrection, the same reaction that is recorded of Jesus' followers on Easter Sunday at the end of the gospel (16:8). The statement that the disciples **did not understand** is not simply a criticism of them, but is meant to pose the question to readers of the gospel: Do you understand any better?

### *Life in the community, 9:33-50*

⁳³ **And they came to Capernaum; and when he was in the house he asked them, 'What were you discussing on the way?'** ³⁴ **But they were silent; for on the way they had discussed with one another who was the greatest.** ³⁵ **And he sat down and called the twelve; and he said to them, 'If any one would be first, he must be last of all and servant of all.'** ³⁶ **And he took a child, and put him in the midst of them; and taking him in his arms, he said to them,** ³⁷ **'Whoever receives one such child in my name receives me; and whoever receives me, receives not me but him who sent me.'**

³⁸ **John said to him, 'Teacher, we saw a man casting out demons in your name,**ᵏ **and we forbade him, because he was not following us.'** ³⁹ **But Jesus said, 'Do not forbid him; for no one who does a mighty work in my name will be able soon after to speak evil of me.** ⁴⁰ **For he that is not against us is for us.** ⁴¹ **For truly, I say to you, whoever gives you a cup of water to drink because you bear the name of Christ, will by no means lose his reward.**

⁴² 'Whoever causes one of these little ones who believe in me to sin,ˡ it would be better for him if a great millstone were hung round his neck and he were thrown into the sea. ⁴³ And if your hand causes you to sin,ˡ cut it off; it is better for you to enter life maimed than with two hands to go to hell,ᵐ to the unquenchable fire.ⁿ ⁴⁵ And if your foot causes you to sin,ˡ cut it off; it is better for you to enter life lame than with two feet to be thrown into hell.ᵐ,ⁿ ⁴⁷ And if your eye causes you to sin,ˡ pluck it out; it is better for you to enter the kingdom of God with one eye than with two eyes to be thrown into hell,ᵐ ⁴⁸ where their worm does not die, and the fire is not quenched. ⁴⁹ For every one will be salted with fire.ᵒ ⁵⁰ Salt is good; but if the salt has lost its saltness, how will you season it? Have salt in yourselves, and be at peace with one another.'

ᵏ Other ancient authorities add *who does not follow us*
ˡ Greek *stumble*
ᵐ Greek *Gehenna*
ⁿ Verses 44 and 46 (which are identical with verse 48) are omitted by the best ancient authorities
ᵒ Other ancient authorities add *and every sacrifice will be salted with salt*

Jesus' teaching of his disciples, which began in verse 31, **33** continues here. Once again Jesus and his disciples are **in the house** (possibly a reference to the later house church), this time in **Capernaum**. Jesus asks the disciples what they were discussing **on the way**. Mention of **the way** makes readers prick up their ears, because they have already been introduced to the way of Jesus which leads to the cross. The way of the disciples is not the way of Jesus at all. **34** Their way is that of greatness, power, and status.

Jesus sits down (this was the posture adopted for teaching **35** by a person with authority) and calls the twelve. The language that is used here strongly suggests that something very important is about to be said, especially since it is directed to those who are regarded as leaders in the community. Jesus says that the one wishing to be first will be **last of all and servant of all**. What he says is a statement of fact, rather than an exhortation as the RSV suggests with its **must**. The word translated **servant** was a common term for those engaged in particular kinds of work in the Christian community. It was work which Jesus himself modelled, since he came not to be served but to serve (10:45).

Jesus places a child **in the midst of them**. This expres- **36,** sion is an intriguing one, since it occurs in later Gnostic **37** (unorthodox Christian) writings, where it is difficult to know what it means. It occurs frequently in Revelation (see 2:1; 4:6; 5:6; 6:6; 7:17; 22:2). In the New Testament, it seems to convey the idea of someone being in authority. Jesus takes the child in his arms, and says that whoever accepts a child such as this in his name accepts him, and, in accepting him, accepts also the one who sent him. The little child represents those of the community who are very young in the faith. It is clear that the early Christian communities were not blissful, harmonious groups, but ones in which tension, division, and status seeking were rife.

Such division seems to be reflected in verse 38. This is the **38** only time in the gospel accounts when words spoken by the disciple John are recorded. Does this section (verses 38-41) indicate a feeling of antagonsim toward the Johannine community on the part of Mark? Is John here speaking as a representative of those Christians in Asia Minor who claimed him as their apostle, just as those in Rome claimed Peter and Paul as theirs? Was there tension between the community of John and that of Mark? John acknowledges Jesus as **teacher**/revealer, and so indicates that what he says he has learnt from Jesus.

John is against the idea of 'Christian' groups casting out demons in the **name** of Jesus when they do not belong to his (John's) group. The gospel of John records no exorcisms at all. In this verse here in Mark the text is very uncertain, but the point being made is the same in most manuscripts. What is not so clear is whether the man is regarded by John as not being a follower of Jesus, or not being a follower of the disciples. In his response, which is no doubt that of Mark as **39** well, Jesus says that it is not possible for someone to do a work in his name and then speak evil of him soon afterwards. A person who is not **against** Jesus is **for** him. The **40** idea expressed here is similar to Jesus' rejection of the suggestion that he is casting out demons in the name of Beelzebul. If this man is casting out demons in the name of Jesus, he cannot be from the side of evil. In fact, Jesus goes **41** on to say, the simple act of giving another Christian a cup of water will not go unrewarded. It is something that is done for Christ and comes from a relationship with Christ. The expression **because you bear the name of Christ** is probably one that was used later, rather than in Jesus' own time.

That there were problems within the Marcan community is clear from verses 42-50. Apparently there were some who thought of themselves more highly than they should have, and so offended the weaker members, becoming a scandal or stumbling block for them. This behaviour meets with Jesus' strongest reprimand. The **millstone** around the neck would mean, of course, that the drowned person would sink to the bottom of the sea, and would thus be denied burial. The fact that this would render the body forever unclean shows what a powerful word of judgment Jesus speaks here. It is as though the stone that was used to cause the weaker person to stumble were to be hung around the offender's own neck.

The references to cutting off a hand or a foot, or removing an eye, are a typical use of hyperbole in order to make a point. It is not clear what the particular sin (or scandal or stumbling block) may have been. The drastic action that is recommended would suggest that it had something to do with the use of one's body. It is worth taking drastic measures in order to enter the new life, the kingdom of God, and to avoid being thrown into hell (or Gehenna) – a thought that corresponds with Jesus' demands on those who follow him. It cost Jesus his life, and the disciple is not greater than the teacher.

**Salt** and **fire** both act as agents of destruction and pain, as well as being able to clean and heal. **Salt is good**, but unless it is used and allowed to have effect wherever it is placed, it is useless, and loses its potency and value. The RSV translates the last section of verse 50 with **have salt in yourselves, and be at peace with one another**, which involves a misunderstanding of the reference to salt here. The use of salt in meals was so common that it could symbolise the meal itself, in much the same way as bread does. To have salt with someone meant sharing a meal with him or her. In Acts 1:4 the verb translated 'staying' or 'eating' can mean, literally, 'having salt together with'. So it would be better to translate here: 'Have salt among yourselves', that is, 'share food with one another', perhaps even, 'have a beer together'! That this is the meaning is made clear from the exhortation that follows: **be at peace with one another**. The Marcan community is experiencing division, arguments and dissension. Mark uses Jesus' words to promote peace and a spirit of service, where the weaker members of the community are not made to stumble as a result of the behaviour of those who regard themselves as being the greatest among them.

## Marriage and divorce in the new community, 10:1-12

¹ And he left there and went to the region of Judea and beyond the Jordan, and crowds gathered to him again; and again, as his custom was, he taught them.
² And Pharisees came up and in order to test him asked, 'Is it lawful for a man to divorce his wife?' ³ He answered them, 'What did Moses command you?' ⁴ They said, 'Moses allowed a man to write a certificate of divorce, and to put her away.' ⁵ But Jesus said to them, 'For your hardness of heart he wrote you this commandment. ⁶ But from the beginning of creation, "God made them male and female." ⁷ "For this reason a man shall leave his father and mother and be joined to his wife,ᵖ ⁸ and the two shall become one flesh." So they are no longer two but one flesh. ⁹ What therefore God has joined together, let not man put asunder.'
¹⁰ And in the house the disciples asked him again about this matter. ¹¹ And he said to them, 'Whoever divorces his wife and marries another, commits adultery against her; ¹² and if she divorces her husband and marries another, she commits adultery.'

ᵖ Other ancient authorities omit *and be joined to his wife*

At first it may appear that this teaching section is a lull in Mark's story of Jesus, the Clean One, going on his way to Jerusalem, to an unclean death. But this is not the case. Questions of marriage and divorce were crucial in the context of the coming kingdom. The kingdom becomes an important theme from now on, as Jesus finally moves out of Galilee and into Judea, but for now still outside the boundaries, among those living beyond the Jordan. Variations in the manuscripts in relation to Jesus' movements indicate that early readers also found Mark's geography difficult to follow. Some manuscripts leave out the word **and** in verse 1, which suggests that Perea is the region that is meant, the second half of the tetrarchy of Herod Antipas. If the **and** is retained, the reference would be to the region of Judea and the other side of the Jordan, that is, the east bank, Perea, but the difficulty with this is that it suggests a single area, whereas Perea and Judea were completely separate areas under separate jurisdiction. The RSV probably correctly understands the author's intention.

The position or status of Jesus as teacher is significant in this section. A question facing the early Christians, espe-

cially those from a Jewish background, must have been:
What is the authority of Jesus as an interpreter of the will
of God in comparison to *the* interpreter, Moses, and those
who have developed the tradition in order to explain Moses?

The Pharisees, who see themselves as being strict observ- **2-4**
ers of the Torah (God's law) and the tradition, come to **test**
Jesus (the same verb as used in 1:13) on the question of
divorce. Jesus' answer to their question suggests a distancing of himself (and therefore also of the Christian community) from Moses. The Pharisees refer to Deuteronomy 24:1,
which allows a man to divorce his wife provided he protects
her by giving her a document of dismissal which frees her
to remarry. Jesus regards this as a concession to human **5**
**hardness of heart**, because the original intention of God,
as expressed in Genesis 1:27 and 2:24, is that husband and **6-8**
wife become one in an indissoluble union. It is quite likely
that what Jesus has in mind here is the common belief that
the original human (Adam) was created by God androgy-
nous, that is, both male and female. What God has joined **9**
together, no-one must separate. What God has created as a
unity must remain united, which is why divorce and polyg-
amy are prohibited. Marriage reflects the unity of God,
perhaps his most fundamental characteristic. Just as there
is no division in God, and no division in his original created
human being, so there is to be no division in marriage. Jesus
may be wishing to underline the fact that both male and
female are created by God, not just the male! Humanity was
created male and female, the two together forming one
human creation. There is no human without both male and
female. It is also worth noting that it is the male, in Genesis
2:24, who is called to leave his parents and become united
with his wife. In our Western culture it has tended to be the
woman who has had to leave, and has gone with her husband wherever he has gone, as symbolised by the wife's
taking of her husband's name.

The scene shifts to the **house**, which again we can under- **10**
stand to represent the Christian community. There in the
house the disciples ask Jesus a question, a common introduction to a statement of revelation from Jesus. Jesus states **11,**
clearly that remarriage of a divorced person is adultery, so **12**
indissoluble is the yoking together of two people in marriage. The fact that this discussion takes place inside the
house indicates that the question of divorce was a real one
for the Christians for whom Mark was writing. It must have
been particularly important for Gentiles who had become

Christian while their partners remained pagan. The question would have been whether there should be divorce in such cases.

Adultery, according to the Jews, consisted of intercourse between a married woman and a man other than her husband. A man could not commit adultery against his wife; he could commit adultery only against another married man. Jesus' answer to the disciples' question, however, shows that he is radically altering this understanding, and is putting male and female on an equal footing in this area. It goes both ways! The equality of male and female, according to Jesus, is based on the original creation. According to Jewish law, Jewish women could not divorce their husbands. Roman women, however, could, and this situation may well have caused debate and division within Christian communities made up of both Jews and Gentiles.

## Let the children come, 10:13-16

**¹³ And they were bringing children to him, that he might touch them; and the disciples rebuked them. ¹⁴ But when Jesus saw it he was indignant, and said to them, 'Let the children come to me, do not hinder them; for to such belongs the kingdom of God. ¹⁵ Truly, I say to you, whoever does not receive the kingdom of God like a child shall not enter it.' ¹⁶ And he took them in his arms and blessed them, laying his hands upon them.**

This episode is introduced rather abruptly, with no explanation of who is bringing the children to Jesus. This indefiniteness is characteristic of Mark and makes for good story telling, because it does not allow readers to distance themselves from the people in the story. They are forced to ask themselves: Is this about us, then?

**Children** here means anyone up to the age of about twelve. The desire for children to be touched by a holy person is still common today – for example, when parents bring their baby to be kissed or touched by the pope. There is no reason given for the disciples' rebuke of those bringing the children. The words 'touch' and 'rebuke' have occurred frequently in this gospel in relation to Jesus' confrontation with unclean spirits and sickness. Is their appearance here coincidental, or is there a deeper significance in it? Jesus' reaction suggests that there is something deeper here (the word

**indignant** is not used of Jesus anywhere else in the gospels). Some manuscripts say that Jesus in turn 'rebukes' the disciples. This word in Mark's gospel usually involves opposition to a serious evil. Could it be that children here represent the future, and that Jesus is saying that there is a future for the kingdom? What the disciples want is the kingdom now, with all the political implications of power and status that it holds for them. Jesus rejects that. Children represent those who are weak, defenceless, and powerless, but the disciples have frequently shown that the kingdom that they desire does not consist of such people.

According to a long and ancient tradition, this story has been commonly associated with baptism, especially that of infants. Jesus says: **For to such belongs the kingdom of God**. This could either mean that it is people who are like little children who make up the kingdom, or that the kingdom itself is like little children: it appears to be weak, insignificant, and powerless. It probably means the former: It is weak and powerless people who are offered the kingdom at the invitation of Jesus.

Jesus goes on to say that **whoever does not receive the kingdom of God like a child shall not enter it**. These words also can be understood in two ways: Either, one must receive the kingdom as one receives a child, because the kingdom appears to be weak and powerless like a child; or, one must receive the kingdom in the way that a little child receives things that are graciously given to it. There are good arguments for both ways of understanding Jesus' words, but the latter is probably the intended meaning.

Jesus takes the children in his arms and blesses them by laying his hands on them, an action which some see as having baptismal connotations. With Mark's community no longer observing the ritual of circumcision (although some Christians may have retained it), the question of whether it should be replaced by infant baptism may well have been an important one for them. Circumcision was performed on Jewish males when they were eight days old. It is likely that some Christians saw baptism as being equivalent to circumcision, and so baptised infants eight days after they were born. This story would have been a favourite one for those advocating this practice. Jesus does not merely touch the children, but shows his love for them and acceptance of them by taking them into his arms. We have noted previously Jesus' willingness to touch and to be touched (see, for example, 1:41; 5:27-31).

*If you are serious, you let it go, 10:17-31*

[17] And as he was setting out on his journey, a man ran up and knelt before him, and asked him, 'Good Teacher, what must I do to inherit eternal life?' [18] And Jesus said to him, 'Why do you call me good? No one is good but God alone. [19] You know the commandments: "Do not kill, Do not commit adultery, Do not steal, Do not bear false witness, Do not defraud, Honour your father and mother." ' [20] And he said to him, 'Teacher, all these I have observed from my youth.' [21] And Jesus looking upon him loved him, and said to him, 'You lack one thing; go, sell what you have, and give to the poor, and you will have treasure in heaven; and come, follow me.' [22] At that saying his countenance fell, and he went away sorrowful; for he had great possessions.

[23] And Jesus looked around and said to his disciples, 'How hard it will be for those who have riches to enter the kingdom of God!' [24] And the disciples were amazed at his words. But Jesus said to them again, 'Children, how hard it is[r] to enter the kingdom of God! [25] It is easier for a camel to go through the eye of a needle than for a rich man to enter the kingdom of God.' [26] And they were exceedingly astonished, and said to him,[s] 'Then who can be saved?' [27] Jesus looked at them and said, 'With men it is impossible, but not with God; for all things are possible with God.' [28] Peter began to say to him, 'Lo, we have left everything and followed you.' [29] Jesus said, 'Truly, I say to you, there is no one who has left house or brothers or sisters or mother or father or children or lands, for my sake and for the gospel, [30] who will not receive a hundredfold now in this time, houses and brothers and sisters and mothers and children and lands, with persecutions, and in the age to come eternal life. [31] But many that are first will be last, and the last first.'

[r] Other ancient authorities add *for those who trust in riches*
[s] Other ancient authorities read *to one another*

Jesus moves on, coming ever closer now to Jerusalem and his cross. A man runs up (literally, 'one runner') and kneels before Jesus, asking for revelation. The question: **What must I do to inherit eternal life?** is a question about entrance into the kingdom of God. Jesus picks him up on his use of the word **good** in addressing him as **Good Teacher**. That quality belongs to **God alone** (literally, the God who is 'one'). Any Jew would have known the answer to the man's question, as stated by Jesus: The inheritance of eternal life depends on one's observance of God's law. Jesus appears to be saying: 'You call me good and ask me a question regarding eternal life. Both goodness and eternal life come from God, through his revealed will which is found in his law. So why do you come to me, calling me good, and asking me about eternal life? What are you saying about me? Who do you think I am?'

It is interesting that Jesus refers only to the so-called second table of the Ten Commandments, which deals with behaviour toward the neighbour. The first table, dealing with attitudes and behaviour toward God, Jesus ignores – or has it been summarised in his statement that **no one is good but God alone**? The command **Do not defraud** is omitted in some reliable manuscripts.

The man now addresses Jesus simply as **Teacher** – 'good' has been omitted this time! His claim: **All these I have observed from my youth**, is not an idle boast. The law could be kept, and the promised blessings enjoyed. Jesus does not criticise his response. Instead, he consciously and deliberately looks at him and loves him. To look at someone face to face and not avert one's eyes is an expression of equality and acceptance. Some have suggested that the word 'love' here refers to a gesture such as embracing or hugging. Nowhere else in Mark's gospel is the word 'love' used of Jesus, so we are obliged to attach significance to its use here. Does this man represent those Jews who are seeking the Christian way, people who are on the run, looking for a better answer to their questions than the ones that are to be found in their traditions? The story certainly indicates that Mark does not see Israel as a nation that is rejecting or opposing Jesus, or that is being rejected by him. The love of Jesus, and his call, go out also to his own people. The Christian community is to show love to those Jews among them who have not yet come to the full understanding of Jesus and his words.

One thing is lacking for this man; it is not necessarily lacking for everyone. Four commands are given by Jesus: **Go**, **sell**, **give** and **follow**. As always in calling people to follow him along his way of discipleship, Jesus calls for a letting go of all that has previously provided security: family, money, business, religious tradition. The man is shocked and appalled at what Jesus says, and goes away sad, because he has many possessions. Jesus has not simply asked him to be charitable, but to give up the very source of his income. This is a very radical demand, and one which clearly caused problems in later Christian communities. Jesus himself, and his disciples, clearly lived a wandering life, without security, relying on the hospitality of friends and supporters. Paul lived a similar life, although he gained some security through the practice of his craft. As time went by, Christians came to be found also in cities, living lives that were in many ways similar to those of their pagan neighbours. Were they also called to give up all that they had? How realistic was the demand of Jesus?

Jesus himself realises the radical nature of what he has said to the man, and so he turns to his disciples (again establishing face to face, or eyeball to eyeball, contact with them) and says what they themselves are thinking: **How hard it will be for those who have riches to enter the kingdom of God**! Some manuscripts have verse 25 before verse 24, and this would make good sense. The disciples are astonished because of the way in which Jesus makes it even more difficult for a person to be saved. 23 24

Much has been written about Jesus' statement that **it is easier for a camel to go through the eye of a needle than for a rich man to enter the kingdom of God**, often to the detriment of the point being made! There is no need to minimise the clear contrast contained in Jesus' picture: he means **camel** and he means **eye of a needle**! However, it is worth remembering that camels were beasts of burden, and that for a camel to get through any low opening, it would have to get rid of its load. The point that Jesus is making is just that: the rich man must get rid of his load before he can enter the kingdom. The disciples understand what he means (for once!), and realise that their own salvation is in grave jeopardy, along with everyone else's, if what he says is true. But salvation is not the result of human effort. For this we can thank God, for whom **all things**, including our salvation, **are possible**! God has the ability to unload for us all the impediments which we bear, which prevent us from walking his way. He unloads them by liberating us from all that is unclean and demonic, all that alienates us from God and from each other, and that destroys human existence. Money is one of the things that potentially has the power to burden people and destroy them. 25-27

Peter begins to reply, but only begins. He argues, as humans do, on the basis of his own actions, which Jesus 28 partly ignores and partly supports. In his reply, Jesus **29** speaks of the security offered by house and family which he calls his followers to leave. In the list of family members that one must be prepared to leave, there is no mention of 'wife'. It is possible that Christians regarded the marriage tie as being so sacred that nothing except martyrdom could justify its dissolution. The absence of 'father' in the list of new family members that the follower of Jesus gains, can be explained by the fact that God is regarded as one's father, and only God. The follower of Jesus leaves his or her phys- **30** ical family, and gains a new community, both in this age and in the new one. The addition of **with persecutions** may indicate that persecution occurred within the Christian community when conflicts of allegiance between family and the community arose. The Christian is called to belong first to the new community of Christ, and one's family is to be always at least second. Instead of the Christian community modelling itself on the family, the family is to be modelled on the community.

This radical call of Jesus must have had social ramifications, and it is quite likely that many Christians did not follow Jesus as radically as he no doubt intended. Family ties were important in themselves, but they also had economical and social implications. Women not marrying, for example, would have meant loss of face for the family, and loss of wealth in many cases as well. These sorts of problems become more evident in certain second century Christian writings such as The Acts of Paul, but there is a suggestion of such problems already in the so-called Pastoral Letters of the New Testament (1 and 2 Tim, Titus). The gospels themselves suggest that there were some people who did follow Jesus according to his radical demand.

Jesus' statement that **many that are first will be last,** **31** **and the last first**, seems to have been a floating saying which the gospel writers attached to various pieces of teaching by Jesus. It stresses here the grace of God, which inverts the values of the social and religious worlds. Being rich is no guarantee of the grace of God, nor is being first among the disciples, as Peter was who had left everything (v 28).

## You can't say you weren't told, 10:32-34

**32 And they were on the road, going up to Jerusalem, and Jesus was walking ahead of them; and they were amazed, and those who followed were afraid. And taking the twelve again, he began to tell them what was to happen to him, 33 saying, 'Behold, we are going up to Jerusalem; and the Son of man will be delivered to the chief priests and the scribes, and they will condemn him to death, and deliver him to the Gentiles; 34 and they will mock him, and spit upon him, and scourge him, and kill him; and after three days he will rise.'**

This is the third prediction that Jesus makes of his passion and his subsequent vindication through his resurrection. The repetition helps readers to focus on what the writer regards as important. It maintains the tension of Mark's cycle of stories, and helps to direct readers toward the climax.

Jesus and his disciples are **on the road**. This calls to mind the beginning of the gospel (1:2,3) with John the Baptist preparing 'the way' of the Lord (the same word that is translated here as 'road'). This reminds readers that what they are called to do is walk the way of Jesus. They are **going up to Jerusalem**. This is very significant, because, from now on, Jerusalem comes very much into focus in the gospel. It was regarded by Jews as the city of God, the centre of the world, the place where God had chosen to dwell in his temple, the place where history found its meaning and its destiny. Going **up** to Jerusalem is a geographical fact, since the city is built on a hill. However, the idea of going up also has other connotations, since mountain tops were seen as places of special revelation (see 9:2-8). In going up to Jerusalem, Jesus is going to the place where he will be lifted up on the cross, and this will be the special revelation of the presence and glory of God.

Jesus walks ahead of the others. What is expected of the followers – that they walk the way that leads to the cross – is undertaken by their Leader. The disciples, as on other occasions, show amazement, while others who are following show fear. These are typical reactions on the part of Jesus' followers in Mark. The disciples are amazed that the Son of God, the Man with all the authority of God, should be heading for Jerusalem and the cross. The more immediate reason for their amazement and fear is that they know what Jesus and they can expect in Jerusalem. Anyone who preaches a message against power-seeking, and against an establishment consisting of people who build walls around the will of God, and who claim to be the only ones who are pure through their keeping of God's law, is bound to be suppressed in one way or another. It did not require divine foreknowledge for Jesus or his followers to be able to predict rejection and even death in Jerusalem.

Amazement and fear are also the reactions of the women at the Easter tomb (16:8), and since the expression 'going before' is used there of Jesus (16:7), (the same word here translated as **walking ahead**), it can be suggested that Mark is hinting at a connection. Jesus is never afraid to cross the boundaries, to go over the lines drawn up by tradition, and here he shows that he is not afraid to face the ultimate boundary, the final line, that of death. In going to Jerusalem, he calls his disciples to follow him, to go with him to the place of rejection and the cross. Later, in his resurrection, he calls them to follow him again, as he goes ahead of them into Galilee, across the lines (see commentary on 16:8). On both occasions – and on many occasions since then in the experience of the Christian community – the response to Jesus' call, and to the direction in which he moves, is one of fear and astonishment.

Jesus takes aside the twelve **again**. **Again** indicates that they have been told all this before, and it underscores their lack of understanding and faith.

In saying: **We are going up**, Jesus includes the disciples in his 'ascension', but he goes on to say that the Son of man alone will suffer at the hands of both Jewish leaders and Gentiles, will die, and will be raised to life again on the third day.

## *On being the greatest, 10:35-45*

[35] **And James and John, the sons of Zebedee, came forward to him, and said to him, 'Teacher, we want you to do for us whatever we ask of you.'** [36] **And he said to them, 'What do you want me to do for you?'** [37] **And they said to him, 'Grant us to sit, one at your right hand and one at your left, in your glory.'** [38] **But Jesus said to them, 'You do not know what you are asking. Are you able to drink the cup that I drink, or to be baptized with the baptism with which I am baptized?'** [39] **And they said to him, 'We are able.' And Jesus said to them, 'The cup that I drink you will drink; and with the baptism with which I am baptized, you will be baptized;** [40] **but to sit at my right hand or at**

my left is not mine to grant, but it is for those for whom it has been prepared.' ⁴¹ And when the ten heard it, they began to be indignant at James and John. ⁴² And Jesus called them to him and said to them, 'You know that those who are supposed to rule over the Gentiles lord it over them, and their great men exercise authority over them. ⁴³ But it shall not be so among you; but whoever would be great among you must be your servant, ⁴⁴ and whoever would be first among you must be slave of all. ⁴⁵ For the Son of man also came not to be served but to serve, and to give his life as a ransom for many.'

**35-37** James and John, whom Jesus had called 'sons of thunder' (3:17), but who are here identified as the sons of Zebedee, raise with Jesus the question about sharing in the glory of his kingdom. The inclusion of this question at this point indicates clearly that Mark sees Jesus' going up to Jerusalem (vv 32, 33) in more than geographical terms: his 'ascension' on the cross will be his coronation and the ushering in of his kingdom. In asking their question, James and John show a misunderstanding which is typical of the disciples, which is why Jesus says: **You do not know what you are asking**. The tradition regarding James is that he was executed by Herod (Acts 12:2). As for John, one tradition records a violent early death, while another records a peaceful death in old age. Jesus speaks of the **cup** that he drinks, and the **baptism** with which he is baptised. The link be- **38, 39** tween Jesus' baptism and his death was hinted at already in 1:10 (see commentary there). The picture of Jesus' death as a cup to be drunk is one that would have been well understood. So, **baptism** here points back to 1:10, and **cup** points forward to 14:36.

**40** This episode contrasts the expectations of some of Jesus' followers (and presumably some communities who followed them) and the expectations of Jesus himself. The followers hope to share in the glory of the Messiah, holding positions of authority in the kingdom. Jesus, however, predicts suffering, rejection, and death, and only then vindication through resurrection. There is a connection between the request of the two disciples to sit, one at Jesus' right hand and the other at his left, and the crucifixion of Jesus, where two revolutionaries are crucified with him, one on his right and the other on his left (15:27). Jesus does not die flanked by his disciples but as a political revolutionary, with revolutionaries on either side of him, misunderstood by his disciples and even rejected by them.

James and John (and their followers?) are not viewed favourably by the other disciples, who are **indignant** at them. But Jesus has something to say to all of them. In relation to the rulers of this world the structures are such that great and powerful people dominate and have power, but it is not to be like that in the Christian community. There, power is not the name of the game, but service by all to all. And what Jesus expects of his communities, he models himself. The Son of man, who has already been identified three times with suffering, rejection, and death, has come **not to be served** like a lord, **but to serve, and to give his life as a ransom for many**. The words **for many** point forward to the meal at which Jesus speaks of his 'blood of the covenant, which is poured out for many' (14:24). But his death is not his only act of service. His whole life is a ministry of service to the unclean, the possessed, the poor, the outcasts, the blind, the deaf, the sinners.

## *Can you see yet? 10:46-52*

**⁴⁶ And they came to Jericho; and as he was leaving Jericho with his disciples and a great multitude, Bartimaeus, a blind beggar, the son of Timaeus, was sitting by the roadside. ⁴⁷ And when he heard that it was Jesus of Nazareth, he began to cry out and say, 'Jesus, Son of David, have mercy on me!' ⁴⁸ And many rebuked him, telling him to be silent; but he cried out all the more, 'Son of David, have mercy on me!' ⁴⁹ And Jesus stopped and said, 'Call him.' And they called the blind man; saying to him, 'Take heart; rise, he is calling you.' ⁵⁰ And throwing off his mantle he sprang up and came to Jesus. ⁵¹ And Jesus said to him, 'What do you want me to do for you?' And the blind man said to him, 'Master,ᵗ let me receive my sight.' ⁵² And Jesus said to him, 'Go your way; your faith has made you well.' And immediately he received his sight and followed him on the way.**

ᵗ Or *Rabbi*

Jesus comes to **Jericho**. We have here again the simple but effective linking of episodes by the movement of Jesus to a new location. At the time of Jesus, Jericho lay to the south of the ancient Israelite town of the same name, and to the west of modern Riha. Herod the Great and Archelaus had redeveloped the city. It was known for its palm trees, and was the seat of a Roman garrison at one stage. No doubt for some readers it evoked memories of the Joshua story. Joshua was the one who led the people into the promised land via Jericho. For Jesus, the new Joshua ('Jesus' is a variant form of 'Joshua'), the way leads via Jericho to the cross.

As Jesus, with the usual **great multitude** of people, leaves Jericho on his way to Jerusalem, blind **Bartimaeus** sits by the roadside begging. Why are we not told his own name, but simply that he is **the son of Timaeus** (the 'bar' of 'Bartimaeus' is Hebrew for 'son of'). In Greek, the man is identified twice: **Bartimaeus** and **the son of Timaeus**. It is possible that this reflects the common idea that, if a person was born blind or disabled, the parents were responsible (see John 9:2). There may be something further: The *son* of Timaeus calls out to the *son* of David. He has inherited from his father, Timaeus, what and who he is as a man. Jesus has inherited all that *he* is from *his* father. But the irony is that Jesus is not only Son of David but also Son of God (see also 12:35-37; 14:61).

The road to Jerusalem via Jericho was the way that was taken by pilgrims. The blind man sits there expecting to receive charity from the pilgrims. He hears that it is **Jesus of Nazareth** who is passing by. This designation of Jesus is significant. He comes from Galilee, the unclean area known for its political and religious rebels. What good thing can come from Nazareth (John 1:46)? Bartimaeus, being unclean himself, calls out to his brother, the Unclean One: **Jesus, Son of David, have mercy on me**! The title **Son of David**, which is used here for the first time in the gospel, becomes significant in the following chapter, where the question of who is David's son is asked and discussed (12:35-37). As he often does, Mark here prepares his readers for further developments later. Blind Bartimaeus is not presented here as being in contrast to the disciples, but as being representative of them. He sees in Jesus of Nazareth the one who is David's Son. The disciples have come to see Jesus as the Christ (8:29). In both cases the perception is very limited. So this story relates closely with the previous healing of a blind man, where he first gained limited sight before having his sight fully restored (8:22-26). **Son of David** could also be seen as a reference to Solomon, who was known at that time as the patron of exorcists, which is what Bartimaeus may have thought Jesus to be. If this were so, it would heighten the irony, since Mark's readers already know that there is much more to Jesus than that. It needs to be noted that Bartimaeus calls Jesus **Son of David** while he is still blind! He represents those Christians who are still blind in the sense that they see in Jesus merely the fulfilment of a national messianic hope. What Mark is saying is that Jesus is much more than that.

Only two healings of blind people are recorded in Mark's gospel, and they are strategically placed. Both episodes begin with **And they came to** (8:22; 10:46). It is well known that oral narratives have a different shape or logical pattern from written narratives. They tend to follow a circular pattern instead of progressing in straight lines. Where the story proceeds in this cyclical fashion, the audience hears the same thing a number of times, but on each occasion is also carried further forward in the story as a whole. It involves repetition (which is a good oral story-telling technique), but a repetition which also contributes to the progress of the story.

Many people rebuke Bartimaeus, commanding him to be **48** silent. He is unclean, in their view, and so should remain silent in the presence of Jesus. But he cries out even more. As noted previously, 'crying out' is a common feature of exorcisms, when an unclean spirit leaves a person (see 9:26). His plea is heard by Jesus, who asks that the man be called. **49** The Clean One calls the unclean, just as he had called the disciples. The people call the blind man, saying: **Take heart; rise, he is calling you**. To all those who are blind, who do not yet understand who Jesus is, the call is given to take heart, to get up, and to hear the call of Jesus to follow his way. The man's cloak may have doubled as his begging **50** bowl, being placed on the ground in front of him to hold gifts of food and money. He leaves his cloak, and enthusiastically comes to Jesus. Jesus responds with his gracious question: **What do you want me to do for you**? Bartimaeus, delib- **51** erately referred to by Mark as **the blind man**, asks of Jesus: **Master** (or Rabbi), **let me receive my sight**. The verb translated 'receive my sight' can also mean 'to look up', and maybe Mark and his readers would have been aware of the double meaning of this word. If one wishes to see again, one needs to look up – up to the Jesus who goes up to Jerusalem, who will be nailed up on the cross, and who will then be raised up from the dead.

Jesus sends Bartimaeus on his way, complimenting him **52** on his trust, a trust which the disciples lacked. That trust, or **faith**, had made him well (the word could also be translated: had 'saved' him). **Immediately** (is this in contrast to the other blind man, who did not immediately see clearly, but needed a second touch from Jesus? [8:22-26]) the man sees again (or, looks up), and, having gained his sight, he follows Jesus. To follow is the action of the disciple. The disciple of Jesus is one who follows him. Significantly, he follows Jesus **on the way** – the way to Jerusalem, to the cross, and, through the cross, to Easter. It is clear that this story asks the reader to see, and in seeing, to follow. As noted earlier, faith is not a possession to be guarded, but involves responding to the call to follow along the way, to make transitions, to let go of the things that give security, and to live hopefully even when faced by the cross.

## PART IV: 11:1 – 13:37

*Long live the king, 11:1-11*

<sup>11:1</sup> **And when they drew near to Jerusalem, to Bethphage and Bethany, at the Mount of Olives, he sent two of his disciples, ² and said to them, 'Go into the village opposite you, and immediately as you enter it you will find a colt tied, on which no one has ever sat; untie it and bring it. ³ If any one says to you, "Why are you doing this?" say, "The Lord has need of it and will send it back here immediately." ' ⁴ And they went away, and found a colt tied at the door out in the open street; and they untied it. ⁵ And those who stood there said to them, 'What are you doing, untying the colt?' ⁶ And they told them what Jesus had said; and they let them go. ⁷ And they brought the colt to Jesus, and threw their garments on it; and he sat upon it. ⁸ And many spread their garments on the road, and others spread leafy branches which they had cut from the fields. ⁹ And those who went before and those who followed cried out, 'Hosanna! Blessed is he who comes in the name of the Lord! ¹⁰ Blessed is the kingdom of our father David that is coming! Hosanna in the highest!'**

**¹¹ And he entered Jerusalem, and went into the temple; and when he had looked round at everything, as it was already late, he went out to Bethany with the twelve.**

**Jerusalem!** For any Jews among Mark's readers, all kinds of thoughts would have been conjured up by this name: thoughts of God, of the temple, of hope, of Israel as a nation and a people. Jerusalem was thought of as being the centre of the world, the gate of paradise. Mark has already identified it as a place of opposition, since Jesus' critics come from there (3:22; 7:1).

The exact location of **Bethphage** is not known. Literally, the name means 'house of unripe figs', and, in the light of verses 12-14, there may be some significance in that. The **Mount of Olives** had deep significance for Jews (especially those who knew the book of Zechariah well) as the place where the Lord would become king of all the earth (Zech 14:4,9). In his passion narrative, which is coming close, Mark quotes from or refers to Zechariah quite often, indicating that it was a significant writing for his understanding of Jesus. In the whole of the New Testament, Zechariah is cited some seventy times.

Jesus' sending of two of his disciples to get the donkey **2,3** shows him speaking with authority, an important theme in the passion story. He seems to be planning his moves, which will be carried out despite the plans of others. This is one of the marks of a prophet. The disciples follow his instructions, **4,5** and find things just as he has said. Jesus sits on the colt, **6-8** which has been covered with his followers' garments. The donkey is portrayed as a kingly animal in Zechariah 9:9 and Genesis 49:11. Mark, however, emphasises the fact that the donkey that Jesus rides on is young and previously unridden. Jesus moves toward Jerusalem as king – that is clearly the point of the story. However, it should be noted that his kingship is applauded by the crowds while they are still *outside* Jerusalem (verse 11 shows that this is the case). Jesus is accepted only outside the holy city. Inside, he is **9,** rejected as king, and as a rejected king he is crucified. **10**

The words of acclamation from the crowd suggest that they are Passover pilgrims singing psalms. Their words come from Psalm 118:25,26. (It is always good to read the wider context of any quotation from the Old Testament. Here, it is quite likely that the crowd sang much more of the psalm than the two verses that are quoted.) The reference to David and his coming kingdom was anticipated in the cry of blind Bartimaeus, who called Jesus 'Son of David'. Here the crowds call David their **father**. If David is their father, then *they* are 'Son of David'! It is possible that there was conflict surrounding this title. Can Christians claim for Jesus what Israel claimed for itself as a nation? The question of who Jesus is builds up to a startling climax in Mark's gospel. References to Jesus as 'Son of David', and as the one who brings in **the kingdom of our father David**, fall far short of Mark's understanding of him. People only half understand who he is, and that is the irony of the story.

Verse 11 records some strange happenings. On coming **11** into the city for the first time, Jesus heads straight for the temple. The word for **temple** that Mark uses here is one that refers also to the forecourt and the wider precincts. Later, in relation to the tearing of the curtain in the temple (15:38), he uses a different word which refers more specifically to the sanctuary. In the temple he looks **round at everything**. What does this action mean? In other passages where Jesus 'looks around', there is often a note of anger or reprimand (see 3:5,34; 5:32; 10:23). It may be the same here. There follows the unusual phrase: **as it was already late**, and then Jesus goes away to Bethany with the twelve. Very mysterious movements indeed! The reference to the late hour probably refers to the fact that the temple was about to close; its gates were shut at dusk. Is Mark suggesting that the temple gates are to be 'shut' in Jesus' death and resurrection? The movement of Jesus into Jerusalem is followed by his going **out** to Bethany. Within a few days he is going to be led out to be crucified as the Outsider.

## *No figs, no temple, 11:12-14*

**¹² On the following day, when they came from Bethany, he was hungry. ¹³ And seeing in the distance a fig tree in leaf, he went to see if he could find anything on it. When he came to it, he found nothing but leaves, for it was not the season for figs. ¹⁴ And he said to it, 'May no one ever eat fruit from you again.' And his disciples heard it.**

This is a rather strange episode. Jesus leaves Bethany 12 and is **hungry**. Here again we have a reference to food and hunger, to not eating (see 3:20; 6:31; 8:14). Seeing from a 13 distance **a fig tree in leaf**, Jesus goes to find fruit on it, but there is none. This is not surprising, since it was not the right time for figs. Jesus responds to this 'message' of the 14 fig tree by cursing it. The disciples hear him speak the curse. An explanation for Jesus' action can be found by seeing it in connection with the episode that follows (the so-called cleansing of the temple). It appears that Jesus sees the fig tree as a symbol of the temple. It is the temple that does not satisfy the hunger of the Clean One from God. The word for **season** that is used here was also used to refer to the seasons of the Jewish religious year. It is Passover festival time when this incident takes place. Jesus himself is the new 'festival time' of God, and, when he comes, the temple is shown to be barren and fruitless. From now on the temple will produce no fruit for Jesus' disciples. Christians and the temple are divorced. There is no obligation on the Christian to look to the temple for revelation from God or for the presence of God. The centre of God's dwelling with his people has shifted to the new temple, which is Jesus himself.

According to some traditions, the fig tree was the forbidden tree in the Garden of Eden. Another Jewish tradition said that the trees of the temple withered when heathens entered the sanctuary, but that they would bloom again in the messianic times. If Mark was aware of this tradition, he seems to be reversing it in relation to Jesus!

Zechariah shapes Mark's passion story to a marked degree. In Zechariah 11:17 a curse is pronounced against the 'worthless shepherd' (the leader of God's people) whose arm will be withered. It may be that Mark had this passage in mind at this point.

## More than a cleansing, 11:15-19

**¹⁵ And they came to Jerusalem. And he entered the temple and began to drive out those who sold and those who bought in the temple, and he overturned the tables of the moneychangers and the seats of those who sold pigeons; ¹⁶ and he would not allow any one to carry anything through the temple. ¹⁷ And he taught, and said to them, 'Is it not written, "My house shall be called a house of prayer for all the nations"? But you have made it a den of robbers.' ¹⁸ And the chief priests and the scribes heard it and sought a way to destroy him; for they feared him, because all the multitude was astonished at his teaching. ¹⁹ And when evening came they[u] went out of the city.**

[u] Other ancient authorities read *he*

Jesus comes again into Jerusalem, and goes into the forecourt of the temple, where he begins to throw out the sellers and buyers, and to overturn the tables of the moneychangers and the seats of the pigeon-sellers. All these people and things were part of the temple's sacrificial system. Daily sacrifices were offered in the temple, and people would also come every day to present their offerings. People were required to pay a temple tax, and money for it was changed so that unclean money would not profane the house of God. Even Jews living outside of Israel, in the diaspora, paid an annual tax for the maintaining of the temple system. Money received from the tax made it possible for the daily public sacrifices to be performed throughout the year in the name of the community of Israel. Only Israelites were eligible to pay the tax and were required to do so. Gentiles, Samaritans, women, minors and slaves did not pay. Exodus 30:11-16 provided the basis for this tax. That passage indicates that the tax was closely related to atonement (verse 16 calls it 'atonement money' [RSV]). So, the moneychangers were essential to the whole sacrificial system of the temple. Jesus' action must therefore have met with astonishment – the man must be mad! Nobody could have possibly understood what he was doing.

Jesus' attack is a rejection of the temple sacrifice system itself. He is not attacking the practice of buying and selling as something wrong, or because there was some injustice being done. It has been suggested that the **tables** with the money for the sacrifices point ahead to another table of sacrifice which Mark will soon be introducing into his story: the table of the Passover, which becomes the table of the Lord who gives himself as a sacrifice on the cross. Jesus is not *cleansing* the temple, but condemning it, together with its cultic and sacrificial practices. Atonement for sin is no longer made through this temple, but through the new 'temple', Jesus, through his body and blood.

**Den of robbers** could also be translated 'hideout for revolutionaries'. The temple was a focal point for many priests with nationalistic aspirations, and it is those priests, especially the younger ones, whom the Jewish historian Josephus blames for the uprising which led to the Roman destruction of the temple in 70 AD. Jesus never chose to go the way of such nationalists, and he certainly rejected using the temple as the place from which God would rescue Israel from Roman bondage.

**16** It is difficult to know exactly what is meant by verse 16. The word translated **anything** could well refer to vessels used in the worship or liturgical practice of the temple. Did Jesus physically prevent anyone from crossing or was it a verbal prohibition? Once again, Mark could well have Zechariah in mind. In 14:21 the prophet looks forward to the day of the Lord, when every pot in Jerusalem and Judah will be holy, and 'there shall no longer be a trader in the house of the Lord of hosts'.

**17** Jesus teaches in the temple, that is, he reveals God's will. He expounds God's law, the Torah, taking as his text Isaiah 56:7 together with Jeremiah 7:11 (this 'con-fusing' of two passages occurs also at 1:2,3). Isaiah's vision was that foreigners, Gentiles, would come to the temple. In Jesus' time, this was not permitted on penalty of death. What Jesus is doing, by quoting the Isaiah passage, is opening the temple to the Gentiles. The term **house**, which occurs twice in the Isaiah quotation, signifies for non-Palestinian Christians their own home-churches. It is the houses of prayer, the houses in which Christians worship, which are the house of God, not the temple in Jerusalem. The houses of the Christians are for all nations. This is what the temple was supposed to be, according to Isaiah, but was not. Temple sacrifice, Jesus is saying, is for Jews only, but his house is **a house of prayer for all the nations**. Prayer, unlike sacrifice, is not bound to a place, or to a system dominated by priests. Prayer provides an opening to God for both Jew and Gentile. By preventing the Gentiles from entering into the presence of God, the temple officials and worship organisers are **robbers**.

The **chief priests** and **scribes** see their whole authority being undermined by this teacher and expounder of Scripture, so they seek to destroy him. Mark builds up tension, although his readers or listeners already know the outcome of these events. They would have smiled to themselves, even laughed, as they watched the opponents plot and plan. Jesus' opposition is afraid of him, because he overwhelms the whole crowd with his teaching. He does not cite authorities, does not quote the sages of the past, but simply speaks in his own name, with his own authority. 18

The reference to **evening** gives significance to a similar reference in verse 11. The time is late for Jerusalem and for the temple – this seems to be the message that Mark is giving. And, since the hour is late, Jesus again goes **out of the city** (as in verse 11). He is the Outsider. 19

### That fig tree again, 11:20-26

**²⁰ As they passed by in the morning, they saw the fig tree withered away to its roots. ²¹ And Peter remembered and said to him, 'Master,ᵛ look! The fig tree which you cursed has withered.' ²² And Jesus answered them, 'Have faith in God. ²³ Truly, I say to you, whoever says to this mountain, "Be taken up and cast into the sea," and does not doubt in his heart, but believes that what he says will come to pass, it will be done for him. ²⁴ Therefore I tell you, whatever you ask in prayer, believe that you receive it, and you will. ²⁵ And whenever you stand praying, forgive, if you have anything against any one; so that your Father also who is in heaven may forgive you your trespasses.'ʷ**

---

ᵛ Or *Rabbi*
ʷ Other ancient authorities add verse 26 *'But if you do not forgive, neither will your Father who is in heaven forgive your trespasses'*

This incident takes place **in the morning**, the opposite 20
of 'late' (v 11) and 'evening' (v 19). The fig tree that was
cursed by Jesus (vv 12-14) has **withered away to its
roots**. The word of Jesus has authority. If the tree repre- 21
sents the temple, as suggested earlier, then this incident
suggests that, at the time that Mark wrote his gospel, the
temple had, in fact, been cut off at its roots. The temple was
destroyed in 70 AD, about 40 years after Jesus pronounced
his curse on the fig tree. Peter remembers Jesus' words from
the previous day. In mentioning this, Mark appeals to the
authority of Peter. Previously he had made a special point
of saying that the disciples heard what Jesus said to the tree
(v 14).

Jesus' reply to Peter's words is addressed to the other
disciples as well. Some manuscripts present Jesus' words
as a command: **have faith in God**, as in RSV, but other 22
manuscripts of equal authority have: 'If you have faith in
God'. Faith is trust and confidence in the God who crosses
the boundaries, who creates life where there is death. When
the believer has trust in such a God, all mountains, all
obstacles are removed, because God is the goal and end of
all faith. It is not the mountain which is the ultimate, but
God. Faith trusts that God will have the ultimate say.

It is also possible to understand 'faith in God' as 'faith of
God', which is what it is, literally translated. This would
mean that Jesus is telling his disciples not only to have
faith, but also to know that God is faithful. So it could be
translated: 'You have the faithfulness of God!' or, 'If you have
the faithfulness of God'. Since God is faithful, the believer 23
can say to the mountain: **Be taken up and cast into the
sea**. The use of the passive voice here could refer to an action
of God, as is often the case. The meaning would then be:
'Since God is faithful, you can say to this mountain: "Let
God take you up and cast you into the sea" '. To move
mountains was a common metaphor for removing great
difficulties. The sea, in Jewish thought, is a place of chaos
and destruction (see 4:37-41; 5:13). **It will be done for him**
suggests that when a person believes that something **will
come to pass**, God is the one who makes it happen, the one
who moves the mountain. What God says, happens. This
the disciple is asked to believe without wavering.

That is why Jesus can now say: **Whatever you ask in** 24
**prayer, believe that you receive it** (there is better manuscript evidence for the past tense: 'have received it') **and**

**you will**. Because God is faithful, the believer can pray with confidence.

For Jesus, the relationship between prayer and forgiveness is very close (see Matt 6:9-15). Some manuscripts include verse 26, but the strongest manuscript evidence is against its inclusion. It is difficult to follow the progression of thought in this whole section. What is the connection between the temple, the fig tree, faith (our faith or God's faithfulness), prayer, and forgiveness? Or are the references to these things just loosely strung together from the tradition that Mark was familiar with? It may be that prayer and forgiveness are seen by Mark as being at the heart of true worship, rather than the temple sacrifices and the contributions made to the temple, which are now seen as bearing no fruit. Where there is prayer, God is present, and where he is present, Jesus, the Clean One, is also present, and where he is present, there is forgiveness. The Christian community which has the authority to pray – that is, to come into the presence of God – also has been given the authority to declare people clean, through the pronouncement of the forgiveness of sin in Jesus' name.

## By what authority? 11:27-33

[27] **And they came again to Jerusalem. And as he was walking in the temple, the chief priests and the scribes and the elders came to him,** [28] **and they said to him, 'By what authority are you doing these things, or who gave you this authority to do them?'** [29] **Jesus said to them, 'I will ask you a question; answer me, and I will tell you by what authority I do these things.** [30] **Was the baptism of John from heaven or from men? Answer me.'** [31] **And they argued with one another, 'If we say, "From heaven," he will say, "Why then did you not believe him?"** [32] **But shall we say, "From men"?'** – **they were afraid of the people, for all held that John was a real prophet.** [33] **So they answered Jesus, 'We do not know.' And Jesus said to them, 'Neither will I tell you by what authority I do these things.'**

Mark is arriving at the climax to his story. With dramatic simplicity he changes the scene to **Jerusalem**, where Jesus is walking about in the temple. Jerusalem and the **temple** – the holy combination! – are the setting for the crucial question about Jesus' authority. The question comes from **the chief priests and the scribes and the elders**, that is, those who are responsible for the temple, the exposition of the law, and the traditions. Note that the Pharisees are not mentioned. The chief priests figure more prominently, since we are now at headquarters, the temple, where the priests do their work. It has been estimated that there were about 1500 priests in Jerusalem in Jesus' time. At least thirty were on duty each day to perform the sacrifices. Many Sadducees were priests.

Jesus stands out from all other rabbis of later Judaism, and from the Old Testament prophets, in that he never reveals the source of his authority. It is his authority that is questioned here. He does not cite the wisdom of earlier teachers, nor does he speak as the prophets did with their 'Thus says the Lord'. Instead, he says: 'Truly I say to you'. He speaks with his own authority. Mark's readers already know, from the beginning of the gospel, that the prophets spoke about Jesus, and that God has given the Spirit of holiness to him and acknowledged him as his Son. Those not 'in on the secret', however, do not hear or see the truth about him. **28**

Jesus' response to his opponents' question simply highlights their deafness and blindness. He asks them about the baptism of John: Was it from God (**heaven** is a circumlocution for God) or was it based on human authority? The questioners are stumped, whichever way they turn. They are forced to confess that they do not know. Their authority is discredited, while that of Jesus is enhanced. **29, 30 31- 33**

## A very pointed story, 12:1-12

<sup>12:1</sup> **And he began to speak to them in parables. 'A man planted a vineyard, and set a hedge around it, and dug a pit for the wine press, and built a tower, and let it out to tenants, and went into another country.** <sup>2</sup> **When the time came, he sent a servant to the tenants, to get from them some of the fruit of the vineyard.** <sup>3</sup> **And they took him and beat him, and sent him away empty-handed.** <sup>4</sup> **Again he sent to them another servant, and they wounded him in the head, and treated him shamefully.** <sup>5</sup> **And he sent another, and him they killed; and so with many others, some they beat and some they killed.** <sup>6</sup> **He had still one other, a beloved son; finally he sent him to them, saying, "They will respect my son."** <sup>7</sup>**But those tenants said to one another, "This is the heir; come, let us kill him, and the inheritance will be ours."** <sup>8</sup> **And they took him and killed**

**him, and cast him out of the vineyard. ⁹ What will the owner of the vineyard do? He will come and destroy the tenants, and give the vineyard to others. ¹⁰ Have you not read this scripture:**
**"The very stone which the builders rejected**
**has become the head of the corner;**
**¹¹ this was the Lord's doing,**
**and it is marvellous in our eyes"?'**
**¹² And they tried to arrest him, but feared the multitude, for they perceived that he had told the parable against them; so they left him and went away.**

Mark does not record many of Jesus' parables. Apart from those in chapter 4 there is only this one, which makes it significant. It is a parable directed against Jesus' opponents. Jesus does not 'teach' them in the same way that he does the crowds and his disciples.

The image of Israel as a vineyard of which God was the owner was common in Biblical times. The owner's son in the parable clearly refers to Jesus himself, since he is called **beloved** (see 1:11). Verse 9 could be a reference to the conquest of Palestine by the Romans, but this is not likely. The reference is rather to Gentiles being taken into the vineyard, which is how the verses that are quoted here by Jesus (Ps 118:22,23) were understood by Christians (see Acts 4:11; 1 Pet 2:7). 1-5

6,7

Verse 8 is central to an understanding of the parable: Jesus, the beloved son, is killed and cast **out of the vineyard**. The very Son of God, declared holy by God, is declared unclean and rejected by Israel. Or is it really a rejection by Israel as such? There are grounds for seeing the rejection as coming from the Sadduccean chief priests and the Pharisees, not from Israel as a nation. *They* are the tenants who kill the owner's son, the builders who reject the stone. 8,9

Jesus quotes Psalm 118:22,23. This psalm, according to some interpreters, is a psalm of David, and therefore messianic. Because it was sung at the Passover festival, this quotation from it here prepares readers for what is soon to come. The Passover will see the rejection of Jesus. Just as David was rejected by Samuel at first as being too young, and was later rejected by Saul, so Jesus is rejected. The **builders** could well refer to the scholars, the interpreters of the Torah (God's law), the builders of the tradition. Jesus' authority in word and deed evokes a response from his opponents: they try to arrest him, but are afraid to do so because of the crowd. The outsiders have been attracted to 10, 11

12

Jesus, and a rebellion in Jerusalem, especially in the temple, is not what the authorities want. They see Jesus as undermining their authority and status, but for now they must leave him and go away. It is not quite the right time yet.

## *The first great question: taxes, 12:13-17*

<sup>13</sup> **And they sent to him some of the Pharisees and some of the Herodians, to entrap him in his talk.** <sup>14</sup> **And they came and said to him, 'Teacher, we know that you are true, and care for no man; for you do not regard the position of men, but truly teach the way of God. Is it lawful to pay taxes to Caesar, or not?** <sup>15</sup> **Should we pay them, or should we not?' But knowing their hypocrisy, he said to them, 'Why put me to the test? Bring me a coin,<sup>x</sup> and let me look at it.'** <sup>16</sup> **And they brought one. And he said to them, 'Whose likeness and inscription is this?' They said to him, 'Caesar's.'** <sup>17</sup> **Jesus said to them, 'Render to Caesar the things that are Caesar's, and to God the things that are God's.' And they were amazed at him.**

<sup>x</sup> Greek *a denarius*

The whole section from verse 13-37 sees Jesus under intense pressure from his opponents as he responds to four of the most crucial questions in Judaism, and probably also in some Christian communities. In some sense, the four questions concern the Messiah and the new messianic age which was expected.

The question of taxes was a ticklish one, both for Jews **13** and for Christians, since the payment of taxes to the Roman government was seen as being inseparable from acknowledging the divine authority of the Emperor or the State. The **Pharisees** were the strict element in Judaism in dissociating themselves from the Gentiles. The Sadducees, on the other hand, belonged more to the ruling class, and therefore tended to make compromises with Hellenistic (Greek) ways and with Roman officialdom. The **Herodians** were people who followed Herod, who had been appointed to power by the Romans.

They address Jesus as **teacher**, indicating that they wish **14** to discuss the law with him. They acknowledge that he is not influenced by people's status or what they think of him, but that he teaches the truth of **the way of God**. This may have been meant sarcastically, especially if it reflects a question that was asked of Christians in Mark's community as much as it was of Jesus himself. Christians called themselves followers of 'the Way', and from a Jewish standpoint did not observe the traditions of the elders, but claimed to be people following the Son of God himself. To pay or not to pay – that is the question that is put to Jesus. If he says 'Pay', that will make him a traitor to the Jews. If he says 'Don't pay', that will put him in the category of the Zealots (radical nationalists) and make him reportable to the Roman authorities. It would be interesting to know if there was any 'dobbing in' of Christians – even by fellow-Christians – in relation to the payment of taxes. Mark's readers would have been acutely aware of the precarious situation facing Jesus.

Jesus asks for a coin, and they produce one. Note the short sentences which skilfully build suspense. Jesus turns the tables on his opponents, and puts the pressure back on them. *They* are now the ones who have to give an answer. Jesus concludes with the well-known words – well-known to us, and probably also to Mark's readers, whether they agreed with them or not: **Render to Caesar the things that are Caesar's, and to God the things that are God's**. **15, 16**

Jesus appears to be saying: 'Whoever uses this coin with Caesar's inscription and image acknowledges Rome as the ruling authority, and is therefore obligated to pay taxes to Caesar'. Christians are not political rebels like the Zealots, who were radical nationalists violently opposed to Roman rule. A similar answer to that of Jesus had previously been given by Jeremiah (see Jer 29:4-14). His advice to the people in exile was that they support their foreign rulers and live a peaceful life. For him, Israel's conquest was a sign from God, but not the final sign, since God would ultimately free his people. Jesus' answer does not imply political acquiescence. What belongs to God must be given to God. Jesus certainly would not stand for any State cult, or any deification of political ideology. The kingdom of God which he proclaims stands in stark opposition to all political systems based on power and oppression. The fact that he dies as a political rebel shows that Rome is aware of the threat that he poses to their whole political system. The waves of persecution that Christians later suffered in Roman courts also strongly suggest that some Romans saw The Way as a threat to their power, and their deification of that power. **17**

## The second great question: resurrection, 12:18-27

¹⁸ **And Sadducees came to him, who say that there is no resurrection; and they asked him a question, saying,** ¹⁹ **'Teacher, Moses wrote for us that if a man's brother dies and leaves a wife, but leaves no child, the man[y] must take the wife, and raise up children for his brother.** ²⁰ **There were seven brothers; the first took a wife, and when he died left no children;** ²¹ **and the second took her, and died, leaving no children; and the third likewise;** ²² **and the seven left no children. Last of all the woman also died.** ²³ **In the resurrection whose wife will she be? For the seven had her as wife.'**

²⁴ **Jesus said to them, 'Is not this why you are wrong, that you know neither the scriptures nor the power of God?** ²⁵ **For when they rise from the dead, they neither marry nor are given in marriage, but are like angels in heaven.** ²⁶ **And as for the dead being raised, have you not read in the book of Moses, in the passage about the bush, how God said to him, "I am the God of Abraham, and the God of Isaac, and the God of Jacob"?** ²⁷ **He is not God of the dead, but of the living; you are quite wrong.'**

[y] Greek *his brother*

The question of whether or not there was a resurrection from the dead was one of the things that divided the Pharisees and the Sadducees (see Acts 23:8). The Sadducees dominated the Jerusalem and temple priesthood. Mark explains to his readers (an indication that some did not know this) that the Sadducees did not believe in a resurrection. It can also be noted that they regarded only the books of Moses (the first five books of the Old Testament) as being the authoritative Word of God. This is why, in their question to Jesus, they speak of what **Moses wrote**.

Deuteronomy 25:5-9 explains what was supposed to happen when a man died childless: his brother was to marry the widow, and any children that they had were to be regarded as children of the dead man. In their question to Jesus, the Sadducees argue that the idea of a resurrection is absurd, since the woman in their hypothetical case would end up having seven husbands after they had all been raised to life again.

Jesus replies that they **know neither the scriptures, nor the power of God**. He seems to put himself in opposition to the Sadducean idea that only the five books of Moses are authoritative. However, even from the books of

Moses it can be shown that God is powerful, and that he is not the God of the dead but of the living. In making this point, Jesus quotes Exodus 3:6. At the time of Moses, of course, Abraham, Isaac and Jacob were dead, but God nevertheless speaks of himself as being their God. If that is so, Jesus argues, then they must still be living. It must be conceded that Exodus 3 clearly does not refer to the resurrection. What we have here is an example of how Jesus and the New Testament writers used the Scriptures to support certain teachings. In referring to the patriarchs, it may be that Jesus has in mind instances where God showed his power to create or preserve life in situations of death: the gift of a child to Abraham and Sarah when they were too old to have children; the rescue of Isaac when Abraham was on the point of offering him as a sacrifice; the rescue of Jacob when his brother Esau wanted to kill him. God has the power to create life where there is death. In the section that follows there is mention of a scribe who regards Jesus' answer as a good one. Earlier in the gospel the scribes were linked with the Pharisees (2:16; 7:1,5), and so we can assume that they accepted the idea of a resurrection.

## *The third great question: love, 12:28-34*

**²⁸ And one of the scribes came up and heard them disputing with one another, and seeing that he answered them well, asked him, 'Which commandment is the first of all?' ²⁹ Jesus answered, 'The first is, "Hear, O Israel: The Lord our God, the Lord is one; ³⁰ and you shall love the Lord your God with all your heart, and with all your soul, and with all your mind, and with all your strength." ³¹ The second is this, "You shall love your neighbour as yourself." There is no other commandment greater than these.' ³² And the scribe said to him, 'You are right, Teacher; you have truly said that he is one, and there is no other but he; ³³ and to love him with all the heart, and with all the understanding, and with all the strength, and to love one's neighbour as oneself, is much more than all whole burnt offerings and sacrifices.' ³⁴ And when Jesus saw that he answered wisely, he said to him, 'You are not far from the kingdom of God.' And after that no one dared to ask him any question.**

In Mark's gospel the scribes are usually portrayed as **28** opponents of Jesus, but here we have 'the friendly scribe', as one scholar calls him. Generally the scribes cannot understand who Jesus is, or accept his authority. It is one of the scribes who now asks Jesus which is the most important of all the commandments of God. Jesus responds with what **29** every Jew knew to be the two greatest commands. The first of these is to love God with all one's heart, soul, mind and strength. God is one, and since love works toward unity, love **30** is to be directed toward God. The second commandment is **31** to love one's neighbour as oneself.

The scribe responds positively to what Jesus says, acknowledging **32** that Jesus knows what he's talking about. The followers of Christ do not reject the law as summed up in its two chief commands. The scribe realises that, in relation **33** to God's will for his people, these commands are central, and that **burnt offerings and sacrifices** are secondary, even dispensable. He knows what the prophets have constantly reminded Israel about: that sacrifices in themselves are not what God asks for, but that what he wants is for people to do justice and to love kindness (Mic 6:6-8).

Because of what the scribe says, Jesus speaks favourably **34** to him: **You are not far from the kingdom of God**. What is still lacking is the man's willingness to fall into step behind Jesus. In the teaching of Jesus, there are no limits to the exercise of love. Love is prepared to accept shame and disgrace for the sake of the other person. This is the way of Jesus, the way of the cross. The exercise of this love is not limited by any laws. To people used to living within limits, this love can seem to be lawless, just as Jesus himself seemed to be a lawless person to many people. There must have been many Jews who saw in the message and life of Christians much that they could support. However, they were not able to leave behind the security of their tradition, to fall in behind Jesus, or to obey his radical call to walk the way of rejection if necessary. Jesus had an understanding of who one's neighbour was which was unacceptable to those who wanted to set limits on who could be included in that term. Many people simply could not accept that love is to be directed also to those who are unclean, those who are beyond the boundaries.

*The fourth question: the Messiah – whose son is he?*
*12:35-37*

**³⁵ And as Jesus taught in the temple, he said, 'How can the scribes say that the Christ is the son of David? ³⁶ David himself, inspired by<sup>z</sup> the Holy Spirit, declared,**
  **"The Lord said to my Lord,**
  **Sit at my right hand,**
  **till I put thy enemies under thy feet."**
**³⁷ David himself calls him Lord; so how is he his son?' And the great throng heard him gladly.**

<sup>z</sup> Or *himself, in*

This crucial question about the Messiah is raised by Jesus **35** in the temple. This is not surprising, since the temple was regarded as the place of revelation. Malachi 3:1 created the expectation that the Messiah would suddenly appear in the temple. The scribes are once more depicted as those who do not understand. They say that **the Christ is the son of David**. Jesus argues, however, that if he is the *son* of David, how can David then call him **Lord**?

Psalm 110, from which Jesus quotes here, was widely **36,** used by early Christians as they attempted to answer the **37** question: Who is Jesus? It appears that here Jesus, and Mark, are rejecting the equation 'Jesus = son of David' as the only way of understanding Jesus as the Christ/Messiah. Jesus' reply to the question of the high priest during his trial (14:61,62) shows that he does not see himself as a nationalist saviour. Jesus is not Messiah-son-of-David, but Messiah-Son-of-*God*, something claimed of Jesus already in the very first sentence of the gospel. Jesus, then, is Lord also of David, which makes his kingship much wider than a nationalistic one.

The message that Jesus is greater than David is heard gladly by the great crowd. It is possible that the great crowd, so frequently mentioned in the gospel, also represents some of those to whom Mark is telling his story. They hear Jesus gladly as he sows the gospel message. We know from both Christian and Roman historians that there were many Jews, particularly from Jerusalem, who placed a high value on genealogical purity, and it is likely that there were some Christians who held similar views. It is known that there were Christians who wished to trace their links with David, and that persecutions were later carried out by the Romans against those Christians claiming direct descent from

David. It could be that Mark records Jesus' words here in order to counteract such claims. The crowds (that is, those who cannot even begin to make such prestigious claims about their ancestry) are very glad to hear Jesus saying, in effect, that having a relationship with him is more important than being related to David.

The four great questions (12:13-37) have been answered. They are end-time questions, questions which were on the lips of many as they waited for the kingdom of God. Mark, in recording Jesus' answers to these questions, is telling his readers that the kingdom is here in Jesus and his words. He is also preparing them for the coronation of the king, and the climax of the kingdom's coming, that is soon to take place on the cross.

## *The scribes and the widow, 12:38-44*

**38 And in his teaching he said, 'Beware of the scribes, who like to go about in long robes, and to have salutations in the market places 39 and the best seats in the synagogues and the places of honour at feasts, 40 who devour widows' houses and for a pretence make long prayers. They will receive the greater condemnation.'**

**41 And he sat down opposite the treasury, and watched the multitude putting money into the treasury. Many rich people put in large sums. 42 And a poor widow came, and put in two copper coins, which make a penny. 43 And he called his disciples to him, and said to them, 'Truly, I say to you, this poor widow has put in more than all those who are contributing to the treasury. 44 For they all contributed out of their abundance; but she out of her poverty has put in everything she had, her whole living.'**

In this section the **scribes** take a pasting from Jesus. **38** They receive respect from the crowds and claim authority as teachers of the law. But they rip off widows under the cover of their piety (**long prayers**). Legally defenceless people, such as widows, made use of the scribes as administrators and guardians, and sometimes entrusted their property to them. The prayers of the scribes are not so much a **pretence**, as the RSV has it, but an *attraction* to widows, **39,** who are taken in by such demonstrations of piety. So their **40** long prayers are not a pretext, but the very thing that attracts the widows. Because of their authority, they will be judged more severely. Jesus' warning, **beware**, suggests that he sees the disciples as being in a similar position as the scribes, since they also are leaders, teachers, people with secret knowledge, and therefore men of power. The danger for the disciples is that they go the same way as the scribes, who have succumbed to the attraction of power and have abused their power, as shown most clearly in their treatment of defenceless widows.

The mention of widows in verse 40 leads on to the account involving a particular widow. This widow contributes her whole livelihood to the temple treasury; others give only out of their wealth. She does what the man who asked what he had to do to inherit eternal life was not prepared to do (10:17-22). **41-44**

The status and role of widows was a concern for both Christians and Jews, since both felt an obligation to help them. In this section, the widow stands in contrast to the scribes. Maybe she is meant to stand in contrast also with the disciples, who are not exempt from playing the power-game and seeking the status given to the powerful. Her action in giving everything she has also points to Jesus himself, who gives his life in service for all. Widows, and unmarried women in general, appear to have been influential in the early church, and were sometimes a problem for certain people, especially certain men (see 1 Tim 5:3-16). They were often examples of Christian faith and piety, people who heeded the call of Jesus to leave home and family, and deliberately did not marry for the sake of the gospel.

## *Apocalypse now? 13:1-27*

**13:1 And as he came out of the temple, one of his disciples said to him, 'Look, Teacher, what wonderful stones and what wonderful buildings!' ² And Jesus said to him, 'Do you see these great buildings? There will not be left here one stone upon another, that will not be thrown down.'**

**³ And as he sat on the Mount of Olives opposite the temple, Peter and James and John and Andrew asked him privately, ⁴ 'Tell us, when will this be, and what will be the sign when these things are all to be accomplished?' ⁵ And Jesus began to say to them, 'Take heed that no one leads you astray. ⁶ Many will come in my name, saying, "I am he!" and they will lead many astray. ⁷ And when you hear of wars and rumours of wars, do not be alarmed; this must take place, but the end is not yet. ⁸ For nation**

will rise against nation, and kingdom against kingdom; there will be earthquakes in various places, there will be famines; this is but the beginning of the birth-pangs.

⁹ 'But take heed to yourselves; for they will deliver you up to councils; and you will be beaten in synagogues; and you will stand before governors and kings for my sake, to bear testimony before them. ¹⁰ And the gospel must first be preached to all nations. ¹¹ And when they bring you to trial and deliver you up, do not be anxious beforehand what you are to say; but say whatever is given you in that hour, for it is not you who speak, but the Holy Spirit. ¹² And brother will deliver up brother to death, and the father his child, and children will rise against parents and have them put to death; ¹³ and you will be hated by all for my name's sake. But he who endures to the end will be saved.

¹⁴ 'But when you see the desolating sacrilege set up where it ought not to be (let the reader understand), then let those who are in Judea flee to the mountains; ¹⁵ let him who is on the housetop not go down, nor enter his house, to take anything away; ¹⁶ and let him who is in the field not turn back to take his mantle. ¹⁷ And alas for those who are with child and for those who give suck in those days! ¹⁸ Pray that it may not happen in winter. ¹⁹ For in those days there will be such tribulation as has not been from the beginning of the creation which God created until now, and never will be. ²⁰ And if the Lord had not shortened the days, no human being would be saved; but for the sake of the elect, whom he chose, he shortened the days. ²¹ And then if any one says to you, "Look, here is the Christ!" or "Look, there he is!" do not believe it. ²² False Christs and false prophets will arise and show signs and wonders, to lead astray, if possible, the elect. ²³ But take heed; I have told you all things beforehand.

²⁴ 'But in those days, after that tribulation, the sun will be darkened, and the moon will not give its light, ²⁵ and the stars will be falling from heaven, and the powers in the heavens will be shaken. ²⁶ And then they will see the Son of man coming in clouds with great power and glory. ²⁷ and then he will send out the angels, and gather his elect from the four winds; from the ends of the earth to the ends of heaven.

This chapter is sometimes known as the Little Apocalypse. An apocalypse is a writing which reveals or uncovers something, usually something about the future. Apocalyptic writings have a language, style, and form of their own, a common 'lingo', as can be seen in such books as Daniel and Revelation, and passages such as 1 Thessalonians 4:13-5:11, and this chapter, Mark 13. There are some common aspects of apocalyptic literature missing here in Mark (visions and journeys into the heavens, for example), but this chapter still fits into that category. Apocalyptic material was written mainly to encourage readers to persevere and endure in the face of hardship and suffering, to 'hang in there', knowing that God would stand by them and would win out ultimately against all evil. It sustained hope, especially among oppressed people or people struggling with transition and change in their world.

It is in the temple that Jesus has given his answers to the great questions of the messianic times (12:13-37). The Jews **1,2** among Mark's readers know that the Messiah will come to his temple (see Mal 3:1). Mark says that he *has* come to the temple, and that he has pointed Christians beyond it, since it no longer bears fruit (11:12-14). As Jesus goes to his cross, the temple figures prominently in the story. So what is the temple's fate? If Mark is writing before its destruction, his readers would have been aware that its fate still hung in the balance. Roman troops could already have been moving toward Jerusalem to quash the rebellion which began in 66 AD and finished with the temple's destruction in 70 AD.

It is difficult for us today to appreciate just what the temple meant for much of Judaism, and probably for many early Christians as well. It was much more than a building, and more than the place where God chose to be present. It was seen as the centre of the cosmos, the symbol of life, the universe, heaven and earth. In the light of this, one can begin to realise how radical the words of Jesus are against the temple, including his claim, repeated by his followers, that he himself is the new temple of God, the new link between heaven and earth, the new axis around which everything revolves, the new centre of the world and of life.

Jesus now leaves the temple. His action suggests that the temple is no longer the place of revelation for the follower of Jesus, no longer the centre of the universe. One of the disciples asks Jesus about its fate, and he replies that it will be destroyed. Mark's readers might have seen this as pointing to the fate of Jesus himself. His body will be destroyed in death, but in three days it will be raised to life again.

Jesus sits (the posture of a teacher, indicating authority) **3** on the Mount of Olives (the mountain from which the Messiah was expected to come) opposite the temple (which has been cursed by Jesus so that it will never produce fruit again [11:14]). The four disciples who were called first ask Jesus what the sign will be that these events are about to occur.

The answer that Jesus gives to the four disciples is by far the longest speech of his recorded in the gospel. It is not interrupted by 'he said' at any point, or by any question from the disciples. The verb here translated as 'to lead astray', and the idea of a deceiver, were common in early Christian literature in relation to questions about the Christ and the messianic time. In Jewish writings after the time of Jesus, one of the most common charges against him is that he was a deceiver or magician. Here Jesus warns that many will deceive and many will be deceived. Many will come in his name, claiming, **I am he!** (literally, 'I am', a title or expression which John's gospel uses of Jesus). Zechariah had spoken of those who 'speak lies in the name of the Lord' (Zech 13:3). The words, 'I am he', could refer to a messianic claim made by these deceivers. Jews claiming to be the Messiah would hardly come in Jesus' name, so we would have to suppose that there will be Christians claiming to be Jesus himself, or the Messiah, who has returned to establish the new age. We know little about Christian movements of this kind, although the claims of Simon Magus and Dositheus (both of them Samaritans who were denounced as heretics by the followers of Peter and Paul) could fall into this category. An answer was needed by some people to what appeared to be a delay in the establishing of the kingdom, and these deceivers provided it. But Mark reminds his readers, through the words of Jesus, that these people are deceivers.

Jesus goes on to say that there will be **wars and rumours of wars**, but these are not the sign to be looked for. **The end**, or goal, **is not yet**. It is true, he says, that **nation will rise against nation, and kingdom against kingdom**, but, like **earthquakes** and **famines**, these are just birth pangs, only **the beginning** of what is to come. Christians will have to appear before **councils** (literally, 'sanhedrins') and will be beaten **in synagogues**. This suggests that Christians continued to maintain links with the synagogues, and in some ways submitted to their authority. On five occasions Paul received the 'forty lashes less one' at the hands of Jewish authorities (see 2 Cor 11:24). If the Christians have completely broken away from Jewish authority, why do they still submit to Jewish law and punishment as this verse suggests? **Governors and kings** are the

Gentile authorities, before whom believers will have to **bear testimony**, or witness. The burning question, 'Are you a Christian?' calls for a person to be a martyr/witness for the name of Christ. It is possible that the phrase **to all nations** belongs with the previous sentence, which would then read: 'You will have to give testimony to governors and kings and to the nations'. **Nations** generally refers to those who are not Jews. The phrase **for my sake** (or, 'on my account') links the fate of the community with that of Jesus. Before the end comes, the **gospel** must be proclaimed. This message of good news, however, no longer includes the temple, which has ceased to be the sign of hope. That hope now rests in Jesus. **10**

Jesus says that when Christians are on trial, they need not prepare any defence, because the Holy Spirit (a better translation might be 'Spirit of holiness') will stand beside them as they testify in the presence of the unclean spirits of State and political authorities, which demand an allegiance that Christians cannot give. The Spirit will enable them to make the Christian confession: 'Jesus is Lord' (1 Cor 12:3). This confession will cause divisions between family members, and maybe even between Christians themselves, because of differing views about Jesus. Christians will be hated simply because of the name that they carry. The question, 'Are you a Christian?' will be the test, and the answer, 'I am a Christian' will condemn them. Jesus' words, **for my name's sake**, show that the fate of the Christian is inextricably bound to the Christ who is confessed. And just as Jesus 'endured to the end' and was saved through the resurrecting power of God, so the Christian community, through endurance, will reach its goal and will be saved by God. **11-13**

The phrase **desolating sacrilege** echoes expressions in Daniel 9:27; 11:31; 12:11. There in Daniel it refers to the desecration of the temple by the Hellenistic ruler over Palestine, Antiochus Epiphanes, who in 168 BC set up an altar to, or image of, the pagan god Olympian Zeus in the temple. Mark here almost certainly refers to the Romans, who more than once had previously set up their standards in areas of the Holy City which the Jews regarded as sacred. There were uprisings and disturbances in 48 and 52 AD, so it was not necessary for a person to have supernatural prophetic power in order to be able to foretell the destruction of Jerusalem and its temple. The aside (**let the reader understand**) probably refers to the person actually read- **14** ing this story for an audience, rather than the private individual reader. Some scholars think that it refers to the reader of Daniel.

The recommendation is that people escape, and that they do so in haste, with no thought of gathering up or going back for belongings, because the destruction will be so sudden and so horrendous. The Jewish historian, Josephus, gives graphic descriptions of the sufferings and atrocities that took place in Jerusalem during the siege that ended in 70 AD. Daniel 12:7 speaks of the horrors lasting for only a fixed period of time. Here Jesus says that since no human being could otherwise survive, the merciful God has decided to shorten the days of suffering **for the sake of the elect**. 15-19 20

It may be that Mark now widens the words of Jesus to include references to events in the end-time, and not simply those connected with the destruction of Jerusalem. It was a commonly accepted sign of the 'last days' that many would come claiming to be the Messiah/Christ. Mark has previously made it clear that Jesus' Messiahship is not based on his ability to perform miracles and wonders. In fact, that he is the Messiah is not the most essential thing there is to be said about him, as is emphasised in his trial (14:61,62). **Signs and wonders** are deceptive, especially for **the elect**. Peter is an example of someone called to be with Jesus who expects signs and wonders, and cannot accept the sign and the wonder which is the cross (8:32,33). **False prophets** predict a golden age; Jesus predicts just the opposite. The phrase **all things** reminds us of the 'everything' of 4:11. Here, as there, the reference is not just to the immediate words of Jesus, but to the whole story about him, which is a mystery and a riddle to those who are 'outside'. The false prophets and false Christs do not see or understand the riddle, which finds its solution in the cross. Jesus' words come true – the mark of a true and trustworthy prophet. The cross is the guarantee of all the words of Jesus. 21 22 23

Apocalyptic writings have a strong element of cosmic catastrophe, and that appears here. The reference to the sun being **darkened** makes one think of Jesus' crucifixion, when darkness covered the earth. The fact that Mark places this apocalyptic chapter hard up against the account of the passion of Jesus, indicates that for him there is a connection between the two. Jesus' death and resurrection, which usher in the last days, are the great tribulation, apocalypse now, the great uncovering of what is secret. Just as Jesus experiences those days so will his community, and, like Jesus, they will ultimately overcome the powers of darkness 24, 25 and alienation and will be vindicated by God. For Jesus, his vindication by God takes place in his resurrection from the dead. For the Christian community, it will take place in the appearing of the Son of man – the one who has authority over sin and sabbath, the one who must suffer and die. The words of verse 26 echo Daniel 7:13, but also point ahead to the words of Jesus at his trial (14:62), a further indication that Mark sees this apocalyptic picture in the light of Jesus' own suffering, death and resurrection.

In the last days, Jesus says, the Son of man will send his messengers to gather the elect from all parts of creation. Once again the authority of the Son of man is underlined. The gathering together of Israel's scattered people was always a strong motif in Israel's hope, a hope which Paul did not discard, but did reshape (see Rom 9-11).

## *The fig tree again, 13:28-31*

**²⁸ 'From the fig tree learn its lesson: as soon as its branch becomes tender and puts forth its leaves, you know that summer is near. ²⁹ So also, when you see these things taking place, you know that he is near, at the very gates. ³⁰ Truly, I say to you, this generation will not pass away before all these things take place. ³¹ Heaven and earth will pass away, but my words will not pass away.'**

The first words of this section can be translated more literally: 'Learn from the fig tree the parable'. There are things that happen in nature that are signs that a change of season is occurring. Jesus says that just as we can tell that summer is approaching when the fig tree starts to come out in leaf, we can know that the goal or end is at hand when certain events occur in history. The Greek text does not actually say who or what is **near, at the very gates**. The RSV suggests that it is the Son of man, but it could also be the 'time'.

Jesus' words, that **this generation will not pass away before all these things take place**, indicate how strong the expectation was that the goal or end would come soon. If the reference is to the 'end of the world', as we commonly use the expression, then that expectation obviously was not met, and we have to either acknowledge that or attempt to explain Jesus' words in some other way. It is not always clear exactly what is meant by the end. In this context, with Jesus' passion imminent, the end could refer to the goal of his ministry: his rejection, crucifixion and resurrection. The **words** of **Jesus will not pass away** – those words which command and rebuke the demonic forces of this world; those words which speak peace where there is chaos and fear; those words which bring life where there is hopelessness, abandonment and death.

## Watch! 13:32-37

> [32] 'But of that day or that hour no one knows, not even the angels in heaven, nor the Son, but only the Father. [33] Take heed, watch;[a] for you do not know when the time will come. [34] It is like a man going on a journey, when he leaves home and puts his servants in charge, each with his work, and commands the doorkeeper to be on the watch. [35] Watch therefore – for you do not know when the master of the house will come, in the evening, or at midnight, or at cockcrow, or in the morning – [36] lest he come suddenly and find you asleep. [37] And what I say to you I say to all: Watch.'

[a] Other ancient authorities add *and pray*

This section appears to speak directly about the last days, with the central thought being the need to watch for the revealed presence of Jesus. For Mark, the kingdom is present already now in Jesus and his cross. Mark does not allow his readers to place their hope merely in 'pie-in-the-sky-by-and-by' or merely in some future action of God. God's future actions cannot be divorced from his actions in Jesus, the crucified one.

Jesus says that no-one knows when **that day or that hour** will be, except the Father. To read into this verse trinitarian problems, as some do, is not being true to Mark, since they are much later theological questions. If Mark (and Jesus) have Jesus' own end in mind (the 'hour' being the hour of his death), then Jesus certainly has to place himself into the hands of his Father. He becomes the 'faithfull' witness, the righteous sufferer, who places his cause into the hands of God.

Jesus' call to **watch** (there is good manuscript evidence for the addition of 'and pray') because no-one knows **when the time will come**, could well be a message to Mark's community to see 'the time' as being connected with Jesus and the events that surrounded his end. Because Christians follow in Jesus' steps, and face an end or goal that is similar to his, they are living in 'the time'. The words 'hour' and 'time' are often used in the Septuagint (the Greek translation of the Old Testament) for the word 'festival'. Jesus' suffering, death and resurrection constitute the great festival of the Christian community. The implication of this is that the call to watch is not a call to idle sitting and waiting, but a call to get up and walk the way of Jesus. A person watches by staying awake, by praying, by struggling with the call of God to go the way of the cross and death. The call to watch is a call to die. As it was for the Master, so it is for the follower.

Like the call to watch, the sudden coming of the master is a common theme in Christian writings about the end. The call to watch was so common that the Greek word for 'watch' became a popular Christian name: Gregory, 'the watcher'. It is possible that Mark is here pointing his readers ahead to the next part of his story, in which the disciples are called to watch with Jesus (14:37,38). Once again the events surrounding Jesus' end are intertwined with the message of the end of all things.

## PART V : 14:1 – 16:20

*The preparation, 14:1,2*

**14:1 It was now two days before the Passover and the feast of Unleavened Bread. And the chief priests and the scribes were seeking how to arrest him by stealth, and kill him; ² for they said, 'Not during the feast, lest there be a tumult of the people.'**

This is the beginning of that part of Mark's story which his readers would have known only too well, and which they would have held in common with all other Christian communities. The death of Jesus and his resurrection were the earliest elements in the Christian tradition, as is shown in the accounts of the preaching of the disciples in the early chapters of Acts, and the tradition mentioned by Paul in 1 Corinthians 15:1-11. This is the climax of Mark's story, to which he has pointed ahead at various times in his narrative.

The **Passover** and the **feast of Unleavened Bread** are **1** identical. The festival involved a seven day feast which began, according to the Jewish calendar, on the 15th day of the month Nisan, at the first full moon after the spring equinox. In saying that it was **two days before the Passover**, Mark is referring to the 13th day of Nisan. The mention of **Passover** would have aroused great emotions in any Jews among Mark's readers. They would have thought of the preparations that had to be made, which involved a strict adherence to requirements about cleansing. Jesus' passion is firmly set in the context of what is clean and unclean. It is precisely at the celebration and remembrance of the event which stands out as *the* saving action of God in Israel's history, that the scribes and chief priests seek to kill Jesus. This is ironical as far as Mark's readers are concerned, because they believe that in the death of Jesus God's **2** great act of salvation is carried out. The leaders seek to kill Jesus, but they agree not to do anything during the feast. The irony is intensified, since the readers already know the outcome, having been alerted to it by Jesus' threefold prediction of his suffering and death. The plans of humans are one thing; the plans of God, worked out through Jesus, are another.

The leaders had grounds for fearing a **tumult**, or riot, during the Passover. The Jewish historian Josephus talks of three million people being in Jerusalem at the time of the festival, and reports a riot that occurred during the reign of

Claudius which led to 30 000 people being trampled to death. Even allowing for typical exaggeration the numbers are still very high. The Passover, which involved the remembrance of God's liberation of Israel from slavery under a foreign power in Egypt, had all the ingredients to incite nationalistic and liberation fervour.

## *The anointing by a priestess, 14:3-9*

**³ And while he was at Bethany in the house of Simon the leper, as he sat at table, a woman came with an alabaster flask of ointment of pure nard, very costly, and she broke the flask and poured it over his head. ⁴ But there were some who said to themselves indignantly, 'Why was the ointment thus wasted? ⁵ For this ointment might have been sold for more than three hundred denarii,ᵇ and given to the poor.' And they reproached her. ⁶ But Jesus said, 'Let her alone; why do you trouble her? She has done a beautiful thing to me. ⁷ For you always have the poor with you, and whenever you will, you can do good to them; but you will not always have me. ⁸ She has done what she could; she has anointed my body beforehand for burying. ⁹ And truly, I say to you, wherever the gospel is preached in the whole world, what she has done will be told in memory of her.'**

ᵇ The denarius was a day's wage for a labourer

Elements of the kingship of Jesus come to the fore in the passion story. In previous chapters Jesus has faced the questions relevant to the coming kingdom (12:13-37), has made his entry into Jerusalem and has come to the temple (11:1-11), and has spoken of the coming of the Son of man in the end time (13:26). Here in this episode he is now anointed 3 – the action that was performed by priests and prophets of God on prospective kings. Mark does not use the actual verb 'to anoint' here, but says that the woman **poured it over his head**. The verb that is used here for 'pour' is similar to that used a little later when Jesus refers to his lifeblood which is 'poured out' (14:24). Is this a clue as to how his kingship is to be understood? His kingship is not that of a nationalistic leader, but of one who goes to death in service for the many (10:45).

Note that here it is an anointing of the **head**, as in Matthew (26:7), whereas Luke and John record an anointing of Jesus' feet (Luke 7:38; John 12:3). This story is radical in its message in that it is a *woman* who acts as a priest and prophet. The woman prepares Jesus for his kingship (not as Messiah, but as Son of God) while the men plot to kill.

Jesus is in a **house** again, here receiving the hospitality of **Simon the leper**. Jesus often associated with lepers. Now he is anointed as king in the house of one who has previously been unclean, and whose nickname refers to what made him unclean. It is ironical that the person who was unclean does not seem to remember his previous condition.

Meal times were open house affairs to some degree, so the woman did not need a special invitation in order to be present. Simon is identified, by name and as a **leper**, but the woman is not identified. There is nothing in the text to link the woman with prostitution, nor is she to be identified with Mary Magdalene (who was not a prostitute either!). However, if the woman was a prostitute, the story has added poignancy. Money gained from harlotry was strictly forbidden to be brought to the temple as an offering to God (see Deut 23:18), but here what is unclean is used as a gift to the Clean One, who in this way is prepared for his own uncleanness (burial). Elsewhere Jesus' body is spoken of as being the new temple. The woman's gift is accepted in this temple. However, there is nothing to suggest that the woman actually is a prostitute.

The expensiveness of the perfume is enormous: **Three hundred denarii** is the equivalent of almost a year's pay for a labourer. The flask itself, which would have been very valuable, is broken, and the precious ointment is poured over Jesus' head, an action which meets with disapproval from the mercenary-minded men. They ask: **Why was the ointment thus wasted**? The translation **wasted** is rather weak; the word has the much stronger idea of destruction or ruin. **4,5**

Jesus stands beside the woman in defence of her. His words about the poor always being present are a direct reference to Deuteronomy 15:11. He understands this woman's action as being a preparation for his Passover: his death and burial. What is the meaning of the words: **She has done what she could**? If the woman's money was tainted in some way, then her gift would not have been accepted in the temple; it could have been used only for some unclean purpose. Is Jesus implying, then, that because the woman's ointment is unclean, all she can use it for is to **6,7** **8** anoint a corpse, the most unclean of all objects as far as Jews are concerned?

Jesus does not accept the objection that the ointment could have been sold and the money used to help the poor. He knows Jewish law, which says that no-one can derive any benefit from the requirements for preparing a corpse for burial. So once Jesus has said that the ointment is for his corpse, the living poor have no claim on it. He also knows, as the woman's detractors must have, that burial of the dead is regarded as a work of charity held in higher esteem than feeding and clothing the living. The expression **a beautiful thing** could be rendered more accurately 'a good work' (so AV). The phrase is a technical term for such charitable acts as visiting the sick, showing hospitality, giving to the poor, and burying the dead.

The action of this woman is at the heart of the **gospel** as Jesus and Mark understand it. She breaks down the barriers, no matter how precious they may be to people in the social and religious setting in which she lives. In this way she imitates Jesus who breaks through the barriers, especially those separating clean from unclean. Her action symbolises the activity of Jesus himself, and so she becomes a model for the Marcan Christian community of what a disciple should be. The power structures, and their inevitable concern for money, are broken by this woman, just as they have been constantly broken by Jesus. The woman, who is a victim of power, sees in Jesus a fellow-victim, and that gives her the perception that Jesus' future inevitably involves death. The valuable flask is broken, allowing the precious contents to pour out over Jesus, to announce him as God's chosen servant and Son/King. In a similar way, the precious body of this King will be broken, allowing his lifeblood to pour out for the cleansing of his people, anointing them as the clean servants of God. This unnamed woman understands what the named disciples do not. She accepts Jesus' fate – that he is to become unclean – and so acts to prepare Jesus for that time. The other 'priests' do not want a Jesus who goes that way. As far as they are concerned, their calling is to be holy, and so to avoid what profanes and makes unclean. This is not the last time in the passion narrative of Mark that the question of the holiness of the priesthood will be raised.

## *Enter Judas, 14:10,11*

**¹⁰ Then Judas Iscariot, who was one of the twelve, went to the chief priests in order to betray him to them. ¹¹ And**

**when they heard it they were glad, and promised to give him money. And he sought an opportunity to betray him.**

That the woman in the previous section is held up as a model disciple is strongly implied by the reference to Judas in this section. He is already known to readers as the betrayer (see 3:19), but here he is expressly called **one of the twelve**. As such, he represents them all. The called men fail to understand who Jesus is, while the nameless woman sees clearly. Her act of anointing Jesus for his burial makes him clean. Burial involves a corpse, and corpses are unclean. Anointing is a kind of washing, a baptism to make clean. Judas personifies the unclean. From now on he figures much more prominently in the story. He represents those in the Christian community who are unclean, and the problem that such Christians cause. He goes to the chief priests and makes plans with them to **betray**, or hand over, Jesus to them, receiving the promise of money in return.

*Everyone is preparing, 14:12-16*

<sup>12</sup> **And on the first day of Unleavened Bread, when they sacrificed the passover lamb, his disciples said to him, 'Where will you have us go and prepare for you to eat the passover?'** <sup>13</sup> **And he sent two of his disciples, and said to them, 'Go into the city, and a man carrying a jar of water will meet you; follow him,** <sup>14</sup> **and wherever he enters, say to the householder, "The Teacher says, Where is my guest room, where I am to eat the passover with my disciples?"** <sup>15</sup> **And he will show you a large upper room furnished and ready; there prepare for us.'** <sup>16</sup> **And the disciples set out and went to the city, and found it as he had told them; and they prepared the passover.**

Many kinds of preparation are taking place: The woman has prepared Jesus for his burial; Judas is preparing to betray Jesus; the disciples prepare to celebrate the Passover; Jesus prepares to die.

The **first day of Unleavened Bread** is the 15th day of the month Nisan in the Jewish calendar. The day on which the lambs that had been bought for the celebrations were killed in the temple, however, was the 14th of Nisan. This means that Mark's dating is imprecise, and this raises the question whether the meal is an actual Passover meal or a pre-Passover meal without the lamb. Preparations for the

Passover meal included the slaughter of the lamb, and the law required that all those intending to eat the lamb were to be present at its slaughtering. There is no mention of the lamb in the meal that Jesus eats with his disciples. The question of the disciples about where they should go to prepare for the Passover looks innocent enough, but in the context of what is about to happen, it again shows up their dullness.

The detailed directions that Jesus gives to two of his disciples seem to be Mark's way of showing Jesus in control. The mark of a genuine prophet was his ability to accurately predict his own destiny. There is an emphasis in these verses on preparation. The disciples are preparing for the Jewish Passover. Jesus, however, is preparing for a different kind of meal. It is interesting that no details are given regarding many of the usual preparations for the Passover. Many common features of the meal are not mentioned, and no reference is made to the very thorough cleaning of the house and household utensils that was required. Could it be that Mark wishes to focus attention, not on the Passover, but on the new meal that is now celebrated in his community in remembrance of their Lord? There may well be an anti-Passover thrust here. One scholar has suggested that this section suggests secrecy, and that the meal was an illegal Passover, deliberately celebrated on a different date, by which Jesus was challenging the Pharisees right in their stronghold, Jerusalem. According to this view, Judas took the morsel of food that Jesus gave him (John 13:26), and then took it to the priests as evidence of the illegality of the meal. However, there is little in the text to support this view. 13-16

The word here translated **guest room** is the same that is used in Luke 2:7, where it is usually translated as 'inn'.

## The meal, 14:17-21

**¹⁷ And when it was evening he came with the twelve. ¹⁸ And as they were at table eating, Jesus said, 'Truly, I say to you, one of you will betray me, one who is eating with me.' ¹⁹ They began to be sorrowful, and to say to him one after another, 'Is it I?' ²⁰ He said to them, 'It is one of the twelve, one who is dipping bread into the dish with me. ²¹ For the Son of man goes as it is written of him, but woe to that man by whom the Son of man is betrayed! It would have been better for that man if he had not been born.'**

This section begins with a reference to the time of day (as **17** in 11:11,19). The RSV translates simply **when it was evening**. A more literal translation would be 'it being late'. It is possible that Mark, rather than merely making a passing reference to the time of day, is suggesting the lateness of the hour for Jesus, for Judas, and for Israel – in a different sense for each of them. The Passover lambs were slaughtered late in the day as well. The disciples in this context are specifically referred to as **the twelve**. They represent the new Israel, with whom a new covenant is about to be established through the blood of Jesus. As in the old covenant between Jahweh and the twelve tribes of Israel, the new covenant is sealed with a meal (see Exod 24:8,11).

Jesus' words, **one of you will betray me**, introduce the **18** theme of uncleanness at the table. Matters in relation to table-fellowship were a serious problem in many Christian communities. Jesus begins with the words that he often uses to introduce an authoritative statement: **Truly, I say to you**. Among those who are with him at the table there is someone who will hand him over to the enemy. Was this something that happened in early Christian communities? Were there Christians who handed fellow-Christians over to the opposition, and then still expected to share in the table-fellowship? Eating with people, or sharing food with them, can make them virtual blood relatives, so strong is the tie created by such fellowship. The story is told of a bedouin who takes in a stranger and shares food with him at his table. The police come, and demand that the visitor be handed over. The host refuses: 'He has eaten with me at my table; I cannot betray him.' He is told that the man is wanted for murder. Still the answer is no. It is then revealed that he is wanted for the murder of the host's son! Nevertheless, the host refuses to hand him over, so strong is the tie created by table-fellowship. Whether the story is true or legendary, the point remains: sharing food with others means identification with them. It means that the guest could expect protection. In sharing food with his disciples, Jesus could expect defence and protection from them. The irony of this would not have been missed by Mark's readers.

So the seemingly innocuous words, **as they were at table eating**, are actually pregnant with meaning! It can be noted that, in the context of the miracle of the feeding of the five thousand, there is the curious expression 'they had no leisure even to eat' (6:31). Here, however, Jesus and his disciples do eat! But Jesus does not enjoy the meal. He knows that it is a travesty of a meal, because among those very disciples whom he has called to be with him, and with whom he shares this meal of 'com-panionship' (from the Latin *com* 'with' and *panis* 'bread'), there is one who is unclean. Ironically, each of them in turn asks: 'Surely, you don't mean me?' (which conveys the meaning better than the RSV: **Is it I?** Compare NIV). They are all convinced that such an action is impossible for them.

Jesus says that it is one of the twelve – one of those especially chosen, one of that group who later claimed authority within their Christian community. It is the one who will dip his hand with Jesus into the dish. For Christians, purity does not depend on the washing of hands, but on the dipping of the hand in the dish, that is, the sharing of food. Dipping is connected with the blood of the Passover lamb (see Exod 12:22). There was apparently a certain etiquette to be followed in relation to dipping food at a meal, with the host and superiors going first. Some have suggested that Judas, by dipping at the same time as Jesus, shows disregard for Jesus' leadership. Motives for any of Judas's actions are difficult to discover. The point here is that the unclean is now found within the Christian community, among those who are very close, those who actually share table-fellowship.

It is true, Jesus says, that the **Son of man** goes to suffer and die as it has been **written of him**, and as Jesus himself has predicted, but that does not remove the guilt and responsibility of the one who actually brings about his handing over. It can be noted that Judas is not mentioned by name at this point. This is probably deliberate on the part of Mark, who wishes his readers to ask the question of themselves: 'Surely it is not I who will hand Jesus over?'

Jesus speaks of the Son of man going **as it is written of him**. Scholars acknowledge that there is no Old Testament passage which speaks directly of the suffering of the Son of man. Therefore Son of man is usually connected with the Suffering Servant of Isaiah, but this connection is quite arbitrary. If we understand the phrase **Son of man** as meaning the Man, or even Adam, then we need look no further than Genesis 3:17-19, which contains the curse of suffering and death placed on Adam. Passages which refer to the 'way of all flesh' could also be relevant here, for example, Psalm 78:39; 90:5; Isaiah 40:6.

*The new covenant, 14:22-26*

²² **And as they were eating, he took bread, and blessed, and broke it, and gave it to them, and said, 'Take; this is my body.'** ²³ **And he took a cup, and when he had given thanks he gave it to them, and they all drank of it.** ²⁴ **And he said to them, 'This is my blood of the<sup>c</sup> covenant, which is poured out for many.** ²⁵ **Truly, I say to you, I shall not drink again of the fruit of the vine until that day when I drink it new in the kingdom of God.'**

²⁶ **And when they had sung a hymn, they went out to the Mount of Olives.**

<sup>c</sup> Other ancient authorities insert *new*

Here the emphasis is placed on the meal: **as they were eating**. Seed (4:3-8), bread, breaking and eating (6:35-44; 8:1-8,14-21), which are common themes in Mark's gospel, reach their climax in this meal. Jesus, as host, takes **bread** (the word can mean any kind of bread, not necessarily unleavened), pronounces the blessing over it (as every host did at every meal), breaks it, gives it to the disciples, and says: **take; this is my body**. It should be noted that the 'words of institution' recorded in the gospels, and in 1 Corinthians 11:23-26, are quite varied in form. There was no common set liturgical form used among the various Christian communities. The reader will find it very interesting to place the passages side by side and compare them. However, it is not the task of this commentary to make such comparisons.

There is no mention of the Passover lamb. Why is Jesus not referred to as the lamb – surely a fitting analogy? Mark is rejecting the Passover as a festival for Christians. It has been replaced by the new festival celebrating the death of Jesus and his coming kingdom. Some scholars have suggested that Jesus, in breaking the bread, deliberately disobeys a prohibition in relation to the Passover lamb that none of its bones be broken. Anyone who did break the lamb's bones was regarded as unclean (that motif surfaces again!). These scholars have made the further suggestion that, since the penalty for this offence was a whipping, the whipping of Jesus which takes place soon afterwards is to be seen as the whipping of one who is unclean, who has acted contrary to the law, the 'lawless' one. This interpretation, however, may involve reading too much into the text. Meals usually began with the host taking bread, blessing it, breaking it, and then distributing it (see 6:41; 8:6).

What is new is the interpretation that Jesus gives to his action of distributing the bread. **Take**, he says. There is no actual command to eat! (Was the command to eat given in those communities where the bread was not eaten by some?) **This is my body**, Jesus says. To what does **this** refer? In Greek it is a neuter word, whereas the word 'bread' is masculine. Nevertheless, the sense is clear: Jesus is referring to the bread, and says that there is a correlation between the bread and his body. It is interesting to note that when the Israelites were about to enter the promised land, they no longer ate the manna with which they had been fed in the wilderness, but ate new food from the land that they were about to enter (Josh 5:10-12). It may be that Jesus' action here reflects what happened on that earlier occasion. The passover meal, which offers food that is equivalent to the manna, is no longer the food of the Christian community. Their food is the bread, the body of Jesus. Just as new food was eaten by the Israelites on their arrival at the borders of the promised land, so this new meal that Jesus provides is the food on which Christian communities live until they finally enter the kingdom. Some have suggested that the word **this** is meant to call to mind the many questions about Jesus: Who is this . . . ? (4:41); What is this . . . ? (1:27); Is not this . . . ? (6:3); Who do men say . . . ? (8:27); and, Who do you say . . . ? (8:29). These are all questions about the identity of Jesus, and here he gives his answer to all those questions. In other words, the true identity of Jesus is seen in the bread (and the cup) of this meal. The bread/body link has been hinted at in various places in the gospel, especially in the feeding miracles (6:35-44; 8:1-9).

After giving the bread, Jesus takes a cup, gives thanks (in contrast to the blessing spoken over the bread. The word *Eucharist* comes from the Greek word used here for 'give thanks'), gives it to them, and they all drink of it. Note that Mark has the disciples drinking from the cup *before* Jesus says anything. Does he wish to combat the practice of some communities where the people did not drink from the cup, or where only some drank and not others? We simply do not know what the practices were, but we do know that they varied from community to community. We also know that some did not drink from the cup at all, because of Jesus' words that he would drink wine again only in the kingdom.

Others drank only water. Was that for ascetic reasons, or did they, too, refrain from drinking wine in order to drink it again at the coming of Jesus? Jews strongly abhorred the drinking of blood. It may be that by separating Jesus' words from the action of drinking, Mark makes allowance for their abhorrence, and softens the thought somewhat. Passages such as Leviticus 3:17 and Deuteronomy 12:23 make it clear that the eating of food with blood in it was totally forbidden. This law even applied to foreigners. It is also possible that Mark separates Jesus' words from the action of drinking in order to focus attention more sharply on the words.

There are several manuscript variations in verse 24. **24** Some lesser manuscripts omit all the words following 'my blood'. Some important manuscripts include the word 'new': 'This is my blood of the new covenant'.

In Jewish thought, blood was regarded as a person's life; the life was in the blood (see Deut 12:23). Jesus says that his blood is **poured out for many**. There is no need to understand this in sacrificial terms; the preposition **for** that is used here does not allow this. A comparison with the Greek text in Matthew shows that he uses a different preposition which is sometimes used in contexts involving sacrifices (Luke 22:20 and 1 Corinthians 11:24, however, have the same preposition as Mark). The preposition that is here in Mark is never used in any passages dealing with sacrifices in the Septuagint (Greek) version of Exodus and Leviticus. Isaiah 53 is often believed to be behind the phrase **poured out for many**, but this does not appear to be the case, since the preposition that Mark uses does not occur in the Septuagint version of Isaiah 53. The preposition means 'for the good of, for someone's advantage'. The only other time that it occurs in Mark it clearly has the meaning of being on someone's side, being *for* a person and not against that person (see 9:40). Jesus' blood is poured out for the advantage of his people. According to Mark's version of the Communion words, Jesus' death is not a sacrifice, and the meal is not a meal of sacrifice, but is a meal of benefit and advantage for the new Israel. For Mark, the sacrificial system is finished. Jesus does not establish a new sacrifice. The new covenant is not based on sacrifice, but on the crucified and resurrected Jesus, who is living and present with his community. If the reading without 'new' is adopted, it suggests that Mark does not even acknowledge the Passover meal as a covenant meal. There is no mixing of the old and the new. New wine is not poured into old skins (see 2:22).

The concept of covenant is central in Jewish thought. God had made his covenant with Israel, a covenant which abides forever. Jesus said many things which shocked his fellow-Jews, but none would have been more shocking than what he says here about his blood being the **blood of the covenant**, whether or not the word 'new' is included. His words raise the question of whether the covenant between God and Israel still stands. It is interesting that it is precisely in the meal of 'communion' that this question becomes significant and important. It is a live question between Jews and Christians still today.

In Old Testament times covenants were often sealed with a meal. Behind Mark's account here stands Exodus 24:11, which speaks of how the covenant between God and Israel was sealed with a meal: 'They beheld God and ate and drank'. Jesus' words also echo Exodus 24:8, which refers to 'the blood of the covenant'. The radical difference, of course, is that Jesus refers to *his* blood as being that which seals the covenant. It is also possible that Mark has Zechariah 9:11 in mind, where God speaks of 'the blood of my covenant'. This connection is likely because of the fact that Zechariah, which is so strongly messianic and concerned with the end-time, is particularly important for Mark. A similar reference is Daniel 9:27, where a messianic figure is spoken of in the context of a covenant. What makes this reference interesting, in the Marcan context, is that it speaks of the covenant being made 'with many'. Who are the **many** referred to by Jesus? The word is often understood to be the equivalent of 'all, everybody', but it may well signify Israel, or, as Christians understood it, the new Israel, the church. In the Essene community of the Dead Sea area the ruling body was called 'the Many'. Rabbinic and Essene literature indicates that it is a covenant term, and therefore in some sense exclusive. Jesus' blood is poured out for a covenant with Israel, but with a new Israel. So the question of who the **many** are would have been a very real one in the early Christian communities. Mark has already made his answer clear: the new covenant is made by God to include the unclean!

The verb **poured out** is sometimes used in the Scriptures in connection with violent death, especially of prophets and martyrs (see, for example, Ps 22:14; Isa 53:12). Mark's readers have been prepared for the violent death of Jesus through the parable of the heir to the vineyard (12:1-12). It is not at all unlikely that Jesus was acutely aware of his impending death, and that it would come violently. He came from Galilee, after all, and taught and acted with an authority which threatened the power and authority structures in both religion and politics. By coming to Jerusalem he knew that he was walking into the lion's den.

Verse 25 is not often included in modern Communion liturgies, in which the Words of Institution are usually based on Paul's version in 1 Corinthians 11:23-26. Jesus' words here speak of a future dimension of the meal. He says that he will not drink wine again until he drinks it new in the kingdom. There is again considerable manuscript variation at this point. Some manuscripts omit the word **again**. Other manuscripts, some with 'again' and some without it, have a different construction altogether, which may be more Semitic in form. Such variations indicate that various communities felt no compunction about modifying the words slightly to suit their own understanding. The idea of drinking abundant wine in the kingdom of God was a common feature of Jewish hope (see Isa 25:6; Joel 3:18). No mention is made here of the participation of the disciples in this future drinking. The Eucharist is a meal which looks forward to that kingdom of God which has been inaugurated by Jesus, and in which all his followers who share this meal with him, and with each other, participate. The meal is linked very closely to the kingdom, which Mark sees as being at the centre of Jesus' message.

The word translated **truly** is actually the word 'amen'. It was the word spoken by Jews in response to the prayers of benediction that were prayed in connection with the Passover meal. Jesus speaks that Amen in the hope of sharing the meal of the kingdom in the future prepared by God. That Amen, and the hope that it expresses, is the Christian community's response to the blessing received in the Eucharist.

At the end of each Passover meal various psalms were sung (Pss 113-118). It is probably these psalms that are the **hymn** that Jesus and his disciples sing before proceeding to the Mount of Olives. Mark has already designated the Mount of Olives as the place of arrival of the coming King (11:1). If the meal that Jesus ate with his disciples was a Passover meal, it must have been quite late at night by this time.

## *The heat is on, 14:27-42*

²⁷ And Jesus said to them, 'You will all fall away; for it is written, "I will strike the shepherd, and the sheep will be scattered." ²⁸ But after I am raised up, I will go before you to Galilee.' ²⁹ Peter said to him, 'Even though they all fall away, I will not.' ³⁰ And Jesus said to him, 'Truly, I say to you, this very night, before the cock crows twice, you will deny me three times.' ³¹ But he said vehemently, 'If I must die with you, I will not deny you.' And they all said the same.

³² And they went to a place which was called Gethsemane; and he said to his disciples, 'Sit here, while I pray.' ³³ And he took with him Peter and James and John, and began to be greatly distressed and troubled. ³⁴ And he said to them, 'My soul is very sorrowful, even to death; remain here, and watch.'ᵈ ³⁵ And going a little farther, he fell on the ground and prayed that, if it were possible, the hour might pass from him. ³⁶ And he said, 'Abba, Father, all things are possible to thee; remove this cup from me; yet not what I will, but what thou wilt.' ³⁷ And he came and found them sleeping, and he said to Peter, 'Simon, are you asleep? Could you not watchᵈ one hour? ³⁸ Watchᵈ and pray that you may not enter into temptation; the spirit indeed is willing, but the flesh is weak.' ³⁹ And again he went away and prayed, saying the same words. ⁴⁰ And again he came and found them sleeping, for their eyes were very heavy; and they did not know what to answer him. ⁴¹ And he came the third time, and said to them, 'Are you still sleeping and taking your rest? It is enough; the hour has come; the Son of man is betrayed into the hands of sinners. ⁴² Rise, let us be going; see, my betrayer is at hand.'

ᵈ Or *keep awake*

Jesus makes the prediction that all his disciples will **fall away**, or, reflecting the actual Greek word that is used, will be 'scandalised' (the same word occurs in 4:17 in reference to those who hear the word but 'fall away' because of persecution). According to Jesus, this is not unexpected, because Zechariah had spoken of the sheep being scattered when the shepherd is struck (Zech 13:7). This is a strange use of this verse, because in its original context it refers to God smiting the shepherd because he has not led the sheep in God's ways. It seems to be quoted here without regard to its original context. Zechariah, which is full of messianic expectations, features prominently in Mark's passion story, which suggests that Mark wants his readers to see Jesus' passion as ushering in the promised kingdom.

In Mark's gospel, being a disciple means following along the way of Jesus. Here Jesus predicts failure for his followers as they stumble on the way. But he goes on to say that after his resurrection (a reference which suggests that the striking of the shepherd refers to his death), he will go ahead of them into Galilee – a prediction that the disciples are reminded of by the angel on Easter morning (16:7). **28**

Peter does not accept what Jesus says, which once again highlights the hardness of heart of the disciples, that is, their inability to see and to hear. He says that even if all the others fail, he alone will not stumble or be offended. Jesus replies with a strong **Truly . . . before the cock crows twice, you will deny me**. It is interesting to note that there is a tradition that while the temple stood there were no roosters in the city of Jerusalem. **29 30**

The irony is heightened (because Mark's readers already know what happens) by Peter vehemently repeating that he will not deny Jesus, even if it means dying with him. Mark records that this is the attitude not only of Peter but of all the disciples. Mark's concern is not merely with Peter, but with all those who call themselves followers of the Way. No matter how strong one's intention is to remain true to Jesus, his way is a lonely way, a way on which one will inevitably stumble. **31**

Like the disciples, whose failure is predicted, Jesus himself faces the test. However, in his handling of the test he stands in marked contrast to them. They all go to Gethsemane, and Jesus tells his disciples to sit and wait while he prays. In the moment of testing, Jesus prays. When the heat is on, he does not place his reliance on his own powers or faith, but throws himself onto the faithfulness of God. His confidence to face the test is not in himself, as was the case with Peter, but is directed toward God. **32**

As on previous occasions, Peter, James and John are taken **with him** (see 5:37; 9:2; 13:3). In those cases, the three were taken aside for the purpose of being given some special inside revelation from Jesus, and there is no reason to understand this situation in the garden any differently. Their actual calling was to be 'with' Jesus (3:14). They now **33** see Jesus **greatly distressed and troubled**. This is one of the few times that Jesus is depicted in psychological terms, as responding to a situation very emotionally. He is suffering in the very depths of his being (his **soul**), to the point of **death**. The verbs used here, **distressed** and **troubled**, and the adjective **very sorrowful**, are very strong in their emotional content. In his loneliness, Jesus calls on his disciples to stay and watch. Here he becomes one with those sufferers who feel overwhelmed. Their cry and their loneliness are his. He prays that, if possible, **the hour might pass from him**. This is the crucial hour for Jesus and his mission, when he performs his great act of service in giving his life as a ransom for many (10:45). This is the hour of testing, when he faces all the fury of the demonic and unclean powers. This is also the hour for the disciples, but for them it is a time of failure. 34 35

Jesus prays, addressing God with the affectionate Aramaic term for 'father', **Abba**, thereby acknowledging his own status as the Son. Possibilities (**all things are possible to thee**) lie outside of himself, with his Father. He asks to be spared **this cup**, the cup symbolising his life which is to be poured out. The cup also represents the judgment of God (see Isa 51:17; Jer 25:15; Ezek 23:33), and it is probably this sense which is dominant here. Jesus is not asking to be rescued from death – he knows how to die! But he asks to be spared the terrible judgment of God: God's withdrawing of himself, his absence. As the Son, Jesus constantly seeks fellowship with his Father. To be God-forsaken, to be abandoned as Son, is what overwhelms Jesus. But he submits his will, in trust and hope, to that of his Father: **Yet not what I will, but what thou wilt**. This is not an action of hopelessness or despair, a last resort, but an action of trust and confidence. He is not resigning himself to blind fate or to the inevitable. It is an act of submission to a Father who has already acknowledged him as his Son, and who will vindicate his Son's suffering and death. We cannot underestimate the struggle that Jesus undergoes here, as if it is somehow easier for him because he is the Son of God. His faith, his courage, his willingness to place his future in the hands of his faithful Father are just as much a risk for him as for us. He, like us, has to place his trust in his Father's faithfulness, and in his promise. 36

Jesus' threefold prayer stands in contrast to the threefold denial of Peter, and also to the sleeping of the disciples. In 37, 38 the time of testing, Mark's readers are encouraged to hear and see their Teacher and Lord, and to walk his way without stumbling. But the disciples sleep, and do not keep watch. Peter is addressed by Jesus as **Simon**. Is Mark indicating that Peter has reverted to what he was before being called and named by Jesus? Peter was called to be *with* Jesus (3:14,16); Simon is the Peter *without* Jesus!

Jesus' words in verse 38 are surely addressed to Mark's readers as much as to Peter (hence the plural form of the verbs, which is indicated by the use of 'ye' in the AV, but is lost in some modern translations). As usual, Mark wishes to involve his audience in the story that he is telling. He does not allow them to divorce themselves from the action. The fact that Jesus goes away and prays again highlights, by contrast, the sleeping of the disciples. Their **eyes** are **heavy**. This has often been the case throughout Mark's story, since they have been unable to 'see' Jesus. When he comes back to them after praying, they do not know what to say to him. They are both blind and dumb. **39, 40**

Verse 41 emphasises the lonely way that Jesus now goes. Sleeping instead of watching for the coming of Jesus is a common New Testament theme. If we accept the RSV reading, **It is enough; the hour has come** (which is probably not the best way of translating this), the idea that is being expressed is that Jesus' death is **the hour**, and that his death is intimately related to his *parousia* (his presence, or return, in the end-time). We do not have to wait for some future time, because the time is here now. In the Christian's time of suffering, and at the time of death, the *parousia* of Jesus has come. The kingdom is not in the distant future, but is right here now, in suffering and dying, in the cross. It is tempting to understand **Son of man** here in the sense of the Human, the one who represents the whole of humanity. At this crucial hour, Jesus, the second Adam (to use Paul's expression), the Human, is handed over to sinners, the Clean One into the hands of the unclean. **41**

The sleeping of the disciples may have further significance for Mark and his community. There is a mid-second century Jewish tradition that, if a member or members of a Passover company doze during the ceremony, the meal can be resumed, but if they fall into a deep sleep, the meal cannot be resumed. At first, the disciples only doze, struggling to keep their eyes open, but eventually they fall into a deep sleep. This means that the Passover cannot be resumed. It is finished. This also helps to explain the verb which the

RSV translates **It is enough**. In its primary meaning the verb refers to the 'receiving in full' of a sum of money, and the issuing of a receipt. It thus refers to the concluding of a business transaction. Jesus is the 'payment in full' in relation to the Passover, which is now brought to an end. **The hour has come**, that is, the time of the new festival is here. This festival has been foreshadowed in the new meal given by Jesus (vv 22-25), just as his burial was foreshadowed by his anointing by the woman (vv 3-9).

In relation to the word translated **It is enough**, some manuscripts have a variation which can be understood as meaning: 'You think the end is far off? The hour has now come'. However, Mark's view that Jesus ushers in a new time supports the explanation given above: that Jesus has made full and final payment in relation to the Passover, and has issued a receipt to mark the end of the transaction. The Passover cannot be resumed. Jesus himself is the new festival. And this festival, it is almost certain, was celebrated not annually, as was the Passover, but weekly, in the Eucharistic meal of the Christian community. However, one can imagine that there were some Jewish Christians who did not want to give up the Passover celebrations.

Jesus calls his disciples to get up and go with him, to face 42 the one who is about to hand him over.

## The unclean is exposed, 14:43-50

**⁴³ And immediately, while he was still speaking, Judas came, one of the twelve, and with him a crowd with swords and clubs, from the chief priests and the scribes and the elders. ⁴⁴ Now the betrayer had given them a sign, saying, 'The one I shall kiss is the man; seize him and lead him away under guard.' ⁴⁵ And when he came, he went up to him at once, and said, 'Master!'ᵉ And he kissed him. ⁴⁶ And they laid hands on him and seized him. ⁴⁷ But one of those who stood by drew his sword, and struck the slave of the high priest and cut off his ear. ⁴⁸ And Jesus said to them, 'Have you come out as against a robber, with swords and clubs to capture me? ⁴⁹ Day after day I was with you in the temple teaching, and you did not seize me. But let the scriptures be fulfilled.' ⁵⁰ And they all forsook him, and fled.**

ᵉ Or *Rabbi*

The point is underlined lest any readers should forget: **43** Judas is **one of the twelve**. Although Judas is mentioned by name, Mark does not see him as standing alone, but as one of the twelve. It is possible even among the leaders of the Christian community for betrayal to occur. The **crowd** (which in Galilee was on Jesus' side, and which flocked to hear him and was taught and fed by him) here in Jerusalem comes to arrest him. They come **with swords and clubs**, and armed also with the authority of **the chief priests and the scribes and the elders**. It is the temple authorities, the religious leaders, who come to arrest him. Those responsible for the purity of the temple arrest the Clean One of God, on whom the 'Spirit of holiness' has descended at his baptism. The **betrayer** (the name of Judas is played down) **44,** gives a prearranged signal, a kiss, calling Jesus **Master** (or **45 Rabbi**) as he kisses him. The word of address literally means 'My Great One'. It was used by students to address their teacher, although there is some doubt about whether it was in use in the time of Jesus. If its use occurred only later, we would have to suppose that Mark's use of the term here has some significance for his readers. We know that a Rabbi Yohanan ben Zakkai was a significant and influential rabbi in Galilee during, or soon after, Jesus' own ministry there. He was one who did not interpret the destruction of the temple as a sign of God's abandonment of Israel. It is claimed by some scholars that the rabbis proved to be the greatest stumbling block for the Christian mission to the Jews. Whether Mark and/or his readers were aware of this is uncertain. Judas's use of the term 'Rabbi' probably serves simply to emphasise his misunderstanding of who Jesus is, and the typical hardness of heart of the disciples as a whole.

A bystander (**one of those who stood by**), presumably **46,** not one of the disciples, draws his sword and cuts off the ear **47** of the servant of the high priest. It has been suggested, as seems very likely, that the servant is not a **slave**, but the chief priest's assistant, that is, someone of quite some importance in the temple and its administration and ritual. The word used for **ear** refers more specifically to the ear lobe. It is hard to imagine a chance swing of a sword slicing off only the lobe! This suggests that the cutting is a deliberate action, and that it has deep significance. A priest with his ear cut would be regarded as unclean, and therefore unable to minister in the temple (see Lev 21:17-23). This incident, then, suggests that the chief priests, the scribes and the elders, who have given orders to have Jesus arrested, are actually unclean.

Jesus does not respond to Judas's kiss and his word of greeting, but he does speak to those who have come to arrest him. His reference to the temple supports the interpretation given to the cutting off of the ear, since the temple was the responsibility of the priests. Jesus says that he taught in the temple day after day. When did this happen? According to Mark, Jesus has not been in Jerusalem at all until this last week of his life. Does the tradition which Mark is using show through here, a tradition which makes a different point from that of Mark regarding Jerusalem and the temple? The word **robber** would be better translated 'political rebel'. The political element in Jesus' arrest and death cannot be ignored, otherwise why was he arrested and ultimately executed on a cross?

Jesus sees these events as the fulfilment of Scripture (**let the scriptures be fulfilled**), although no specific passage is mentioned. Perhaps passages from Zechariah are in mind.

All Jesus' followers leave him and run away. So much for the bravado of the disciples. Possibly the **all** includes others besides the twelve. The shepherd is struck, and the sheep are scattered (v 27). Jesus must now walk his way alone.

## *The naked 'vicar', 14:51,52*

**⁵¹ And a young man followed him, with nothing but a linen cloth about his body; and they seized him, ⁵² but he left the linen cloth and ran away naked.**

These two verses are meant to be read with the preceding paragraph. The young man is one of those who left Jesus and fled. He is a mystery figure, and much thought has been given to his identity. He is said to have **followed** Jesus. In Mark a very closely related verb is often used to refer to those who are followers of Jesus. He has thrown a **linen cloth** over his naked body. Together with Jesus he is arrested. But leaving his linen cloth behind, he flees **naked**.

The emphasis in the story seems to be on the linen cloth and on the young man's nudity. Linen was worn by the priests (Lev 6:10; 16:4,32; 1 Sam 2:18; 2 Sam 6:14). Daniel has a vision of a heavenly messenger dressed in linen (Dan 12:6). Linen is also used in Jesus' burial (15:46). The word translated **young man** can also mean 'servant'. It is the word used of the messenger at Jesus' tomb on Easter morning (16:5), which suggests a possible link between this incident and the resurrection. However, if Mark is trying to give us a clue, it is not one that is very helpful. It may be better to identify the young man as a priestly servant – not a slave, but an assistant of the high priest – who is a follower of Jesus, but now, under pressure from Jesus' opponents, is left naked, without his linen cloth. Just as we call clergy 'men of the cloth', the priests were 'men of the linen'. According to this interpretation, the service of the priests is now shown to be unclean (as was implied also by the cutting off of the ear of the high priest's servant), since nudity involves uncleanness in Jewish thought. Exodus 28:42 makes it clear that the very purpose of the 'linen breeches' for the priests was 'to cover their naked flesh'.

It was the priests who had the authority to decide who and what was clean or unclean. It is significant that the very next verse records how Jesus is taken away to the high priest, to be subsequently charged with being unclean by profaning the name of God. So the context strongly suggests that the naked young man is a priest, or the assistant to a priest. Like the other disciples of Jesus, this priest also flees. **52**

Most interpreters see this young man as a disciple of Jesus, or as a representative of all the disciples. He flees when stripped naked, in contrast to Jesus who is also stripped naked, but who still goes the way of the cross. Some scholars have seen a reference to baptism here. According to this interpretation, the young man is an initiate who is naked and therefore ready to die, but Jesus dies instead. In Jesus' resurrection, the initiate is clothed again with white garments (16:5). While it is possible to see this baptism symbolism here, there is little support for it in the rest of Mark.

## *Jesus is on trial, 14:53-65*

**[53] And they led Jesus to the high priest; and all the chief priests and the elders and the scribes were assembled. [54] And Peter had followed him at a distance, right into the courtyard of the high priest; and he was sitting with the guards, and warming himself at the fire. [55] Now the chief priests and the whole council sought testimony against Jesus to put him to death; but they found none. [56] For many bore false witness against him, and their witness did not agree. [57] And some stood up and bore false witness against him, saying, [58] 'We heard him say, "I will destroy this temple that is made with hands, and in three days I will build another, not made with hands." ' [59] Yet not even**

so did their testimony agree. ⁶⁰ And the high priest stood up in the midst, and asked Jesus, 'Have you no answer to make? What is it that these men testify against you?' ⁶¹ But he was silent and made no answer. Again the high priest asked him, 'Are you the Christ, the Son of the Blessed?' ⁶² And Jesus said, 'I am; and you will see the Son of man seated at the right hand of Power, and coming with the clouds of heaven.' ⁶³ And the high priest tore his garments, and said, 'Why do we still need witnesses? ⁶⁴ You have heard his blasphemy. What is your decision?' And they all condemned him as deserving death. ⁶⁵ And some began to spit on him, and to cover his face, and to strike him, saying to him, 'Prophesy!' And the guards received him with blows.

Jesus is taken to the **high priest** and to the assembly of **chief priests, elders**, and **scribes**. The high priest's name is not mentioned, which implies that Mark is not thinking of a particular high priest, but of high priests in general, or the office. In relation to the previous two sections it has been suggested that the role of the priests may well be very much in Mark's mind in connection with Jesus' passion. It can also be noted that there were some Jewish traditions which saw the priesthood in messianic terms. In Leviticus 4:5,16 where the phrase 'anointed priest' occurs, the Septuagint (the Greek translation of the Old Testament) uses the word 'Christ' (the Greek equivalent of the Hebrew 'Messiah') for 'anointed'. In Zechariah 4:14 (a book that appears to have special significance for Mark) the high priest and the king are referred to as 'the two anointed'. The *Testament of Judah* (a Jewish writing) has the Lord setting the office of king beneath that of priest. The idea was common that the Messiah would be a descendant of Aaron, that is, would come from the priestly line. In all these traditions, the Messiah is seen as a human figure, a divinely sanctioned leader of Israel. It is possible that the priests rejected Jesus because they saw him as a threat to their messianic hopes, or because he did not meet the priestly criteria for a messiah. No wonder they condemn him when he claims to be, not the nationalist Messiah that they expect, but the Messiah who is Son of God!

The sanhedrin (the highest Jewish council) to which Jesus is brought, appears to consist of three groups: the **chief priests**, the **elders**, and the **scribes**. A majority of the scribes would have been Pharisees. The sanhedrin consisted of 71 members. However, there were other groups with legal and judicial authority, also called sanhedrin, which consisted of much smaller numbers.

Peter, who is soon to feature in the story again (vv 66-72), is introduced at this point. He follows Jesus (the verb is the one that Mark uses of a disciple) but **at a distance**. He comes to the highpriest's courtyard, and sits with the servants (rather than **the guards** as in the RSV) warming himself. The last we had heard of him he had fled, together with the other disciples, but now he has followed Jesus after all. People hearing this story for the first time might have had their hopes raised at this point: Peter is going to be true to his word after all. The others might be keeping far away, but not Peter. He is bigger than that. He is prepared to follow. He will stand firm and be 'with' Jesus, as he was called to do (3:14). So Mark, in good story-telling fashion, raises a glimmer of hope for Peter, and therefore also for those who are listening to or reading this story, who are meant to see themselves in Peter. 54

Meanwhile, the council tries to find witnesses against Jesus, but cannot make any of their accusations stick, because the false witnesses disagree among themselves. The picture of Jesus as the Righteous One is developed from here on, since he is shown to be innocent in both the Roman and the Jewish court of law. Later Christian communities understood this to mean that they did not deserve the death penalty demanded for them by various courts. What the false witnesses testify is that Jesus has spoken against the temple, but even in this there is disagreement. The accusation that they make against Jesus is another example of irony. The witnesses speak the truth, but they do not understand what they are saying. Those hearing or reading Mark's story would have been 'in the know', and would have chuckled to themselves at this point. They understood themselves to be the temple **not made with hands**, since they belonged to the resurrected and vindicated Son of God, and had received the Spirit of holiness through him. The claim of Christians to be the temple of God must have seemed very radical, not just to followers of Judaism, but to Christian Jews as well. The temple was regarded as the very centre of the cosmos, the very basis for Jewish existence, the link between heaven and earth. The destruction of the temple was a reality, as was also the destruction of the body of Jesus 55, 56 57 58, 59 through death. The vindication of God, however, is given not to the building, but to the body of Jesus through his resurrection.

The high priest stands up **in the midst**, which is the position of authority (see Rev 1:13; 7:17), and gives Jesus the chance to respond to the accusations that have been made, but he is silent. He leaves it to God to defend him and to see that justice is done. In his silence, Jesus stands alongside all the powerless victims of oppression and injustice, who are brought before courts where charges are laid which have no basis in fact, and where prisoners' rights are withheld. His silence pronounces the judgment of God on all such injustice.

There now comes the crucial question, asked by the high priest: **Are you the Christ, the Son of the Blessed?** This is another way of asking: 'Are you the Christ, the Son of God?' It is common to place a comma between **Christ** and **the Son of the Blessed**, as the RSV does. However, it may be better to omit the comma, in which case the question is about what kind of Messiah Jesus is claiming to be: a Messiah who is son of David, or one who is Son of God? The first of these two claims could be tolerated, but the second could not. To claim to be the Messiah was not blasphemous, but to claim to be the Son of God was. The fact that Jesus breaks his silence at this point indicates that this is a crucial question for Mark. Jesus answers with the words **I am**, which are the name by which Yahweh reveals himself to Moses at the burning bush (Exod 3:14). **Son of man**, which Jesus uses here, is simply a term with which he claims authority for himself, rather than a title for himself, or a reference to some other figure. To sit could be to assume the position of authority. The **right hand** was also the place of authority. Jesus shares in the authority of God, who is here called **Power**, and is symbolised, as often in the Bible, by **clouds**. This authority, Jesus says, will be seen, something which has not been possible so far for Jesus' disciples or his opponents.

This claim to an authority which belongs to God alone is too much for the high priest. In genuine distress he tears his clothes (see 2 Sam 1:11; 2 Kgs 18:37) at this blasphemy. The robe of the high priest had come to be regarded as having a special sanctity. On occasions, the procurators of Rome had taken the robe and locked it away as a security against disturbances, and had allowed it out again only for ceremonial purposes. The hope of Israel was symbolised by the robe. So there is irony in the action of the high priest. As a result of his tearing of the robe, the hope of Israel now rests no longer in the robe, but in Jesus. According to Leviticus 10:6 and 21:10, the high priest was not to tear his clothes.

The judgment of the high priest against Jesus is supported by the members of the council, who pass the death sentence on him. According to Mark, they have power to do that. According to John's gospel, only Rome had that authority (18:31). Jesus is spat upon and humiliated. He had used **65** his own spittle for the purpose of healing (7:33), but here spit is used in order to harm him. The mocking demand, **Prophesy**! calls to mind Jesus' predictions that he would be handed over to the Jewish authorities, and that he would suffer many things at their hands. One of the marks of the true prophet was the ability to accurately predict the circumstances of one's own death. There is irony in this insult. Jesus has just prophesied that the Son of man will be seen coming in the presence of God, a prophecy that is rejected as blasphemy. While Jesus is being ridiculed in regard to his ability to prophesy, Peter is denying Jesus, just as Jesus had prophesied! The one who accurately prophesied the actions of Peter can be trusted to bring to fulfilment his prophecy that he will be seen as Son of man in the presence of God.

Jesus' trial is a travesty of justice. As such it allows Jesus to be the Symbol for all those who suffer injustice, especially at the hands of courts, whether religious or political.

## *The heat is on Peter, 14:66-72*

**⁶⁶ And as Peter was below in the courtyard, one of the maids of the high priest came; ⁶⁷ and seeing Peter warming himself, she looked at him, and said, 'You also were with the Nazarene, Jesus.' ⁶⁸ But he denied it, saying, 'I neither know nor understand what you mean.' And he went out into the gateway.ᶠ ⁶⁹ And the maid saw him, and began again to say to the bystanders, 'This man is one of them.' ⁷⁰ But again he denied it. And after a little while again the bystanders said to Peter, 'Certainly you are one of them; for you are a Galilean.' ⁷¹ But he began to invoke a curse on himself and to swear, 'I do not know this man of whom you speak.' ⁷² And immediately the cock crowed a second time. And Peter remembered how Jesus had said to him, 'Before the cock crows twice, you will deny me three times.' And he broke down and wept.**

ᶠ Or *fore-court*. Other ancient authorities add *and the cock crowed*

Jesus stands in stark contrast to Peter, who goes through his own trial. Mark's readers are meant to learn from Jesus, not from Peter. The pillar of the church fails the test. The Christian's confidence is not to be placed in Peter and his authority, but in Jesus, even if his authority appears to be weak and comes under attack from the power structures in society. There may well have been people in Mark's community who were put to the test, and who found it safer to identify themselves as Jews than as Christians. Probably one of the greatest temptations for Jewish Christians was to go back to the ways of Judaism, and to identify as Jews, religiously, socially and politically.

Peter is **below**, just as John the Baptist was a lesser person than Jesus. He is questioned by one of the young women servants of the high priest. In Jewish law the testimony of a woman was not accepted in court, but this woman's testimony is too much for Peter! It can be noted that while here it is the testimony or witness of a woman that brings about Peter's downfall, it is also the witness or testimony of a woman that later brings about his restoration (16:7). The young woman realises that Peter has been with Jesus, **the Nazarene**. The phrase **with the Nazarene, Jesus** is full of irony. Jesus had called Peter to be 'with him' (3:14), and, according to Matthew, in Gethsemane he had asked him to watch and pray 'with' him (Matt 26:38,40). Peter, however, fails to live up to that calling. Here he denies any association with Jesus. Jesus had said that being a disciple means denying oneself (8:34). It is therefore ironical that Peter, the leader of the disciples, instead of denying himself (he wants to save his own skin), denies the one who called him to walk the way of the cross. It is also ironical that he should say that he does not **know** or **understand** what the girl is saying, because, in a sense, that is true! It is a point that Mark has regularly made: Peter does not understand. Some manuscripts include here the words 'and the cock crowed', but they are not in the better manuscripts. 66 67 68

Peter is seen again by the girl, who comments to the bystanders: **This man is one of them**. Again he denies it. Mark's readers, like readers today, would have squirmed at this trial of Peter. In Mark's community there would have been those who had faced similar situations, and who had perhaps replied in a similar way to Peter. 69 70

Those who are standing around are convinced that Peter is **one of them** – after all, they can tell from his accent that he is a Galilean. Maybe Peter now wishes that he had been silent, like Jesus! As far as people in Jerusalem are concerned, the fact that Peter comes from Galilee means that he comes from rebel territory, from the area of those who are unclean, impious, and 'lawless' (not true followers of God's law). And he opens his mouth again to prove it! In the strongest possible terms he rejects **this man**, who has just claimed, as **Son of man**, to have the authority of God. He rejects the Son of man who, when he comes in the glory of his Father, will be ashamed of those who have been ashamed of him (8:38). 71

The rooster crows, and Peter is reminded of Jesus' prediction. This memory produces tears. Peter's threefold denial stands in contrast to Jesus' threefold prediction that he would suffer and be put to death, and his threefold prayer in Gethsemane. Jesus is the righteous and faithful witness; Peter is not. 72

### Roman justice, 15:1-15

<sup>15:1</sup> **And as soon as it was morning the chief priests, with the elders and scribes, and the whole council held a consultation; and they bound Jesus and led him away and delivered him to Pilate. <sup>2</sup> And Pilate asked him, 'Are you the King of the Jews?' And he answered him, 'You have said so.' <sup>3</sup> And the chief priests accused him of many things. <sup>4</sup> And Pilate again asked him, 'Have you no answer to make? See how many charges they bring against you.' <sup>5</sup> But Jesus made no further answer, so that Pilate wondered.**

**<sup>6</sup> Now at the feast he used to release for them one prisoner for whom they asked. <sup>7</sup> And among the rebels in prison, who had committed murder in the insurrection, there was a man called Barabbas. <sup>8</sup> And the crowd came up and began to ask Pilate to do as he was wont to do for them. <sup>9</sup> And he answered them, 'Do you want me to release for you the King of the Jews?' <sup>10</sup> For he perceived that it was out of envy that the chief priests had delivered him up. <sup>11</sup> But the chief priests stirred up the crowd to have him release for them Barabbas instead. <sup>12</sup> And Pilate again said to them, 'Then what shall I do with the man whom you call the King of the Jews?' <sup>13</sup> And they cried out again, 'Crucify him.' <sup>14</sup> And Pilate said to them, 'Why what evil has he done?' But they shouted all the more, 'Crucify him.' <sup>15</sup> So Pilate, wishing to satisfy the crowd, released**

**for them Barabbas; and having scourged Jesus, he delivered him to be crucified.**

Once again the three groups comprising the council, and making up the opposition to Jesus, are mentioned: the **chief priests, elders,** and **scribes**. While they certainly act with hostility toward Jesus, that response stems from an even deeper problem: their hard-heartedness. For Mark, the real problem with any opposition to Jesus is the lack of perception or understanding of who he really is. Jesus is now taken to Pilate, and so moves a step closer to the cross. He is **delivered** to Pilate. The word that is used here occurs ten times in the passion story, but is translated in various ways. Political disturbances, and those who initiated them, were an embarrassment to those Jewish leaders who wanted to remain in the good books of Rome and so retain power. For the sake of peace, the easiest thing to do was to hand potential rebels over to the Romans and let them deal with them. This also helped to keep favour with Rome.

**Pilate** was procurator, or governor, of the Roman province of Judea from 26-37 AD. His official residence was in Caesarea, but he came to Jerusalem at the time of the Passover festival in case of trouble. He apparently ruled with a heavy hand, and tried on several occasions to break the relative autonomy of Jerusalem. He failed in an attempt to bring Roman standards into Jerusalem. He made use of temple money for the building of an aqueduct. There are no historical records that give any further information about him following his recall to Rome. Christian tradition has generally portrayed him as a great wrongdoer, and the inclusion of his name in the Apostles' Creed has made him go down in history as the one who supervised the miscarriage of justice in relation to Jesus. Some Christian traditions, however, portray him as a person who repented, became a Christian saint, and died a martyr's death.

Jesus stands before Pilate, who represents Rome and its power. An important question for the Christian community was the political implications of their relationship to this world power. Understandably, Pilate can think only in terms of power, so he asks Jesus: **Are you the King of the Jews?** **King of the Jews** has not been mentioned at all in any of the charges brought before the Jewish court. In the Greek the question has a touch of sarcasm about it, with an emphasis on **you**. Jesus' answer, **You have said so**, is ambiguous: it is neither an acceptance nor a rejection of the title. Further charges which are not stated, but presumably are serious, are laid against Jesus by the chief priests. However, when Pilate gives Jesus a chance to defend himself against the charges, he does not answer. This causes Pilate to respond with wonder. Jesus stands before the representative of one of the best legal systems in the world, whose heritage has lasted into our own times. It is a system supposedly based on justice and civil rights, but one which cannot handle the one who does not defend his own rights. Jesus stands before Pilate as the representative of all those who suffer injustice and deprivation of human rights in courts of law, even where those courts are supposedly part of the finest legal systems in the world. In the face of this, Pilate, representing all legal systems, can only marvel and wonder. **3**  **4,5**

The practice of releasing a prisoner at the time of the Passover festival is not mentioned in any Roman or Jewish writing, although releasing prisoners during festivals was a known practice among the Greeks. **Barabbas** has been imprisoned for his part in a recent uprising, presumably in Jerusalem, during which he **committed murder** There were Jewish political revolutionaries who believed the kingdom would come only if they took forceful and violent action. Jesus stands in contrast to them, by attacking the very root of the social and political system. This system uses its power, which Jesus knows to be demonic and anti-God, to oppress people. Because of what he stands for, Jesus is more threatening to Rome than the political revolutionaries, and he suffers the consequences. **6**  **7**

In Jerusalem **the crowd** is not pro-Jesus as it was in his home territory of Galilee. They come to Pilate and ask him to continue the practice of releasing a prisoner. Pilate asks whether they want the **King of the Jews** released, a question presumably asked out of ignorance about Jesus. His ignorance increases the irony of the fact that the crowd does not want the 'King of the Jews', but prefers a political rebel. It also places Pilate in a less negative light: he acts out of ignorance, while the Jerusalem crowd acts as it does as a result of a conscious rejection of Jesus. Note, however, that in Mark it is never said of the Jews collectively that they handed Jesus over. Those groups of people who are mentioned – the chief priests, the scribes, the crowds – are never collectively referred to as 'the Jews'. Mark has no anti-Jewish feeling. Pilate thinks that the crowd may want Jesus released because he has been on their side against the **8**  **9** authority of the priests. He thinks that they have handed Jesus over **out of envy**, because he has been eroding their authority among the people. In thinking this way, Pilate is partly right! But Jerusalem – both the priests (who still have effective power) and the crowd – is against Jesus. They choose Barabbas rather than Jesus, the one who makes a grab for power rather than the one who works to undermine the power structures.

Verse 12 shows the 'innocence' of Pilate, who wishes to have Jesus released. Whether Pilate himself calls Jesus **King of the Jews**, or whether he is referring to what he thinks the crowds and/or the priests call him, is unclear from the manuscripts; both readings are possible. The response of the people to Pilate's question is clear: **crucify him**. According to Roman law, to claim to be king was a political crime for which the punishment was death. Crucifixion was reserved by the Romans as the means of execution for political criminals. It was a crude form of execution, and one that was an embarrassment to some Greek and Roman citizens, such as Cicero and Tacitus, who were more enlightened and humane. According to the Jewish historian Josephus, after the death of Herod the Great the Roman governor of Syria crucified some 2000 Jewish rebels. Crucifixion was also used in putting down the rebellion of 66-70 AD. Christians had to come to terms with the fact that their hero had been put to death as a political criminal. This is something that they had to explain to their erstwhile pagan fellow-Christians. The cross – the symbol of a political rebel's death – was what Paul wished to preach (1 Cor 1:17,18,23). The follower of Jesus was also expected to take up the cross (8:34), which meant bearing the political implications of following Jesus. The essential meaning of the cross contrasts sharply with any grasping for power. Jesus' death poses for us the question: Why was he executed? What political factors, if any, were involved?

Pilate's question: **Why, what evil has he done?** again exonerates him. Christians pose no political threat to Rome: Rome finds no evil in them. For Mark's community this would have been a message for local magistrates as well. Jesus may have died as a criminal, but the verdict against him was not that of Rome but of Jerusalem. Jewish unrest in areas under Roman administration was notorious. Mark is distancing Christians from this unrest. Marcan irony surfaces again: Jesus, who is not a political rebel, is crucified as such, while Barabbas, who is a revolutionary, goes free.

Pilate plans to give the crowd some power or authority (this is closer to the intended meaning than **wishing to satisfy**), and so releases Barabbas to them. At the same time he 'delivers' Jesus (that word again) to be whipped prior to crucifixion. Whipping was a very painful punishment, lacerating the body and stripping the skin. It was the prescribed punishment for breaking the Passover lamb's bones. It makes Jesus unclean. So begins the defilement of Jesus, the one who was declared clean in his baptism. His death is his ultimate defilement – and our cleansing.

## *Crowned by soldiers, 15:16-20*

**¹⁶ And the soldiers led him away inside the palace (that is, the praetorium); and they called together the whole battalion. ¹⁷ And they clothed him in a purple cloak, and plaiting a crown of thorns they put it on him. ¹⁸ And they began to salute him, 'Hail, King of the Jews!' ¹⁹ And they struck his head with a reed, and spat upon him, and they knelt down in homage to him. ²⁰ And when they had mocked him, they stripped him of the purple cloak, and put his own clothes on him. And they led him out to crucify him.**

The soldiers lead Jesus away to the **praetorium**. Mark's knowledge of Jerusalem may have been a little shaky, since such a building is not known from other sources. When he was in Jerusalem, Pilate stayed either in the palace of Herod or in the Antonia fortress. The **battalion** (literally, 'the whole cohort', which would have been about 600 soldiers, although numbers varied) carries out a mock coronation of this **King of the Jews**. As has been the case throughout Mark's story, no-one understands who Jesus is. **Purple** is a colour commonly associated with royalty. The **crown of thorns** is no delicately formed circle, but more likely a bush pulled out of the ground and forcibly pushed down on Jesus' head. Once again, Romans act out of ignorance. In one sense, Christians could join in the mocking, because they do not see Jesus as king of the Jews, either. The words, **And they led him out**, are poignant. The one who calls his followers to follow him as he leads the way is now led out by Roman power to be executed as a revolutionary.

It is important to note that Jesus is led **out**. He is the Outsider. He is expelled from Jerusalem, the holy city, as the Unclean One. Crucifixion is the death of one who is unclean: 'Cursed be every one who hangs on a tree' (Gal 3:13; Deut 21:23).

## The Man is tested, 15:21-32

**²¹ And they compelled a paser-by, Simon of Cyrene, who was coming in from the country, the father of Alexander and Rufus, to carry his cross. ²² And they brought him to the place call Golgotha (which means the place of a skull). ²³ And they offered him wine mingled with myrrh; but he did not take it. ²⁴ And they crucified him, and divided his garments among them, casting lots for them, to decide what each should take. ²⁵ And it was the third hour, when they crucified him. ²⁶ And the inscription of the charge against him read, 'The King of the Jews.' ²⁷ And with him they crucified two robbers, one on his right and one on his left.ᵍ ²⁹ And those who passed by derided him, wagging their heads, and saying, 'Aha! You who would destroy the temple and built it in three days, ³⁰ save yourself, and come down from the cross!' ³¹ So also the chief priests mocked him to one another with the scribes, saying, 'He saved others; he cannot save himself. ³² Let the Christ, the King of Israel, come down now from the cross, that we may see and believe.' Those who were crucified with him also reviled him.**

ᵍ Other ancient authorities insert verse 28, *And the scripture was fulfilled which says, 'He was reckoned with the transgressors'*

The original readers and hearers of Mark's story would have been very familiar with this climax to the story. It stood at the heart of their existence as a Christian community, as followers of a Christ who was executed by crucifixion.

No-one from Jerusalem is willing to walk Jesus' way and to carry the cross with him, so a stranger from out of town is forced to do so. **Simon** is a Jew, but from the diaspora and not a local. An outsider helps the Outsider. It would appear that his sons were well known to Mark's readers. **Alexander** and **Rufus** are non-Jewish names, which suggests that, even though they were Jews, they recognised and accepted that they were part of the pagan world in which they lived. Simon is from **Cyrene**. According to Acts 6:9, Jews from Cyrene, together with others, had a synagogue of their own in Jerusalem. The location of **Golgotha** cannot be identified with accuracy today. Mark follows his habit of giving a translation of the name, presumably for the benefit of his non-Aramaic-speaking audience. The name is used in relation to the burial of Adam in some late Jewish traditions.

Jesus refuses the pain-killing drug of wine mixed with myrrh which the women of Jerusalem used to offer to those about to be executed. It appears that Jesus' last meal was the one he had with his disciples. From then on he fasts. The report here is startlingly brief, the sentences short. The climax to Mark's story is here. **23**

Some scholars have suggested that the account of Jesus' death parallels the story of Adam: whereas Adam took the food offered by the woman, Jesus refuses the drink that is offered to him. Since Mark sees Jesus' death as his ultimate defilement, but also his ultimate exorcising of the demonic, it may well be that Jesus' refusal of the drink is meant to be seen as a reference to that first testing of humanity by the unclean and demonic powers.

The link between Jesus and Adam is developed by Paul, and is part of early Christian tradition (see, for example, Rom 5:12-19), but it is possible that a Jewish tradition is also reflected here. Some of the Jewish traditions regarding Adam bear a remarkable resemblance to Mark's account of the death of Jesus. According to these traditions, Adam was created on a Friday, and sinned and was expelled from the garden on the same day. He was also said to have died on a Friday. Similarly, Jesus is crucified and dies on a Friday. Adam was said to have been stripped of the glorious garment that he had before the Fall. Jesus is stripped of the purple cloak (v 20). Adam's fall was said to have triggered an eclipse of the sun and a darkening of other cosmic lights. Jesus' death is accompanied by darkness (v 33). The forbidden fruit, in some Jewish traditions, was grapes. Eve was supposed to have crushed the grapes for Adam and given him wine to drink. Jesus is offered wine by the women, which he refuses. Adam was regarded as a kingly figure. Mark has some fifteen references to Jesus as king in this chapter. It was said to be the ninth hour when Adam was commanded not to eat of the fruit of the tree. It is the ninth hour when Jesus undergoes his greatest test: a sense of the absence of God (v 34). Adam was known as son of God. Jesus is confessed as truly being Son of God. There is also a tradition which associates Adam's death and burial with Jerusalem and Golgotha. Admittedly, many of these traditions appear in post-Jesus writings, such as the Talmud, but there is no reason to suppose that they were fabricated, and **24** they could well be an expression of much older traditions. There is considerable evidence that Mark sees Jesus as the Second Adam, in a way that is not very different from Paul's understanding. The understanding in this commentary of the phrase 'Son of man' also supports this view (see commentary on 2:10).

**And they crucified him.** Crucifixion was considered to be barbaric by both Greeks and Romans, but it was a widespread form of execution in the ancient world. It was used for political and military rebels, and the intention was to utterly humiliate the person involved. The corpse was often not buried, but was left for wild animals and birds to feed on. Death was slow and agonising, the person finally dying from asphyxiation, being unable to raise the chest enough to take in air. The skeleton of a man called Jochanan, who had been crucified, was found in Jerusalem in 1968. Among other things, it confirmed that the nails were driven through the wrists, and not through the palms of the hands as artists have usually depicted it. The wrist bones offered support, whereas the palms would simply have ripped under the body's weight.

The soldiers take Jesus' garments and cast lots for them. Although it may offend our sense of modesty, it is quite likely that Jesus was crucified naked, which would have increased his shame, since nudity was shameful for Jews. Jesus dies as the Unclean One. Mark again specifically mentions the hour: the **third**. A Jewish tradition regarding Adam suggests that it was at the third hour that his limbs were shaped. Is Jesus' crucifixion at **the third hour** meant to be seen as involving the 'shaping' of his limbs? If so, Jesus is again being portrayed as the Adam, the Human.

The epigraph (the word comes from the Greek word that is used here) above Jesus' head states the crime for which he is being executed: the claim to be **the King of the Jews**, which is seen as a political challenge against Rome. The idea of Jesus as king is a common theme in Mark's passion account. To emphasise the political nature and the irony of this execution, Mark records that two revolutionaries are crucified with Jesus, one on either side of him. As was the case with Barabbas, these two political rebels stand in contrast to the radical Rebel of God, who does not bring in a political kingdom based on power and on ethnic and religious foundations, but who brings in the kingdom of God, which calls its citizens to abandon the quest for power and the suppression of the outsiders, and to strive for justice and freedom for the poor and alienated.

It is therefore ironical that Jesus is executed as a political rebel, when in fact he is bringing in the kingdom of God. There is also irony in the fact that Jesus is not crucified with the two disciples who wanted to sit on his right and left in his kingdom (10:35-45), but with two men who had been hoping for a political liberation. The best manuscripts omit verse 28.

Those who pass by – those who have never 'seen' or 'heard' the true Jesus because of their hardness of heart, and therefore have never walked along his way – again demonstrate their inability to see. They mock Jesus by referring to his prediction about the temple being destroyed and then rebuilt. The irony is that this prediction refers to his own resurrection. The destruction of the temple building is predicted in the death of the temple which is the body of Jesus. For Christians, Jesus is the new temple, a belief validated by the resurrection of his body from death. For Jews, this is the real blasphemy, not the one that he was accused of in his trial before the high priest (14:61-64). **Save yourself, and come down from the cross!** is the taunt. Something similar may have been the taunt made to Christians facing execution: 'Look, forget about this following of the way of Jesus, which leads to the cross. Forget his call to take up your cross and follow him, and you can get yourself out of this predicament.'

The chief priests and the scribes join in mocking Jesus, saying to one another that **he saved others but cannot save himself**. Their demand that he come down from the cross so that they **may see and believe**, indicates their inability to 'see' who Jesus is. They think of him as the **Christ, the King of Israel**, whereas Mark has clearly shown that to 'see' Jesus and to believe in him is to acknowledge him, not as a political national Christ, but as the Christ, the Son of the Blessed (see 14:61,62), not the son of David, not the King of Israel, but the Son of God. The term **King of Israel** here is probably to be understood in a religious rather than a political sense. Israel is the name used of the people of God as a worshipping community, and it was frequently used in association with ideas about the end-times (see, for example, Acts 1:6). A reference to the end-times may also be present in the verb **see** (see also 13:26 and 14:62, where the word occurs in relation to the *parousia*, the presence or return of Jesus). What the priests are saying is: 'OK, Jesus, if you are bringing in the kingdom of the end-times, let's see it. Surely you don't expect us to believe in a Christ who is hanging on a cross!' It is important to note that the leaders make the link between **Christ** and **King of Israel**, a link which Jesus and Mark have constantly rejected and seen as a sign of hardness of heart. Their words stand in ironical contrast to those of the Gentile centurion, who sees the 'king' as Son of God (v 39).

The call to **come down** could suggest that the cross is like 'the mountain', the place where Jesus calls his followers (3:13), the place of revelation (9:2), the place of assignment for mission (Matt 28:16). The temptation is always to abandon the cross as the place for such vocation, revelation and mission, and to find a more secure, more socially and politically acceptable starting point.

Those crucified with Jesus are as blind as the others, and join in mocking him. The loneliness of Jesus is accentuated: he does not fit in even with the rebels. He is totally unclean, totally alien, totally rejected.

## *The final exorcism, 15:33-41*

**33 And when the sixth hour had come, there was darkness over the whole land[h] until the ninth hour. 34 And at the ninth hour Jesus cried with a loud voice, 'Eloi, Eloi, lama sabachthani?' which means, 'My God, my God, why hast thou forsaken me?' 35 And some of the bystanders hearing it said, 'Behold, he is calling Elijah.' 36 And one ran and, filling a sponge full of vinegar, put it on a reed and gave it to him to drink, saying, 'Wait, let us see whether Elijah will come to take him down.' 37 And Jesus uttered a loud cry, and breathed his last. 38 And the curtain of the temple was torn in two, from top to bottom. 39 And when the centurion, who stood facing him, saw that he thus[i] breathed his last, he said, 'Truly this man was the Son[j] of God!'**

**40 There were also women looking on from afar, among whom were Mary Magdalene, and Mary the mother of James the younger and of Joses, and Salome, 41 who, when he was in Galilee, followed him, and ministered to him; and also many other women who came up with him to Jerusalem.**

[h] Or *earth*
[i] Other ancient authorities insert *cried out and*
[j] Or *a son*

The demonic powers of the unclean are in full cry. Such is 33
the picture that Mark paints as **darkness** covers **the whole
land** from the sixth hour to the ninth. There have always
been strong traditions about supernatural signs in the heavens at the birth or death of a great person. But it is likely
that Mark, in speaking of this darkness, has in mind the
'end' as predicted by Jesus in 13:24. Jesus' death brings
humanity and all human history to its end and goal. With
his resurrection a new humanity and a new time have their
beginning.

**At the ninth hour** Jesus is in the depths of his struggle 34
with the unclean forces and the demonic powers. It was
noted, in relation to verse 24, that it was a Jewish tradition
that it was at the ninth hour that Adam was commanded
not to eat of the fruit of the tree in the Garden of Eden. The
language here is highly significant. Crying out **with a loud
voice** is the language of possession by an unclean spirit,
demon-possession, and exorcism. Here, in this darkest hour,
the Son of man, the Human, is possessed by all that is
unclean, all that is demonic. He bears the unclean powers
in his own body, his own spirit. In his struggle with these
powers that possess him, Jesus sings Psalm 22, a psalm
sung so often before then and so often since by the victims
of injustice and dehumanisation, by those who have felt
abandoned by God. Only the first line of the psalm is
recorded here, but this could be Mark's shorthand way of
saying that Jesus sang the whole psalm. Jesus sings the
psalm in **a loud voice**, just as demon-possessed people and
unclean spirits had called out when he had used his authority to exorcise them (see 1:26; 5:7).

The **bystanders** are 'blind', and misunderstand what 35
Jesus says. They think that he is calling on Elijah, the one
who in Israel's hopes for the messianic age was expected to
come and prepare people for the coming of the Messiah. He
was also a 'patron saint' of those in trouble. Someone tries 36
to relieve Jesus in his agonising struggle by giving him
**vinegar** to drink. The people wait to see whether or not
Elijah (or God) is on Jesus' side. The scribes had previously
reached the conclusion that Jesus was in league, not with
God, but with Beelzebul (3:22). His death now proves the
point for them. The Son of man, who was supposed to have
authority on earth to forgive sins (2:10) and to be lord of the
sabbath (2:28), has been handed over by God to the powers
of the world, and has been abandoned by God.

Jesus, uttering (literally, 'leaving' or 'letting go') **a loud** 37
**cry**, expires (literally, 'expels the spirit'). The **loud cry** is
characteristic of a demon being expelled (see 1:26; 5:7). The

demon is exorcised, the unclean spirit is driven out. The
unclean spirit leaves, screaming, as the demons so often did
when challenged by the authority of Jesus. Jesus' crucifixion
is the result of unclean and demonic hostility. But in his
death, in his ultimate defilement, he exorcises the demon of
uncleanness, and breaks its dehumanising power. His cross,
his death, breaks the powers – those powers which belong
to political, social and church systems – which alienate
people, destroy their dignity, and make them powerless. But
his death is one that involves his being possessed by the
unclean spirit of death, by the demon's diabolical power.
Like the boy who is freed from the unclean spirit only after
a struggle that leaves him as if dead (9:26), the Son of man
struggles so violently with the unclean spirit on the cross
that he is left spirit-less, lifeless, as a result of the struggle.

Jesus' death tears open **the curtain of the temple**, in **38**
this way profaning the temple, and making it unclean, by
exposing it to those not permitted to enter there. The word
for **temple** that Mark uses here (a different word from the
one used previously) refers particularly to the Holy of Holies, the inner sanctuary, which was entered only once a
year, by the High Priest, on the Day of Atonement. Just
when the body of Jesus is being profaned by the chief priests
and scribes, who are linked to the temple, the covering of
the temple is torn away so that it is profaned. The leaders
of the temple worship had mockingly asked for a sign (v 32).
Here it is. Just as there was the sign of the heavens being
torn open, and the voice of God declaring Jesus to be his Son
at his baptism, so now the curtain of the temple is ripped
from top to bottom, and the presence of God is revealed. The
temple stood for the presence of God with his people. The
temple worship was for Israel and Israel only. But now all
of that is torn open, and the presence of God is on public
display – on the cross. In the crucified Jesus even the pagans
can now 'see' the Son of God, the Clean One, the Holy One
of God.

The curtain is ripped **in two, from top to bottom** (literally, 'from above to below'). Jesus' death exposes to the public
eye the presence and glory of God. The centurion's acknowledgment of who Jesus is may relate to verses in Psalm 22
(Jesus' song from the cross) which speak of the acknowledgment of God by all the nations of the world (Ps 22:27,28).
The centurion, who is from the powerful nation of Rome, **39**
'sees'. He does what the disciples and the Jewish leaders

have not been able to do: they are blind, but he sees. He is **facing** Jesus, or more exactly, is standing before Jesus, in his presence, like a priest standing before God (the wording here is important). He sees how Jesus cries out, and how he 'breathes out' in dying; that is, he sees how Jesus, the Clean One, exorcises all the powers which profane and demonise. His 'seeing' causes him to exclaim: **Truly this man was the Son of God**! His words can also be translated: Truly this man was a son of God, or, Truly this man was Son of God. The centurion's reference to Jesus as **this man** might again suggest that Jesus is the Man who is the Son of God. It is clear, from Mark's story as a whole, that the centurion's words are meant to confirm God's own pronouncement about this man: He is my Son (1:11; 9:7). What God had said of this man, a Gentile soldier now sees to be true. This seeing is possible only when one stands before Jesus at his cross. Only when one stands in the light of the cross (the darkness of the cross?) does one stand in the presence of God, the Holy One.

Note the past tense: 'Truly this man *was* the Son of God'. This does not mean that Jesus is no longer Son of God, but emphasises that only at the cross can one look back on the life of Jesus and come to the conclusion: He was Son of God after all. The cross is God's answer to Jesus' own question: Who do you say that I am? (8:29). The cross replaces the temple as the ladder or bridge between heaven and earth, between God and his people. The sacrificial worship activities of the temple are replaced by the Son of God himself, who gives his own body and blood to feed his new community, which is made up of people from all nations.

This episode with the centurion must have been a real surprise to many hearing or reading this story for the first time. The centurion would have been a much-travelled and highly experienced soldier, whose responsibility it would have been to see that executions were carried out, and to maintain and enforce discipline among the men under his command. More importantly, he would have to have taken the oath of allegiance to the Emperor, and to have made offerings to the Emperor as part of the religious ceremonies in which the Emperor was honoured as a divine being. Mark's point is that even the powers of Rome, and the allegiance demanded by that State, are broken by the name of Jesus. What is so shocking, so incredible, is that such a switch of allegiance can be brought about at the cross, as the centurion, in this case, stands facing the one who has been condemned and executed by that Roman legal and military system.

There has recently been an increasing realisation of the important status and role of women in the gospel story. They are the ones who model true and faithful following of the way of Jesus, who remain with him right up to his death when his male followers have all left him. The women here are **looking on from afar** (it could also be translated 'women from afar were looking on', that is, women who did not come from Jerusalem but from Galilee, as indicated by the next verse). Among them is **Mary Magdalene**. There is not the slightest suggestion in Mark that she was a prostitute. That idea comes from arbitrarily identifying the woman of Luke 7:37 (who is described as 'a sinner') with Mary Magdalene who had seven spirits cast out of her (Luke 8:2). Male imagination has identified those seven spirits as the seven deadly sins, one of which is lust. **Mary the mother of James the younger and of Joses** has no further identification. The text here can be read in various ways. It is possible that Mary, instead of being the mother of both James and Joses, is the mother only of Joses, and the sister, or wife, of James. In addition, it is uncertain how many women are being referred to. It is possible that there are actually four: Mary Magdalene, Mary the wife/daughter of James, the mother of Joses (not named), and Salome. The first verse of chapter 16, however, suggests that there are only three. Mark clearly identifies these women as followers of Jesus who **ministered** to him (the same word, translated 'serve', is used in 10:45 of Jesus himself as the Son of man). They had followed him **in Galilee**, and had then gone with him along 'the way' to Jerusalem. **Many other women** also came up to Jerusalem with Jesus. The women reading this section, or listening to it being read, would have been smiling, because they would have been aware of their special status and ministry in Mark's community.

## Bury the unclean, 15:42-47

**⁴² And when evening had come, since it was the day of Preparation, that is, the day before the sabbath, ⁴³ Joseph of Arimathea, a respected member of the council, who was also himself looking for the kingdom of God, took courage and went to Pilate, and asked for the body of Jesus. ⁴⁴ And Pilate wondered if he were already dead;**

and summoning the centurion, he asked him whether he was already dead.ᵏ ⁴⁵ **And when he learned from the centurion that he was dead, he granted the body to Joseph.** ⁴⁶ **And he bought a linen shroud, and taking him down, wrapped him in the linen shroud, and laid him in a tomb which had been hewn out of the rock; and he rolled a stone against the door of the tomb.** ⁴⁷ **Mary Magdalene and Mary the mother of Joses saw where he was laid.**

ᵏ Other ancient authorities read *whether he had been some time dead*

It is late (**evening**) on **the day before the sabbath**. The reference to the time of day, so common in Mark's passion narrative, may be understood as a reference to the 'lateness' of the sabbath. Jesus is bringing in a new sabbath rest through his resurrection. Jewish law forbade the leaving of hanged people at the place of execution overnight (Deut 21:22,23). The disciples are conspicuous by their absence. **Joseph**, from a place called **Arimathea**, a wealthy man (Matt 27:57), is one who is waiting for God to bring in his kingdom. Is Joseph a member of the sanhedrin, the Jewish council, of which all the members had condemned Jesus (14:64)? Mark calls him **a respected member of the council**, or 'respected councillor', using a word not used previously for the sanhedrin. There is nothing explicit in Mark to suggest that Joseph is a follower of Jesus. He may wish to bury Jesus' body simply as an act of piety to ensure that the sabbath is not defiled. Burial of the dead was regarded as a more charitable act than the provision of food and clothing for the living. Joseph dares to ask for the body of Jesus, that is, for the body of a condemned and executed criminal, which is regarded as utterly unclean and not worthy of burial.

Pilate wonders (as in 15:5) that Jesus is already dead: death by crucifixion could take days. He summons the centurion – presumably the same one who had 'seen' (v 39) – and asks whether Jesus has, in fact, **been some time dead** (alternative reading, RSV footnote). This verse seems to be making the point clear to any doubters: Jesus is well and truly dead! But there is no need to see behind this verse later Christian heresies which denied the reality of Jesus' death. Nor is there an apologetic here against the opponents of Christians. Rather, Mark is doing what he so often does: readying his readers for some future event, in this case the resurrection. Once again, those reading or listening to this account, who were in on the 'joke', would have enjoyed this confirmation by Pilate of the reality of Jesus' death.

When Pilate finds out from the centurion that Jesus is in fact dead, he gives the **body** ('corpse' would be a better translation, with greater significance) to Joseph. A corpse, particularly that of a criminal, was regarded as the most profane of objects. The word that is used here can mean a *mutilated* body, which, if it were possible, would be even more unclean. The Holy One of God has become totally unclean. Joseph takes Jesus' body **down** (from the cross, presumably) and wraps it in a **linen shroud** which he has bought. The garments worn by priests were made of linen. Is Mark making the point here that Jesus is actually a priest, right at that point when, as a corpse, he is most unclean? He would then be the real priest of God, in contrast to those other priests who have been rendered unclean (see commentary on 14:47-52). Or is the wrapping of the unclean corpse in a priestly garment meant to indicate that the status and function of the priesthood has come to an end? Mark seems to have something like this in mind, since he overlooks the fact that it is unlawful for anyone to buy anything on the first day of Passover.

The corpse is laid in **a tomb which had been hewn out of the rock**. Corpses of criminals were normally buried first in a common grave, and then removed some days later and buried in a family plot. Jesus is certainly not buried in his family's plot, and there is no indication at all that members of his family are remotely interested in his body. Nor does Joseph bury him in his own family plot. There is no anointing of the body: that has taken place already prior to his death (14:3-9). A **stone** is placed at the entrance to the tomb, as was the custom. Since no burials were allowed inside the holy city, the tomb would have been outside. The women are again mentioned as spectators at these events, which prepares readers for their great discovery and their great message on Easter morning. The men see to the burial; the women announce the living Jesus.

*The resurrection, 16:1-8*

**16:1 And when the sabbath was past, Mary Magdalene, and Mary the mother of James, and Salome, bought spices, so that they might go and anoint him. ² And very early on the first day of the week they went to the tomb when the sun had risen. ³ And they were saying to one**

another, 'Who will roll away the stone for us from the door of the tomb?' ⁴ And looking up, they saw that the stone was rolled back – it was very large. ⁵ And entering the tomb, they saw a young man sitting on the right side, dressed in a white robe; and they were amazed. ⁶ And he said to them, 'Do not be amazed; you seek Jesus of Nazareth, who was crucified. He has risen, he is not here; see the place where they laid him. ⁷ But go, tell his disciples and Peter that he is going before you to Galilee; there you will see him, as he told you.' ⁸ And they went out and fled from the tomb; for trembling and astonishment had come upon them; and they said nothing to any one, for they were afraid.**

This section has attracted more discussion and a greater variety of opinions than any other in Mark's gospel. The main question is about the ending to the gospel: how did the original gospel end? The manuscript evidence shows that from an early time there were problems with the ending. The best manuscripts, however, suggest that the original ending to the gospel was at verse 8. Anything that comes after verse 8 can be seen as an attempt to overcome the problem of a gospel in which the last words are about being afraid. This commentary regards verse 8 as the original ending of the gospel.

The resurrection begins **when the sabbath is past**. Not **1,2** only does this comment give the time that the resurrection occurs, but it also implies that a new sabbath is about to dawn. For the Christian community the sabbath is now past. Mark makes three references to the sabbath: the day before the sabbath (15:42); the sabbath itself (16:1); and the day after the sabbath (16:2). The mention of these three days confirms the prediction of Jesus that he would be killed but raised to life on the third day (8:31; 9:31; 10:33,34).

The women, who were introduced at 15:40 in preparation for their role in the proclamation of the Easter message, are mentioned by name again. It was customary for friends and relatives to visit the grave of the deceased for three days after the death, partly because of the belief that the person's soul stayed around for that period of time. After three days, death was regarded as irreversible. The women bring **spices** to **anoint** the corpse, as was the custom. However, they do not get to anoint the body, because an unnamed 'priestess' has already performed that duty (14:3-9). Anointing slowed down the process of decay. Mark wants to say that it is not anointing which prevents the decay of the Clean One, but it is God himself, who raises his clean Son from the uncleanness of death and the grave.

**The first day of the week** became the day when Christian communities met together for worship (see 1 Cor 16:2; Acts 20:7). Mark has the women asking the question: **Who will roll away the stone for us?** One would think that they would have thought about that before they set out! Mark wishes to show that *God* is the one who is in action here in the raising of his Son. The women's concern about the size of the stone draws attention to this. The women look **up**, and they see that the stone has been moved. The word for 'see' here is the same one that was used of the women in 15:40,47. Our English word 'theatre' comes from this word. It does not refer to the seeing of faith, but simply to observing. The statement that the stone **was very large** draws attention to that fact that someone else (God) has acted here.

The women enter the grave and see **a young man sitting on the right side, dressed in a white robe**. (Here the word for 'see' is the one that can imply understanding and faith.) The symbolism here is strong. **Young man** may be a reference back to the young man who fled naked without his priestly garb (14:51,52). Now he is clothed, not as a priest, but as a messenger of Easter. He sits (the posture of a teacher, of a person with authority) **on the right side** (also the place of power and authority, as well as of victory and favour). The **white robe** may refer back to Jesus' transfiguration, where his clothes became whiter than any bleach on earth is capable of producing (9:3). That revelation of Jesus' glory was a foreshadowing of his resurrection. Disciples of Jesus now share in the glory of Jesus' resurrection, which involves a transformation for them too. No wonder that the women are **amazed**. (This translation is not strong enough. The word conveys that they are utterly astonished, to the point of being alarmed.) But the message to these faithful women who have stood by Jesus, and who now stand in the presence of the great miracle of the resurrection, is: **Do not be amazed** (or alarmed). Is it the role and position of women to be in the presence of such authority and to receive such revelation? Mark says yes.

The women need not be alarmed, because **Jesus of Nazareth, who was crucified ... has risen**. **Jesus** is given emphasis in the Greek by being placed first in the sentence (the name, which is a form of Joshua, means 'God saves'). The reference to Jesus as **Jesus of Nazareth** (or the

Nazarene) takes readers back to the beginning of the gospel, to Galilee, the area which was seen by Jerusalem Jews as being 'beyond the boundaries'. Jesus is referred to as the one **who was crucified**. The form of the Greek verb (which might be better translated 'who has been crucified') indicates that Jesus' crucifixion has continuing relevance and significance. **He has risen** would be better translated 'he has been raised'. The passive form of the verb refers to an action performed by God. The young man continues: **He is not here; see the place where they laid him**, which recalls the earlier statement that the women 'saw where he was laid' (15:47). The verb 'see' which is used here is the one that refers to the seeing of faith, the seeing of the insider who understands the mystery of Jesus.

The women are commanded to go and tell the disciples that Jesus is going before them to Galilee. They become the apostles of the resurrection to the disciples and especially to Peter. This is a remarkable calling that these women have as the first witnesses to the resurrection. It is their message which restores Peter, the representative of the disciples, later to become leader of some Christian communities. As the word of a woman had reduced him to shame-filled tears (14:66-72), so the testimony of the women restores him to union with the living Jesus.

The message that the women are to take to the disciples is: **he is going before you to Galilee**. The Jesus who originally came out of unclean Galilee to join with Israel in the return to the desert (1:9), who there heard the call to be Son of God (1:11), and who then proclaimed the kingdom of God to the people of Galilee (1:14), now returns to that area as the Living One. Life is found with Jesus beyond the borders of Jerusalem, and the disciples are called to follow him there. The way of Jesus does not come to an end at the cross. Instead, the cross provides the way through to a new life. The form of the verb (perfect tense) translated **who was crucified** conveys that the crucifixion is a present reality with continuing significance. This means that following Jesus does not end at the cross, but involves going through the cross. Jesus goes **before** them, or ahead of them. He is still present with his community as the crucified one, leading his people like a shepherd leading his sheep. His going to **Galilee** involves the total rejection of Jerusalem as the place of divine revelation. There is to be no restoration of Jerusalem or the temple. The risen Jesus will be found by his followers not in Jerusalem, but in second-class Galilee.

The message for the disciples continues: **there you will see him, as he told you**. Before the crucifixion they could not see Jesus, because their hearts were hardened, but now, having gone through the cross, they can see and understand who he is. The message of Mark is clear: there can be no understanding of Jesus, no 'seeing' of him, except through the cross, and by seeing him as the Living One. This is true for the generation of people for whom Mark writes, who have not, of course, seen Jesus in the flesh. Nor can there be any following of Jesus unless one is prepared to cross the borders, to go into unclean areas.

Mark's account of the resurrection ends very strangely: the women leave the tomb and flee (the same word is used of the disciples in 14:50). They flee from the tomb, that place of death and burial, with **trembling and astonishment** (the word for **astonishment** is the one from which our word 'ecstasy' comes). They say **nothing to any one**, because 8 they are **afraid**. Their reaction is like that of the people who were amazed at Jesus' authority over death (5:42) and those who experienced fear because of his power (4:41; 5:15; 10:32). Previously, people who had been healed by Jesus were told not to tell anyone about what had happened, a command which was disobeyed (1:44; 7:36). Here, in contrast, the women are commanded to speak, but they remain silent (**they said nothing to any one**)! Some interpreters suggest that their silence lasts only while they are fleeing from the place of death to bring the news of life. According to this view, it is the thought of the sacredness of their obligation to deliver a message from the living God that reduces them to silence. However, the message that they are asked to carry is not actually that Jesus is risen, but that he is going ahead of his disciples, especially Peter, to Galilee. According to Mark, the risen Jesus does not make special appearances, as in the other gospel stories, but is the one who is present with his community in Galilee. He will be seen in Galilee. The verb **see** is often used in relation to the *parousia* (the presence or return of Jesus at the end of time). Just as Jesus came from Galilee and not from Judea, so now he is present and will finally be seen in that 'outside' area. This is the message that the women are to carry. This is how the gospel ends, at least according to the best manuscripts.

The gospel, which began with authority and power, and with dynamic language, ends with fear and silence. Some interpreters understand this to be the fear and silence associated with bearing the authority of the one who has authority over the ultimate uncleanness, the final separation from God: death and the grave. The women, like Paul, feel the burden of that great apostolic commission that they have received. There is no appearance of Jesus – to anyone. All there is, is a messenger. This reflects the situation of Mark's community. They live a generation or so after Jesus, and probably also a short time after the death of Peter and Paul. The only witness that they have is the word of the apostles' followers. Their hope now is in that word, that message. Mark may well be emphasising this at a time when there is beginning to be a desire to find out more about Jesus' resurrection, and about the resurrected life of Christians. Or perhaps Mark's ending is meant to turn Christian thought away from the physcial presence of Jesus, to confidence in the tradition and message that have been handed down.

Galilee is to be the place where mission begins. Does Mark leave the ending of his gospel open as an encouragement to his readers to carry on that mission, with the promise that Jesus goes ahead of them?

The women's fear can also be seen in relation to other instances of fear in Mark's story, where fear is the response to a Jesus who breaks through the barriers of clean and unclean, the response of those who cannot come to terms with a Jesus who associates with outsiders (11:18). In his resurrection Jesus remains the same Jesus, and continues to call his followers to make the transition that he has made. His resurrection, then, is a transition similar to the ones that he made with his disciples on the sea (4:35; 6:45), on the mountain (3:13; 9:2), and in the desert (1:12; 6:31). His followers are afraid, because they have yet to take the step themselves. So the gospel ends with Jesus going ahead. He is across the borders already, he has already made the transition. He has cleared the way by the expulsion of all evil spirits and demons, and has even overcome the power of death. Those who have read the gospel, or have listened to it being read, go away knowing that Jesus waits for them to follow. He is in Galilee, and now he calls: 'Are you coming?' That call still evokes fear, and calls for courage, daring and faith.

So there is no glory road for Mark's community. The Jesus they follow is the Jesus of the cross. The way is hard and tough. There are still the evil powers which threaten, and there are still those who want to stay on the land and who refuse to make the crossing (4:35; 6:45). There is still division within and pressure from without. There is still failure, hard-heartedness, blindness and deafness. There are still systems which are corrupt and which dehumanise. In the face of all this there is nothing for the Christian community to do except to take up the cross and follow Jesus into Galilee.

## Alternative endings, 16:9-20

⁹ Now when he rose early on the first day of the week, he appeared first to Mary Magdalene, from whom he had cast out seven demons. ¹⁰ She went out and told those who had been with him, as they mourned and wept. ¹¹ But when they heard that he was alive and had been seen by her, they would not believe it.

¹² After this he appeared in another form to two of them, as they were walking into the country. ¹³ And they went back and told the rest, but they did not believe them

¹⁴ Afterward he appeared to the eleven themselves as they sat at table; and he upbraided them for their unbelief and hardness of heart, because they had not believed those who saw him after he had risen. ¹⁵ And he said to them, 'Go into all the world and preach the gospel to the whole creation. ¹⁶ He who believes and is baptized will be saved; but he who does not believe will be condemned. ¹⁷ And these signs will accompany those who believe; in my name they will cast out demons; they will speak in new tongues; ¹⁸ they will pick up serpents, and if they drink any deadly thing, it will not hurt them; they will lay their hands on the sick, and they will recover'

¹⁹ So then the Lord Jesus, after he had spoken to them, was taken up into heaven, and sat down at the right hand of God. ²⁰ And they went forth and preached everywhere, while the Lord worked with them and confirmed the message by the signs that attended it. Amen.

Other ancient authorities add after verse 8 the following:

But they reported briefly to Peter and those with him all that they had been told. And after this, Jesus himself sent out by means of them, from east to west, the sacred and imperishable proclamation of eternal salvation.

As most modern translations indicate, the best ancient manuscripts end the gospel at 16:8. However, some manuscripts include additional verses which we will briefly look at here.

**Mary Magdalene** was obviously a significant figure in the early church, and in all the gospels she is shown as a witness to the resurrection, and the first apostle of the resurrected Jesus. It is only later writings which portray her as a prostitute who was forgiven by Jesus, partly on the basis of verse 9, which says that Jesus had cast seven demons out of her. The **seven demons** became identified with the seven deadly sins, one of which is lust, and in this way Mary Magdalene became identified with the woman of Luke 7:37. But here we have the tradition which highly regards Mary as the **first** one to whom Jesus appeared. It is important to note that the resurrection of Jesus is not announced directly to the male disciples but to the women. Mary goes to the weeping and mourning disciples, who do not accept her news (**they would not believe it**). This is consistent with the Marcan tradition, which sees the disciples as blind, deaf and hard of heart when it comes to recognising the essential nature and status of Jesus. **10, 11**

The incident recorded in verses 12 and 13 could well be a reference to the episode in Luke 24:13-35 of the two disciples going to Emmaus. Luke, however, does not have the reference to the other disciples not believing what had happened. **12, 13**

Jesus appears (no appearances of Jesus are recorded in the original text of Mark) to **the eleven** (presumably Judas is the one who is missing). There is nothing in Mark's gospel about the fate of Judas, and so this reference to the eleven adds weight to the rejection of this passage as part of the original text of the gospel. Jesus appears to them while they sit **at table**. This is in harmony with accounts in other gospels which portray the resurrected Jesus as being present with his disciples at a meal, probably seen as a Eucharistic meal (Luke 24:30,41-43; John 21:12,13). Jesus' rebuke of the eleven for not believing those who saw him after he had risen, suggests that the author of this addition accepted the authority of the women as apostles of the resurrection. **14**

The disciples are commanded to go and preach the gospel. The mention of baptism suggests that the Matthew 28:18-20 tradition, if not the whole text of Matthew, was known to the author. The **whole creation** refers not only to all people, but to the whole created order. The gospel is not the property of one group of people, but is to be proclaimed to all people, the whole of humanity. At the same time, it is something that belongs not only to people, but also to the whole cosmos, the whole of God's creation. **15, 16**

Many theological arguments have centred on verse 16, especially in regard to the relationship between faith and baptism. Some have argued that since faith is mentioned first, baptism is only for believers, and therefore only for adults. Some have also argued, on the basis of this verse, that baptism is not necessary for salvation, since it is said here that it is only unbelief that results in damnation. Others would say that adult baptisms are always the norm in missionary situations, and that adults were often baptised with their families, which included children. Baptism, according to Paul, joins to Christ, and to the very centre of Christ's mission: his death and resurrection (see Rom 6:3,4, for example). Baptism is therefore essential for salvation, since Christ, and union with him, is essential. This is not the argument of the text here, which simply connects faith, baptism and salvation.

The signs mentioned in verses 17 and 18 have also been held by some to be central to Christian life and faith. They certainly do not fit with the central understanding of Mark's gospel. Acts indicates that the disciples were able to perform great works and signs, as evidence that God had vindicated Jesus by raising him from the dead and by appointing him to be Judge and Lord of all. Drinking poison is not mentioned anywhere else in the New Testament. The laying on of hands is a very ancient practice which is believed to convey blessing and healing. God's own hands are hands of blessing and healing.

Verses 19 and 20 are an abbreviated form of a larger tradition in regard to Jesus' ascension. **The Lord Jesus** is not a Marcan expression; in fact, Mark seems to consciously avoid the title **Lord** in relation to Jesus. Clearly these verses, like the others in this section, have been added by a later editor in an attempt to tidy up the ending of the gospel. The **right hand of God** is his powerful, ruling hand. To sit with someone is to be regarded as that person's equal. Jesus sits at the right hand of God because he shares in God's power and authority. The disciples now go and preach the gospel, with Jesus providing the assurance and the power. This is in contrast to the depiction of the disciples in Mark's gospel, which shows them as still being fearful even after the resurrection. There they were called to take risks by going into Galilee, into unclean areas, and to do that without being given any appearance of the living Jesus, but simply on the basis of his command, his promise, and his example.

Another shorter ending also exists in some manuscripts, which simply states that the women reported **to Peter and those with him**, and that they were then sent out by Jesus with the message of salvation.

# FOR FURTHER READING

1. The following commentaries, which can be recommended, are more popular in style, and do not require much technical knowledge of the reader:

   Nineham, D.E. *Saint Mark*. Penguin Books, London, 1963.

   This is a standard work which has been well received. It provides helpful summaries along the way, and gives closer comment on many individual verses, but not on each verse. It looks at whole sections at a time, rather than giving a verse-by-verse commentary.

   Williamson, L. *Mark*. Interpretation Series. John Knox Press, Atlanta, 1983.

   This is a readable commentary displaying good, sound exegesis. Each section is concluded with a paragraph or so on the significance of the passage within its own context and also in the context of the modern preacher.

   Schweitzer, E. *The Good News According to Mark*. SPCK, London, 1971.

   Harrington, W. *Mark*. New Testament Series. Michael Glazier, Wilmington, Del., 1979.

   Cole, R.A. *The Gospel According to St Mark*. Tyndale Press, London, 1961 (and other editions).

   Juel, Donald H. *Mark*. Augsburg Commentary on the New Testament. Augsburg, Minneapolis, 1990.

2. The following commentaries are more scholarly, requiring more technical knowledge of the reader:

   Taylor, V. *The Gospel According to Mark*. Macmillan & Co., London, 1963 (and later editions).

   This is a standard work on Mark using the old textual critical approach, which does not always make for easy reading. It is valuable for its close textual work, and for some informative notes. It is a book for the scholar more than the preacher.

Mann, C.S. *Mark*. Anchor Bible 27. Doubleday, Garden City NY, 1986.

3. The following studies also contain useful material on Mark's gospel:

Kingsbury, J.D. *Jesus Christ in Matthew, Mark and Luke*. Proclamation Commentaries. Fortress Press, Philadelphia, 1981.

Kingsbury writes clearly and is easy to read. He gives a very neat and helpful summary of Mark's gospel, and particularly of the presentation of Jesus in Mark. The book deals in a similar way with Matthew and Luke, and so is good value.

In the same series is:

Achtemeier, P. *Mark*. 2nd ed. Fortress Press, Philadelphia, 1987.

This is a very sound and useful introduction to Mark as literature, to the Marcan understanding of Jesus, and particularly to the theme of discipleship in Mark. It is not a commentary, but provides a summary view of the gospel.

Juel, Donald H. *An Introduction to New Testament Literature*. Abingdon Press, Nashville, 1978.

This is an introduction to the New Testament from a literary point of view. Amongst other things, it provides a useful guide to questions about relationships between the gospels, and what a gospel is as literature. His material on Mark is generally very helpful.

Best, E. *Disciples and Discipleship: Studies in the Gospel According to Mark*. T & T Clark, Edinburgh, 1986.

The theme of discipleship is strong in Mark, and Best has published many of his writings on that subject. His books tend to be collections of papers and lectures, which means that one can pick and choose the sections to read rather than having to read the whole book.

Kingsbury, J.D. *Conflict in Mark: Jesus, Authorities, Disciples*. Fortress Press, Minneapolis, 1989.
This is a good book, in Kingsbury's typically lucid style. He provides an overview of the portrayal of Jesus, the disciples, and the authorities in this gospel, which is valuable in itself without the added theme of conflict between them.

www.ingramcontent.com/pod-product-compliance
Lightning Source LLC
Chambersburg PA
CBHW060602230426
43670CB00011B/1939